ADVANCE PRAISE

"What Jarie has put together here is really incredible. If you're on the edge of entrepreneurship or are already in it and just need some reassurance that you're not in this alone, you should read this book. *The Entrepreneur Ethos* breaks entrepreneurship down by sharing real stories and insights from dozens of entrepreneurs. It's a deep and refreshing read that shows that entrepreneurship isn't just what you see on Shark Tank."

- Joel Runyon, CEO of IMPOSSIBLE

"*The Entrepreneur Ethos* is a book which combines the essential mindset required for success, along with the practical steps required to get there. Bolander draws on the experience of entrepreneurs from around the world to give the reader a rare insight into the habits you need, challenges you'll face, and the thrill of overcoming that comes with being an entrepreneur. Highly recommend to anyone that wants to be an entrepreneur."

- Nathan Rose, CEO of Assemble Advisory

"Jarie has stitched together a beautiful narrative through honest interviews with entrepreneurs. This book is an amazing case study for the struggles, enlightenments, and successes in the world of 'applied creativity'. *The Entrepreneur Ethos* is a must read for anybody, veteran entrepreneurs or someone new, looking to enter the world of entrepreneurship."

- Ravi Kurani, CEO of Sutro

"*The Entrepreneur Ethos* is a wonderful read. It's well researched with lots of real-world examples of how following the Ethos leads to success. We as a community need to hold ourselves to a higher standard and *The Entrepreneur Ethos* perfectly captures that high standard. A must read for all entrepreneurs."

- Ajay Malik, CTO of Lunera

"The external challenges for entrepreneurs are clear and obvious, and there's a wealth of valuable advice out there to help you with those.

But every entrepreneur has to win an inner game as well as the outer one. And the challenges here are not so clear or so obvious. Many entrepreneurs with seemingly sound business plans have been tripped up by their inner doubts and demons. And there isn't so much advice out there that's tailored to the specific needs of entrepreneurs.

Jarie Bolander has filled this gap with an inspiring and instructive guide to building the mindset and character that are critical to achieving your business goals. Full of real-life stories from entrepreneurs who stayed the course, as well as Jarie's own hard-won wisdom, *The Entrepreneur Ethos* deserves its place on the bookshelf of any aspiring entrepreneur."

- Mark McGuinness,
Coach for Creative Entrepreneurs
and host of The 21st Century Creative Podcast

THE ENTREPRENEUR ETHOS

How to Build a More Ethical, Inclusive, and Resilient Entrepreneur Community

By Jarie Bolander

Published by BookLocker.com, Inc., St. Petersburg, Florida.

Printed on acid-free paper.

BookLocker.com, Inc.
2017

First Edition

http://theentrepreneurethos.com

DISCLAIMER

This book details the author's personal experiences with and opinions about entrepreneurship and business

The author and publisher are providing this book and its contents on an "as is" basis and make no representations or warranties of any kind with respect to this book or its contents. The author and publisher disclaim all such representations and warranties, including for example warranties of merchantability and entrepreneurship and business advice for a particular purpose. In addition, the author and publisher do not represent or warrant that the information accessible via this book is accurate, complete or current.

The statements made about products and services have not been evaluated by the U.S. government. Please consult with your own legal or accounting or business professional regarding the suggestions and recommendations made in this book.

Except as specifically stated in this book, neither the author or publisher, nor any authors, contributors, or other representatives will be liable for damages arising out of or in connection with the use of this book. This is a comprehensive limitation of liability that applies to all damages of any kind, including (without limitation) compensatory; direct, indirect or consequential damages; loss of data, income or profit; loss of or damage to property and claims of third parties.

You understand that this book is not intended as a substitute for consultation with a licensed medical, legal or accounting professional. Before you begin any change in your lifestyle in any way, you will need to consult a licensed professional to ensure that you are doing what's best for your situation.

This book provides content related to entrepreneurship and business topics. As such, use of this book implies your acceptance of this disclaimer.

DEDICATION

To Jane. My muse, my best friend, my soulmate, and my partner-in-crime. Our time together was too short. Rest easy, my love. You are always in my heart.

TABLE OF CONTENTS

FOREWORD

I first met Jarie Bolander in the spring of 2017 after a fellow Founders Network (FN) member, Barbara Tien (August 2012 Cohort), introduced us.

Barbara, a Silicon Valley veteran and founder of Ponga.com, had heard Jarie give a talk on startup public relations at Galvanize in San Francisco. She was impressed by his presentation and stuck around to have a conversation with him. She learned about Jarie's 20-plus years in Silicon Valley's tech industry including six startups, $6M in funding, and $750M in exit value. The very next day Barbara sent an email connecting us and making an enthusiastic nomination for him to apply to Founders Network.

Shortly thereafter, Jarie and I grabbed lunch in the Jackson Square neighborhood of San Francisco and hit it off instantly. In Jarie I found a peer who, like me, was making a career in Silicon Valley working in and around startups and who shared many similar values and beliefs.

During that first meeting we covered a lot of ground. In big ideas, we talked about the importance of maintaining and strengthening Silicon Valley's collaborative culture, especially as the tech startup industry globalizes and attracts new entrants from different industries with different cultural norms. We also talked about the problems with the existing culture, from "tech bros" to sexual harassment and discrimination in venture capital land to the need for a more inclusive ethos. I shared stories about founders who had joined FN over the years and the wide variety of expectations for how the industry operates and just how much work they had cut out for them. For every anecdote I shared, Jarie had a similar one, and so the conversation went on.

We also talked about life. Jarie openly shared about his wife's recent passing and I shared about losing one of my best friends in a natural disaster. We talked about the grieving process and his plans for honoring his late wife's memory, and more. While it was immediately obvious we were working towards similar ends and motivated by the same passion for helping people realize their dreams, it was these personal conversations that made me realize we shared the same values of authenticity, reciprocity, humility, and respect.

Since that meeting, Jarie applied—and was accepted—into Founders Network, a peer mentorship community of over 600-plus tech founders worldwide that I founded over seven years ago. Unsurprisingly, he's been a fantastic member, and in a short time has made a big impact on the community. He's helped his fellow FN'ers find the best pitch events, get featured on startup podcasts, discover resources on SaaS metrics, and even gave away free tickets to a growth conference he advises.

Like our first lunch meeting, *The Entrepreneur Ethos* covers a lot of ground. In broad-brush strokes, Jarie provides an excellent survey of the forces that impact entrepreneurs, both external and internal, as well as what it takes to be successful. The language is simple and easy to understand – written by a practitioner, for practitioners. Jarie draws on the depth of his own experience and the wider industry to accompany each topic with numerous anecdotes that illustrate his point while simultaneously providing the reader with a primer on key tech startup industry events, organizations, and news.

That is why I believe *The Entrepreneur Ethos* is especially valuable to aspiring entrepreneurs who are brand-new entrants to the tech industry. The chapters on battling the status quo are especially poignant to new entrepreneurs and the chapters on traits, values, and beliefs are critically important for those who are new to Silicon Valley or starting up in one of the numerous emerging tech hubs around the world. Bottom line, if you're interested in becoming an entrepreneur or have already taken the leap, this book should be required reading. Likewise, if you've been around and are a serial entrepreneur like Jarie, this book is a great refresher.

In that first lunch meeting, Jarie and I talked about the need to codify Silicon Valley culture to help more founders around the world better understand and adopt the ethos that led to the success of this region. We need a shared culture that cuts across national boundaries and unifies this special class of workers, eases collaboration, learns from one another, inspires camaraderie, and ultimately accelerates the pace of progress towards a better future. *The Entrepreneur Ethos* is a step in that direction.

Kevin Holmes

CEO, Founders Network

July 2017

INTRODUCTION

Thousands of companies get started each year to buck the trend, disrupt the market, change the paradigm, and put their own dents in the universe. Friends, family, and others often ridicule the people who start these companies because they don't believe they have what it takes to succeed. Who are these people who dare to believe they are creating the next Facebook, Twitter, Tesla, or insert your favorite unicorn (company with > $1B valuation) here? Most of these new companies will fail, but thousands will try anyway, even though the odds are stacked against them.

The people who start these companies are entrepreneurs.

My own 20-plus-year, six-company journey with entrepreneurship has given me some valuable lessons and insights. Those lessons, additional research, and interviews with dozens of entrepreneurs form the basis of *The Entrepreneur Ethos*. Some of these lessons and insights have been painful to learn.

Like the time my boss and I had to shut down the California division of Adaptive Solutions. We had to liquidate all our equipment, find someone to sub-lease the office, and box up all the important documents to send to the corporate office. I was among the last to leave, and even locked the door for that last time. That was painful because just two years earlier we had gone public. The difficult and humbling lesson I learned from that experience was that, no matter how important you think you are, you can always be let go. In the end, Adaptive Solutions went bankrupt after a failed pivot a year later. I guess I was lucky I got out when I did.

Other lessons have been easier.

Like the time I spent at Ion Torrent where we were building the next generation of DNA sequencing machines. Our CEO, Jonathan Rothberg, would always tell us, "You can print money, but you can't print time." This was an invaluable lesson about how to evaluate the cost of taking action versus spending money. As an entrepreneur, time is never on your side, and if you can accelerate any type of learning by spending money, it's money well spent.

Those are two examples of how lucky I was to get invaluable professional life experience, and have great people around me showing me the way. Their knowledge and insights are sprinkled throughout this book, along with the interviews of other entrepreneurs about their journeys. I was also lucky to be at some great companies and some not-so-great companies. But all of this has provided a practical education in formulating *The Entrepreneur Ethos.*

Hindsight is a great teacher. As I reflect back on the past 20 years, I have come to the conclusion that the entrepreneurial journey is not for everyone. That is one of the motivations behind writing this book. I want to capture the spirit of the entrepreneur culture so that, if you really want to give it a shot, you should know what you're in for.

I also want to give those who are already entrepreneurs a framework in which to evaluate themselves and their peers, so we can hold ourselves to a higher standard. A community that does not have high standards will never continue to improve and thrive. Just look at the recent sexual harassment scandals at Kleiner Perkins, Uber, Binary Capital, and 500 startups, to name a few.

All of those situations are the antithesis of an Ethos that is ethical, inclusive, and resilient. The sad part is that this biased and unacceptable treatment of women investors and entrepreneurs has been going on for years. Even worse, when some women did speak up, they were marginalized or rebuffed. We as a community can and must do better.

A community that does not look at both its successes and failures will never grow into a culture where merit matters more than your gender, or who you know, or where you went to school. This is why I was compelled to write *The Entrepreneur Ethos* so that the entrepreneurial community can better take on the challenges that the 21st century has in store.

This book will describe the challenges that the status quo (Part One) presents to entrepreneurs, and then detail the Traits (Part Two), Values (Part Three), and Beliefs (Part Four) that successful entrepreneurs must engender and embrace to overcome the many challenges they will face in creating the great ideas, products, and services that will make our world a better place (Part Five).

The thing to realize is that, without entrepreneurs, many of the greatest and most significant innovations we rely on daily would not exist – mobile phones, streaming audio and video, online software, electric cars, self-driving cars, etc. Even corporate "failures" like AltaVista, Webvan, and Pets.com paved the way to make our lives better. That's why it's critical to set forth an Ethos that provides a framework to enable all entrepreneurs to have a shot at success.

For most entrepreneurs, success is not measured by the size of their bank account or by being on the cover of *Fast Company*.

All those perks are great, but they are fleeting.

In fact, most will never see the stellar returns of an Apple, Microsoft, Facebook, YouTube, or Instagram.

That's reality.

Success for most entrepreneurs is being able to create their own lives on their own terms. It's more about freedom, creativity, and overcoming challenges than money, fame, and prestige. The true reward of entrepreneurship is being able to do your own thing in your own way.

That's not to say that every entrepreneur does not want stellar returns for their investors or a shot at creating a unicorn. In reality, the odds of doing that are stacked against them, no matter how smart, how well funded, or how connected they may be.

To help you on the journey through *The Entrepreneur Ethos*, let me give you a little more detail on each of the parts.

Part One will explore the *Challenges to the Status Quo* that get in the way of an entrepreneur's success. These challenges are yourself, friends and family, talent, technology, technique, timing, customers, competitors, investors, and government. Each and every one of these will challenge you at some point. The many and varied battles against the status quo are what every entrepreneur must overcome and win to have a shot at becoming successful.

Part Two is about the *Traits* of entrepreneurs. I started with traits because those are the most outward-facing characteristics of successful entrepreneurs. These traits are what we most often admire from afar and try to emulate.

Part Three goes through the *Values* that entrepreneurs must embrace and hold dear. These values are what define the culture and show how entrepreneurs can hook into it. These values provide the personal framework in which entrepreneurs operate.

Part Four details the *Beliefs* that entrepreneurs should adhere to. A belief system is at the core of the Ethos and, without a solid understanding of what entrepreneurs believe, it will be difficult to understand how to navigate ethically and operate successfully.

Part Five is called *Dents in the Universe* from a famous Steve Jobs talk about how entrepreneurs aspire to make their own mark on the world. This part includes examples of how entrepreneurs have applied the *Traits, Values,* and *Beliefs* to overcome the challenges that got in their way. It will also show how *The Entrepreneur Ethos* is relevant, necessary, and sufficient in a wide variety of real-world situations.

Along with successes, I have also included examples of times when entrepreneurs failed or strayed from the Ethos. These examples are used to emphasize the importance of holding ourselves to a higher standard. I chose these specific topics because they are easily identifiable and most readers will already have some knowledge about them.

I'm glad you have chosen to join me in this journey to explore what it means to be an entrepreneur. You will discover why it's important that the entrepreneur community have an Ethos—a set of guiding principles—to believe in, adhere to, and prosper from.

By holding ourselves to a high standard, we can not only create fantastic businesses but also better serve the communities in which we live in with honor and integrity. It is up to all of us to ensure that the entrepreneur culture is a positive force in the world and that our community is teaching the next generation of entrepreneurs how to behave ethically, how to benefit from the power of inclusion, and how to be resilient to the rapid pace of change.

I have also compiled my Source Notes in the back of this book, organized by chapter. I did this because I did not want to distract from the flow and narrative of the book by including footnotes. The sources of facts, figures, and stories should be clear from the source note descriptions—if not, my apologies.

To start our journey off on the right foot, I have put *The Entrepreneur Ethos* in the prologue. This will be our guide star as we explore the challenges entrepreneurs will face, the traits, values, and beliefs they must have and use to overcome those challenges, and the ways they can make their own dents in the universe.

Now, let's get after it!

Jarie Bolander
Silicon Valley
July 2017

PROLOGUE
The Entrepreneur Ethos

In today's world, there is a rare breed of person who challenges the status quo. This person pursues an idea with a zest and furor that rivals the greatest accomplishments of society. They have grit, tenacity, and confidence that all envy yet few will ever aspire to.

I am that person.

I take calculated risks to seek knowledge and to solve the world's problems. Through hustle and collaboration, I create something that has never existed before. I have unparalleled creativity, focused resolution, sound reasoning, and an unwavering self-belief in my ideas, even though the odds of success are small.

1. Failure is an option, but never the end result.

I demand integrity from my team and myself, no matter how tough a situation may be. All under my leadership are given equal and unbiased opportunities to succeed. I lead myself and my company so that everyone involved is safe from harassment, bullying, and exploitation. My word is my bond.

2. Integrity is my middle name.

I must always remain nimble and flexible. Markets will change, technologies will shift, and investors may not understand my vision. These challenges do not deter me, because I am self-aware enough to know that I don't always have all the answers.

3. Seeking the truth will guide my decisions.

I know that each day I must earn the loyalty, respect, and trust of my team and my community. Without them, my vision will never become reality. Although fame and fortune may come to me, I am not motivated by material things. At times, trying to change the world will be a lonely and difficult endeavor. There are rarely any Eureka Moments. I accept this as part of the life I have chosen. I do what I do to create an independent life that completes me.

4. The journey is my reward.

My goal is to make a positive difference in the world with my ideas and deeds. This is an honor that I take seriously. I will do this with aggressive actions, pure intentions, and a determination to never give up until my vision becomes a reality. When others look to me for guidance, I will step into the void and help make things happen.

5. Being an entrepreneur is an honor I must earn daily.

PART ONE
Challenging the Status Quo

The one undeniable truth that my entrepreneurial journey has taught me is that, no matter how much you prepare and how hard you work, challenges will constantly arise on a daily basis.

These challenges take many forms and may cause you to wonder whether you're actually running a company or just playing a game of whack-a-mole. Pushing against the status quo and trying to bring the world around to your point of view will continually pit you against these challenges. You will need to marshal all your resources to stay in the battle day-in and day-out to create a successful company.

The many ways that challenges present themselves are what we will tackle in the first part of *The Entrepreneur Ethos*. It's vital that before we can set off on the entrepreneurial journey, we need to know what we are up against.

The first challenge to the status quo we'll explore is you: the entrepreneur. This is the first battle all entrepreneurs face. Without first overcoming our own fears, uncertainties, and doubts, we won't ever have the courage to start and carry on our life's work. The rest of the challenges are presented in roughly the order you'll have to face them. Let's get started.

ONE

Yourself - The Struggle Within

"When there is no enemy within, the enemies outside cannot hurt you."
— Winston Churchill, former British Prime Minister

In his book *The War of Art*, Steven Pressfield writes of the struggles of the creative process and how "The Resistance" takes hold and sabotages the artist's ability to create. This "Resistance" is every excuse you can think of to not create and make progress. Entrepreneurs, the artists of the business world, face the same fate and must first overcome the challenges within themselves.

The entrepreneur's end goal is to create something that did not exist before. This drive to build a mere vision into a commercial success requires a lot from an entrepreneur. Making money is one of the major measuring sticks of entrepreneurial success and can lead to long nights of endless toil. This effort can raise serious questions about whether all the pain and suffering is worth it. This "struggle within" is the first challenge to the status quo every entrepreneur needs to face and overcome.

Joel Runyon, CEO of IMPOSSIBLE, knows a thing or two about the struggle to work on things that matter and what it takes to keep creating:

I feel that there is a grit or resilience factor that is needed to make an idea into reality. Any time you create a product or service, it's something ambitious. It's important to get up and try new things along the way. Keep trying new and different things. Keep going when things are not going well, even when you don't want to. If you don't do that, you'll be beaten every time.

Joel's advice to "keep going" is one aspect of believing in yourself. By and large the most problematic source of doubt is the little voice inside our heads. All entrepreneurs feel that inner doubt—no matter how successful they have become. That doubt manifests itself in thoughts like *"Am I good enough?"* or *"Is my idea good enough?"* and it can drive entrepreneurs to either succeed or stall. Compounding the problem is that entrepreneurs are never satisfied with what they have accomplished so far or might yet accomplish. They are always looking for the next challenge to overcome, even at the expense of stalling on a current one.

It's healthy to have a modest amount of internal dialog that questions your motivations, skills, direction, ideas, or techniques. What can be problematic and destructive is when those fears, uncertainties, and doubts rule your every waking moment. When those moments occur, Pressfield's "Resistance" is in full swing and can gnaw away at you to the point of madness.

Melissa Hanna, CEO of MCH Ventures, an entrepreneur in the online healthcare space, who has been an entrepreneur since she was 11, has a unique perspective on how to push past "The Resistance":

> An activist and an entrepreneur are closer than you might think. It's too simple to say that I wanted to make money because money never comes that easy. You can't be afraid of making money and doing good. You can have both if you realize that the love of money is the root of all evil and will drain you. That's why you have to have an activist mindset. The cause is always bigger than the individual, and that makes it easier to deal with the setbacks and struggles.

The entrepreneur as activist is an interesting concept. Entrepreneurs can choose to adopt an activist mindset to help them make the necessary changes happen. With this mindset entrepreneurs can then take their efforts to a higher level because the cause becomes greater than themselves.

All activists believe in the cause.

They fight for an idea.

They have a clear concept of how they want the world to look.

They have a solid *Why* (more on that in a second).

It's never easy for the activist or the entrepreneur. It's this idea of your idea being bigger than yourself that is one way to battle the internal struggles that will try to sabotage your efforts.

Activists, like entrepreneurs, have to fight against the never-ending current of challenges that will constantly be in their way. It's the ultimate fight against the status quo. Only through commitment, determination, and a true belief in the cause do they sustain enough stamina to move the needle forward. In some cases, it may take decades of effort to move the needle enough to make an impact. But when you believe in what you are doing and that belief transcends yourself, the wait for results becomes more tolerable.

Like an activist, the entrepreneur has to convince people to join the cause. As most people know, new causes are hard to get off the ground for the exact same reasons a new company is hard to start. What a movement or a new company needs is a great idea that leads to an overwhelming groundswell of support. It takes a critical mass of people to create a movement. This reality can compound the internal struggle since it's hard to think of yourself as charismatic enough to sway others, but sway others you must—starting with yourself.

The internal struggle every entrepreneur faces will overcome them in if they let it. Of course, external factors can always make the struggle hard, sometimes even impossible, but those challenges pale in comparison to the internal battle against yourself that never goes away, never sleeps, and is always lurking in the corner, ready to ruin your day.

The ultimate fear that entrepreneurs face shows itself in the one act, the one single moment, where it all comes together. This moment is the point where the internal struggle is the most intense. It's when the entrepreneur's courage is tested the most. The moment I'm talking about is shipping or launching your product.

When you ship, your creation is now ready for the world to see.

There is no place to hide.

No more excuses.

No more hiding.

To all entrepreneurs, that's downright scary—no matter how many companies or products they have launched.

In his book *Do the Work*, Steven Pressfield sums up why shipping is such a big deal:

> Why does Seth Godin [best-selling author and marketing genius] place so much emphasis on "shipping"?
>
> Because finishing is the critical part of any project. If we can't finish, all our work is for nothing.
>
> When we ship, we declare our stuff ready for prime time. We pack it in a FedEx box and send it out to the world. Our movie hits the screens, our smartphone

arrives in the stores [and] our musical opens on Broadway.

It takes balls of steel to ship.

Yes, it takes balls of steel to ship, because at that point you're vulnerable to the critics. They will waste no time jumping on every single flaw, every pixel that is off, every typo, or every product issue. Get past all that and you'll be able to overcome the struggle within more often than not.

Chris Klundt, CEO and founder of StudyBlue, an entrepreneur in the education space, has an interesting approach to the attitudes it takes to fight the struggle within and play the entrepreneur game:

> You have to be naive. Actually, stupid or even childlike. You have to be able to say, "I can go do something and disrupt the world." If my 22-year-old self knew it would take ten years to be successful, I'm not sure I would do it, but now I can't see myself doing anything else.

Doing the work along with a level of childlike naiveté will go a long way to quieting the inner demons. It's this level of commitment that allows entrepreneurs to ship, but that's not enough.

The inner demons will always be there. They will chip away at your confidence. They will strike when you are at your lowest point. That's why it's vital to have a strong *Why*. A strong *Why* will be a powerful weapon against the naysayers in your head and out in the world who will tell you that your idea is a fool's errand.

Your *Why* is the internal reason you are doing what you are doing. It's independent of the fame or fortune that may be bestowed upon you. It's your internal compass. It's something that needs to transcend the external world and be for you and only you.

It's vital to understand how you're making the decision in your life to pursue the particular path you choose. It's your *Why* that guides your decisions.

Have a solid *Why* and you can slay any dragon.

In order to formulate your *Why*, you need to take a look at your motivations.

There are two types of motivation: intrinsic (internal) and extrinsic (external). Can you guess which one is the most important? I'll give you a hint. The most important type of motivation is one that you control.

Intrinsic motivation is your inner drive to complete a task. It's a motivation that does not change with the changing external world you find yourself in—thus the reason it's under your control. Extrinsic motivation comes from rewards that are out of your direct control. Things like fame, fortune, praise, company profit, or getting an investment. Those are all great but, again, out of your control.

As an entrepreneur, you have to have a higher purpose. Your *Why* has to be something that drives you and your team to get things done even when the going gets tough.

When things get challenging, those extrinsic motivators can fade away since they are distant, fleeting, and, again, out of your control. If your primary motivation for starting a company depends on those extrinsic motivators, then your self-determination will dwindle. Entrepreneurship is full of struggles and challenges that can only be overcome with a strong *Why* to find a solution even when the obstacles are great.

Determining your *Why* can be tricky since a lot of us think we know why we do things, but in reality, our motivations are a mix of ego and pride with some altruistic motivations thrown in for good measure.

The best way I have found to determine your *Why* is to ask yourself the aptly named "5 Whys" series of questions. This is a common technique to get to the root cause of an issue. The theory goes that you keep asking why until you can't ask why anymore. Once you get to the last why, that's your *Why*. Let me give you an example.

Question: I want to form Lab Sensor Solutions to solve the problem of preventing perishable items from spoiling.

Why #1: Spoiled perishable items waste time and money.

Why #2: If a patient is given a spoiled item, it could lead to complications. Complications waste time and money and are a potential liability issue. I have seen this firsthand.

Why #3: Spoiled perishables are not as effective and it's hard to know what is spoiled or not spoiled. My wife Jane was subjected to this when she was being treated for leukemia.

Why #4: There is no inexpensive way to monitor perishables.

Why #5: No one has yet spent the time and resources to make a solution that works both economically and systematically.

Within the "5 Whys" you can see a lot of reasons to intrinsically want to solve this problem, including preventing patients from getting sicker. From this exercise, I can then form my *Why*:

> I feel that monitoring perishable items can save lives and also save money. I know this because when my wife Jane was going through her leukemia treatment, I saw firsthand the mistakes made. This made me realize that I had the talent and opportunity to make a big impact. This realization drives me every day to solve the problem of how spoiled perishables are negatively impacting the lives of patients.

Your *Why* needs to be inside you so that it cannot go away. This is important because, when "The Resistance" pays you a visit, the temptation to regress back to drinking bad corporate coffee will be strong.

A strong *Why* will resist this self-doubt and will allow it to pass.

Entrepreneurship is a way of life. If you don't enjoy the journey, the goals are meaningless. That's why entrepreneurs like Elon Musk, Mark Zuckerberg, Larry Ellison, and Reed Hastings, who have each made billions, continue to get up every day and grind it out on the next new thing.

It's the journey and not the destination that's important, which sounds like a cliché, but it's absolutely true.

The struggle within is the scariest part of being an entrepreneur. That's why building a strong *Why* will benefit you greatly. This struggle within oneself always needs to be respected because it will manifest as that voice in your head that keeps saying "stop" when things get tough. This is the first barrier to success every entrepreneur will face. It will prevent you from persevering if you let it. We'll explore later how the traits, values, and beliefs of entrepreneurs can help you slay this struggle within.

TWO

Friends and Family –
The Company You Keep

"How delightful to find a friend in everyone."
— Joseph Brodsky, poet

Once you get past the doubts within yourself or at least come to terms with them, your friends and family will be your next barrier to success. I have never met an entrepreneur who has not asked friends and family for advice or money. It's part of the vetting process all good entrepreneurs use. If your wacky idea can't get money or a "that's a great idea" from a close friend or your rich aunt Betty, then it might not be worth doing.

Friends and family will always be a mixed bag. They have an emotional vested interest in your success or failure. In some cases, friends and family might even try to dissuade you from taking the risk of starting your own company, unless they are as crazy as you are. Then, watch out, they might ask *you* for money.

Jonathan Shih, CEO of Decisive Health and an entrepreneur in the digital health space, sums up the conflict and the responsibility:

Friends and family are essential to making your company successful. My dad always wanted to go to grad school then start a company, but he had to support his family. So, in a sense, I'm living his dream and don't want to let him down.

Jonathan's experience is a common one. The mix of legacy and money can create a sense of duty and tension in a friend or family relationship. There is usually a large emotional investment that friends and family put into a founder.

These investments range from the simple to the complex. The simple could be an encouraging word, an intro to a company, or a late-night call. The complex could be financial support, sacrificing vacations, or even working to support you.

All these investments will take their toll on a relationship if expectations are not set ahead of time. Entrepreneurship is beyond a full-time job—it's a lifestyle that everyone involved has to agree to. And I would even venture to say that any such agreement between friends and family should be written down. That way, there is no debate about what is expected.

Eric Eggers, an entrepreneur in the healthcare industry, knows that it takes buy-in from everyone in your life to have a shot at being a successful entrepreneur:

If you want to go down an entrepreneurial path, you need to get buy-in from your friends and family because they will be by your side during all the ups and downs of doing a startup. If they don't realize that they will also have to sacrifice, it's going to create a lot of tension. Buy-in matters a lot.

It's true that buy-in matters and, in order to get buy-in, you need to not be afraid to work at it. An important thing to consider is that friends and family may not understand why you want to risk a safe job to pursue some crazy idea. Their doubts may manifest by putting fear, uncertainty, and doubt in your head, even if you think you have them convinced.

The struggle to launch a company will go through many highs and lows. It's at both the high and low points where the support of dedicated friends and family will be the most critical. It's at these times where your mettle as an entrepreneur will be tested—even during good times. Let me explain.

During good times, everyone will be excited and confident that you'll be one of the lucky ones. The truth is, the good times are often when major mistakes happen, and these can amplify the bad times. The expectations set during good times can come back to haunt you during bad times, and cause questions like "Didn't you say when you hit X revenue, that you would get paid more?" or "Can we now take a vacation?" or "How come you are taking another pay cut?" These are tough conversations to have.

All these good-time expectations need to be set and managed beforehand or your friends and family will start to doubt you. Once doubt sets in, it will be harder and harder to convince them your idea is a winner. This will chip away at your motivation in all sorts of ways.

Dale Beerman, CEO of Pacifica, a company that helps people cope with stress and anxiety, has some great advice on setting expectations:

> Know that it's going to be slog. Be in it for the long term and not to get rich quick because it will never happen. Be honest with your family about how hard it will be. Manage expectations. Be open when things go bad and go well. Your family is a big part of your team.

One thing that founders often overlook is Dale's astute observation that "your family is a big part of your team."

No one else will be with you through all the evolutions that your company may take. Your family will have a front-row seat to the drama of pivots, payroll challenges, direction changes, frustrations with co-founders, and the growing pains of hiring people. Treating them as key advisors will make the journey much more enjoyable and manageable. Leave them out at your peril.

Of course, not all friends and family are equal. We all have certain family or friends that we look to for advice. These trusted advisors will make up our Kitchen Cabinet and form the foundation from which we will make decisions. These are the ones to get buy-in from.

Arry Yu, an entrepreneur from Seattle, wrote in an April 2016 *Huffington Post* piece about what her mother taught her about business:

> My mother used to say that most people don't work as hard as they can—so if you always give your best, you'll beat out most people in whatever you want to do. Hard work means you'll get better each time and accomplish something you're proud of. Without hard work, you'll end up with regrets. Whatever you do—from work to friendships to marriage—give it your all.

Arry's experience makes an important point about the people you surround yourself with. First, your friends and family are your first line of mentors, coaches, and role models. You look to them to show you how to handle situations. These people will help and bolster you when things get tough. If they don't believe in you, then it's harder for both them and you, and the challenge to succeed increases. Remember that it will take a lot of hard work and effort to get them onboard and keep them on your team.

My own family does not understand why I choose to be an entrepreneur over a safe corporate job. This primarily comes from my dad since he spent his entire career (33 years) working for United Airlines. Ironically, he was retired early in the aftermath of 9/11—so much for a "safe" corporate job. My mom is the same way. She worked at a big company and just cashed a paycheck. My brothers have a similar attitude and both work for local governments. If you can't tell, I'm the black sheep of the family.

There will be entrepreneurs who don't have supportive family or encouraging friends. Overcoming that will take much more effort. Worse yet, actively unsupportive friends and family can lead to a host of frustrations, including isolation, self-doubt, and a lack of motivation. If you don't have support, you will need to get it from somewhere, like other entrepreneurs, mentors, teachers, and coaches. You, like every other successful entrepreneur, will need others—people who believe in your vision, encourage you to explore it, and help you keep the flame alive.

THREE

Talent - Finding the Crazy Ones

"United We Stand, Divided We Fall."
— Aesop, Greek fabulist

Once you overcome the struggle within and get buy-in from your friends and family, it's time to find the crazy ones who will join you on this long, strange trip called building a company. It's time to find some talent.

Talent is the single most important factor in determining the success of a startup. It even trumps your original idea, because many startups will pivot away from that over time. Don't believe me? Here are some examples.

Twitter started out as a podcasting company and pivoted to 140-character updates.

Flickr started out as an online game and is now a photo sharing website.

Nintendo started out as a playing card company and is now a game console company.

The list goes on and on.

Those pivots were successful because the team that came up with the original idea was talented enough to realize it was not going to work or there was an even better idea to pursue. That's an important skill and here is why.

Out of all the things that could go wrong in a startup, the number one reason a startup fails is due to founder conflicts. *CNN Money* put it perfectly in a 2014 article:

> In fact, 65% of high-potential startups fail as a result of conflict among co-founders, according to Noam Wasserman, a professor at Harvard Business School who studied 10,000 founders for his book, *The Founder's Dilemma*. Pairs and groups bring a variety of skills, but there is also more potential for conflict—over leadership, money, strategy, credit, and blame.

Can you see now why finding the right talent is so important?

Sixty-five percent is a huge number, and that's only with co-founders. Just image when you throw in bringing employees onboard. Those co-founder conflicts will seep into the hearts and minds of the employees who are working hard to bring your vision into reality. It's a founder's worst nightmare, yet it can't be easily fixed by just not having co-founders—more on that in a second.

Jason Cohen, founder and CTO of WPEngine, has a similar take on Professor Wasserman's, but with a twist:

There are well-understood traits of entrepreneurs. Determined. Gritty. Hubris. In retrospect, you can't always tell the difference between success and failure. It's not true that everyone should be an entrepreneur. Some may be more fulfilled just staying in the corporate cocoon.

This brings us back to the "challenge of yourself" chapter. When you are picking talent for your startup, start with yourself. Ensure that you are actually up to the task, and not doing it just to chase the dream of becoming the next Elon Musk.

The natural next question is whether to just go it alone and avoid the hassles of hiring talent in the first place. That's not a good idea either since it's also known that startups with single founders tend to fail more often. Why, you may ask?

There are many variables that need to go right to succeed. Most of us are not ten out of ten in each one of the traits, values, and beliefs of successful entrepreneurs. We'll go into more depth later about all three. As a result, we'll need others to fill in the gaps.

Investors know this and that's why most want a company to have more than one co-founder. Investors will want to size up the founders, the team, and the company they keep.

Los Angeles-based venture capitalist (VC) Mark Suster sums up the criteria he looks for in a founder in a May 2016 piece on his blog, *Both Sides of the Table*:

As a starting point, I have to believe the founder has the attributes of an entrepreneur that matter most to me: tenacity, resiliency, inspiration, perspiration, attention-to-detail, competitiveness, decisiveness, risk tolerance and integrity.

I have to believe the founder is cost-focused, mission-driven, and aligned on cultural values with me, which mostly relates to integrity and how to treat other people.

Wise words indeed!

It's easy to get lured into an enterprise with a brilliant asshole founder with a record of success. It's tempting to overlook those personality issues and crass attitudes towards underlings and just charge ahead. Given Professor Wasserman's findings and Mark Suster's advice that would be a big mistake.

People make a company.

The right people make a great company.

Choosing the wrong people will make it harder to recruit others and more challenging to build a world-class company. Why make an already challenging task even harder?

Of course, this is easier said than done. It's always going to be a challenge to get along with any group of people under stressful circumstances. Humans are often messy, irrational, emotional, selfish, and sometimes mean. We as a species have complex emotions that can get in the way, especially when under intense pressure to perform. That's why it's important that entrepreneurs act with integrity to earn the trust and respect of their teams daily—an important part of *The Entrepreneur Ethos.*

Geoff Zawolkow, CEO of Lab Sensor Solutions, sums up how he approaches building his team:

> The most important aspect to get right is working style. Your team has to have a compatible work style or all sorts of problems can occur. Of course, everyone has to be able to do the job, but the way they do the job matters as well. Teams with incompatible work styles will have more conflict.

Geoff's advice makes a lot of sense. You must realize that a fast-paced startup environment is going to create tensions that will test each person on the team. Throw in work style differences and miscommunications are bound to happen. These miscommunications can lead to infighting and wrong assumptions that make it hard to zig and zag when conditions change.

It's tempting to jump right into an awesome idea with a smart team of people. I did that with one of the companies I formed to create a technology that would track all the blood tubes in the world. We had over 20 "founders" and this made it that much more challenging to manage. We had to fire one founder because of work style and direction differences. It was clear early on that this person was not a fit yet we chose to ignore it. This led to a lot of tension and even a coup attempt. Thankfully, with some cool and calm management discussions, we averted an ugly situation.

That last point is an important one. Too often, a young startup team only wants to hire technical doers and neglects to secure the needed management skills to keep the whole thing together. It's a common trap to fall into, even for successful companies like Google.

Google has had to change the way it evaluates candidates and manages their teams. Google was famous for experimenting with completely eliminating middle management. This threw the entire company into disarray. What Google finally figured out was that managers were as important as team composition.

Project Aristotle was a research project that Google took on to figure out how to build the perfect group. The researchers noticed two behaviors that all the good teams generally shared:

> First, on the good teams, members spoke in roughly the same proportion, a phenomenon the researchers referred to as "equality in distribution of conversational turn-taking."

> Second, the good teams all had high "average social sensitivity"—a fancy way of saying they were skilled at intuiting how others felt based on their tone of voice, their expressions, and other nonverbal cues.

These studies and experiences highlight the importance of choosing your co-founders and initial employees with caution. The challenge of resolving employee issues and changing hearts and minds once you get going will make it that much harder to succeed. This reality even transcends an important metric like salary.

Talent wants to make an impact and do interesting work that challenges them. No amount of money can fix that. Waymo found that out the hard way.

Waymo is a self-driving car company that is part of Alphabet (parent company of Google). Back in 2009, it was started as the Google Self-Driving Car Project and has racked up over two million self-driving miles.

So it was a shock when top employees started fleeing Waymo in droves when it spun out in December of 2016.

The answer as to why may surprise you.

It turns out that Google put in some stellar incentives to make the self-driving car a reality. These incentives, according to a February 2017 *Bloomberg* article, backfired:

> Early staffers had an unusual compensation system that awarded super-sized payouts based on the project's value. By late 2015, the numbers were so big that several veteran members didn't need the job security anymore, making them more open to other

opportunities, according to people familiar with the situation. Two people called it "F-you money."

Let me explain what F-you money means. F-you money is the amount of money you need to tell the company, "F-you, I'm outta here." This may surprise some of you since you might wonder why people wouldn't continue to stick around for those super-sized paydays.

In the Waymo case, the answer was that key people were frustrated with the lack of progress. For entrepreneurial people, this is a fate worse than death because lack of progress means their vision is not being realized. Couple that with a legitimate way out to go try something better and you get a mass exodus of talented people with pockets full of F-you money.

Waymo's talent time bomb illustrates the perfect storm of figuring out how to attract and retain top talent. Most new ventures won't have the Waymo problem with too much pay. Rather, they will more likely run into the too little pay problem. As John Gruber over at Daring Fireball puts it in a February 2017 blog post:

> Talent retention is one of the hardest problems in the whole industry. Pay employees too little and they'll leave. Pay them too much and they'll leave. And if they get bored, they'll leave.

The secret to the whole pay problem is to pay your talent fairly and according to market conditions. It's also important to always be open and honest with how the company is progressing. There should never be any surprises.

As an entrepreneur, talent attraction and retention will be a constant struggle. There are no easy answers, yet it's the most important thing to get right.

Finding the crazy ones who will join your startup is a mix of having interesting things to work on, being paid fairly, making progress, and having a sense that what they're creating will change the world. That's why it's vital to act with integrity and earn the respect of your team daily. It's the easiest thing within your control that you have to offer.

FOUR

Technology – Then Magic Happens

"Any sufficiently advanced technology is indistinguishable
from magic."
— Arthur C. Clark, science fiction writer

So far, we have confronted our self-doubts, made the case to
our friends and family that our idea is good, and are on the
lookout for some talent. The next challenge to the status quo
is figuring out if your idea is technically feasible. To put it
another way, it's now time to overcome the challenge of "is
your idea just science fiction?" or "does it have a chance to
become science fact?"

All companies rely on technology and it's vital that the right
technology is picked to solve a problem. A lot of time is spent
looking at high-tech solutions, but low-tech solutions can be
just as important. As an entrepreneur, you need to look at
both because if you pick the wrong technology, you'll never
get over the finish line.

Companies in Silicon Valley are inundated with all sorts of
timesaving, crush-your-competitors, sign-up-for-our-free-trial
technologies that come and go with the San Francisco Bay
tides. It can be daunting to pick the right technology stack to
make your business thrive. So hard, in fact, that a company

called Stackshare allows you to see what all the best companies use all in one place. At the time of this writing, there are thousands of stacks with thousands of pieces of software to choose from. A stack, for those of you who don't know, is the set of software pieces that you put together to build your product or service. For a new startup trying to figure out how to build a new software solution, it's daunting.

This drive to assemble and/or create the best technology to solve problems is critical. Despite the availability of building blocks, this quest for technology dominance is rife with fits and starts. Choose the wrong path and the future of your company could be in jeopardy, but that's not the whole story. Sometimes other things get in the way.

Kodak was the Google of its day. Founded in 1880, it dominated the camera and film business. By 1976 Kodak accounted for 90% of the film and 85% of the camera sales in America. But by 2011 it had filed Chapter 11 bankruptcy. By 2012 they announced that they would only focus on the corporate digital imaging market.

At its peak, Kodak employed over 140,000 employees and had a high stock price over $90. Today Kodak's stock is in the mid-teens and employees hover around 5,000. What on earth happened?

Digital photography happened.

Ironically, Kodak had invented the digital camera back in 1975, but did nothing with it.

So why did Kodak drop the ball on the single biggest innovation in photography since, well, photography? Like all blunders in history, hindsight is 20/20.

Speculation suggests that Kodak did not realize what it had in the digital camera. Furthermore, its myopic management vision, focused on the high-profit film business, could not get out of its own way. Yet Kodak had the opportunity to catch back up later, but chose not to take its "Kodak moment." Love that slogan!

Steve Brachmann from IPWatch did a fantastic write-up of the demise of Kodak and why being vigilant on not only technology but also its application is more than just science:

> Addicted to the profits generated by its 35mm film, Kodak would do nothing that it saw as endangering the success of this business. A lack of early investment in digital photography during the 1970s brought a double-whammy during the 1990s, as the giant corporation was not only laid low by smaller firms like Sony and Canon, but the entire film photography industry created by the company was finally relegated to second-class status behind digital by the 2000s.

Classic innovator's dilemma—nimble upstarts disrupt the low end (since digital was not as good as film) and eats away at the high end. However, that was not when the fall started. It actually happened much sooner with a bunch of unfortunate blunders in choosing which technologies to invest in. Back to Mr. Brachmann's piece:

> Digital photography as the sole reason for Kodak's failures makes a good story [but] it was not the first major technological disruption in the company's history. Instant photography had been invented by 1950 and Polaroid was able to develop the cameras needed to capture this segment of the market.
>
> Throughout the 1980s, a major shift in the film market was sparked by Japanese photography company Fujifilm, which was able to sell mass-produced film to huge retailers like Wal-Mart for a price less than Kodak's film, a move which dramatically undercut Kodak's profits.

The challenge for any company, be it a startup or an established one, is to analyze the technology trends and invest in those that will make you successful. Those investments need to align to your core competency or failure is inevitable, as Mr. Brachmann explains:

> In 1988 Kodak paid $5.1 billion to acquire American pharmaceutical company, Sterling Drug. The company hoped to utilize its [Kodak] expertise in chemical engineering to create drugs with high profit margins, but lacked the ability and resources to apply that knowledge in creating patented pharmaceuticals or extremely cheap generic medications. Kodak dismantled the Sterling operations and sold off the remainder of their pharmaceutical business for less than $3 billion only six years after acquiring Sterling.

Kodak is one example of how an early innovator can stumble when faced with a technological disruption. It's true that Kodak had a pretty good run. It's been around over 100 years. Still, for anyone who needs technology to be successful, Kodak is a cautionary tale to choose wisely and align that technology to your core values.

Kodak could have done a lot of things and the results might have been different. What we can learn from Kodak is that, no matter how good you think your technology lead is, someone will disrupt you. Chances are the disrupter will be a startup that's better, faster, and cheaper.

The speed of innovation is increasing at a rapid rate. Companies that were startups a mere 10 or 15 years ago are now being disrupted. Take Google, for example.

Google did not invent search—it perfected it. Recall that Alta Vista was one of the leaders in search when Google hit the scene. Even Yahoo was ahead of them. In fact, Yahoo could have bought both Google and Facebook yet they chose to blaze a trail on their own—that's a whole other book in itself.

What I'm getting at is if you were to look at search now, there would be no way you could ever imagine that Google would or could be disrupted. How could it? It has a huge lead and is the *de facto* verb for looking something up on the internet. But why did Google form Alphabet and branch out into home automation (Nest), robots (Boston Dynamics), and self-driving cars (Waymo)? Simple.

Search is maturing and, as a growth market, slowing. Upstarts like DuckDuckGo are capturing users who want anonymous search—something Google has, but which completely disrupts its AdSense-based revenue model, which relies on knowing your search history. To some, including me, being tracked on the internet is a double-edged sword of convenience and concern. For Google, their argument for tracking you is: How can you serve up a targeted ad if you don't track what a particular user is searching for? Answer: You can't. But privacy advocates would say, tough. Figure it out.

Social media companies like Facebook are starting to see technologies that will disrupt them if they don't change with the times. Messaging and the use of chatbots (automatic ways to answer user queries—think customer support phone tree, but in a browser) are now creating opportunities that were not there two years ago, and finding better and cheaper ways to interact with customers.

In an April 2016 article, *Forbes* described what messaging means to CMOs (Chief Marketing Officers):

> More important for brands, think mobile. Overall, mobile usage passed desktop usage in 2014 and its lead continues to grow. At the same time, brands in the West have struggled to advertise effectively in mobile, where 50% of all ad taps appear accidentally. And they fare little better with commerce. By one often-cited study, mobile shopping cart abandonment rates top 97%.

Forbes makes an important point that a company needs to look beyond its home market to see where the trends may be coming from to disrupt its technology. No other technology has shown that like mobile messaging.

Messaging apps such as Facebook Messenger, WhatsApp, Line, and SnapChat dominate mobile, currently accounting for six of the top ten most used apps globally. In China, apps have also evolved into powerful brand and commerce tools. There, 50% of all e-commerce occurs on a phone or tablet, with messaging apps accounting for a big percentage of transactions. For example, apps like WeChat also double as a mobile payments system. This makes apps a one-stop app for doing everything from booking a ticket, hailing a cab, buying a car, and getting a loan.

Over time, I'm sure some new-fangled technology startup will come out and change the way we live, work, or recreate. Kind of like SnapChat is starting to do right now.

SnapChat provides a mobile experience where you can send Snaps (short videos) to friends that then disappear once you view them. They invented the means of putting all sorts of filters on these Snaps so you can look like a cat or a dog or have a crown of flowers on your head. I honestly don't get it, but what do I know? I did not get Facebook at first either. I think that's why it's important to look at what SnapChat and other messaging apps are disrupting. To me, it's the social media noise in your "feed." With messaging apps you can curate your interactions and see only what you want to see.

That's a powerful feature that disrupts the whole social media paradigm, which relies on those feeds for ad revenue.

All of the companies we discussed had a moment where they got all the pieces just right. Once this happened, then science fiction became science fact. That's why it's important to be open-minded, collaborate with others, and seek the truth about the dynamics of technology—you just never know what crazy idea may just be the next Uber, Facebook, or Amazon.

FIVE

Technique - Practice Makes Perfect

"The most perfect technique is that which is not noticed at
all."
— Pablo Casals, cellist

Talent and technology are not enough to be successful, since
it's the application of both that brings great ideas to life.
That's why the techniques you use will play such an important
role. By techniques, I'm referring to things like your product
development process, hiring process, and go-to-market
strategy—all the things that apply talent and technology to
the problem you are trying to solve.

Entrepreneurs usually overlook technique. Most fall in love
with their product so much that all the rest of it becomes
"boring stuff" that gets little or no attention. That is a recipe
for disaster and is a major challenge to overcome. Out of all
the challenges we have covered so far, this one sneaks up on
you and can be deadly. Webvan is a great example of this.

Webvan was one of the high-flying internet startups of the
2000s. Its demise is a case study on how not to scale. Many
business schools feel that Webvan's downfall was their rush to
go public. Yet, others feel that it could be attributed to
building their own infrastructure from scratch and rolling it

out in too many places all at once. Using different techniques is fine if you have figured out your product market fit, but was too much for Webvan to handle. In my mind, Webvan's demise came because back then, it was not common to shop online for most things. This made it hard to convince shoppers that online shopping was both safe and convenient. Without the critical mass of shoppers being "trained" to shop on line, it was hard to attract new customers. A better technique would have been to partner with a local grocery store chain until they gained market traction.

Grocery home delivery is still a good idea. Instacart and Postmates have been successful by using stores as their warehouse. Plated, Blue Apron, and Luke's Local (in San Francisco) have their own warehouses and ship directly to consumers. So far, these techniques have proven to be a lot more scalable. Only time will tell if one of these will enable a particular company to win the home delivery market.

Chris Klundt, CEO and founder of StudyBlue, an entrepreneur in the education space, knows that technique starts with the "boring stuff":

> For me, I see it as the struggle to do the work on your desk. The boring stuff is the challenge. Get it done. Get through your stack of stuff to do and that will go a long way to success and quelling the internal debates about whether you can do it. 90% of the time, success is getting through the stack on your desk.

Do the boring stuff and things will get done. It always seems to be that the grind of a startup is all about the little things.

A feature here.

A deal there.

A better way to deploy.

A little more yield.

A better way to on-board customers.

Yes, it's the little details that matter, yet most entrepreneurs want to chase after the fun, world-changing stuff.

Technique is an often overlooked aspect of how a company functions. Magic does not happen by stocking the lunchroom with free food, providing all the coffee you can drink, and hanging some inspiring art from Hugh MacLeod (Gapingvoid inspirational cartoons). The chaos of a startup needs structure and, dare I say, process.

Yes, process is important even at a startup.

Process forms the basis of technique because your overall strategy on how you build your company is built on the processes that each of your departments use.

Process could be that dirty little word that convinced you to shed the corporate chainmail and venture off into the entrepreneurial forest to slay the market dragon, along with your wit and wisdom, of course. Good for you. Let's hope your name is not Don Quixote.

I jest, but I do want to make a point.

Even if you don't have a process written down even if you don't need TPS reports even if your organizational structure is as flat as the famous Woodside, CA, Bucks short stack, realize that you need to have process. Those processes build into techniques and that is how you build a company, and not end up tilting at windmills. The sooner you realize that, and get your team on the same page, the better.

No other business exemplifies the importance of technique more than the hospitality business. Entrepreneurs can learn a lot from how a hotel is run.

Catherine Bartolomei-Smith, who started and runs a worldwide, top-rated hotel in northern California, understands the importance of technique:

> We understood from minute one that we are the best in the world and we executed towards that. We are only 25 rooms yet rank top against big hotels worldwide. We get the People's Choice award all the time. We have been so consistent because we communicate expectations. We build on that and learn from it.

We have a clear vision of who we are and what we want to be. Core values are our guest experience. Snapshots of perfection are what we strive for. You can't have a nick in a wall. Every moment has to be perfect. Attention to detail is paramount. It has to be perfect all the time and we strive for that every minute of every day.

A few things stick out of Catherine's experience that all entrepreneurs can learn from.

The first is "we communicate expectations." This is critical because the team has to know what standards they need to adhere to. These expectations set the framework for how work gets done. Your company has to have clear and consistent expectations. Without that, the hope that any old technique will get the job done is false. This is what is meant by the passage in the Ethos that reads:

I know that each day, I must earn the loyalty, respect, and trust of my team and my community.

Communicating expectations will bring you a long way in accomplishing all three of these traits.

The second is "it has to be perfect all the time and we strive for that every minute of every day." This is a clear and concise expectation in order for Catherine's business to be successful. It's this standard by which her business is measured. This will dictate the techniques she and her staff will use to make the customer experience wonderful. The same goes for any business—set a standard and always strive for it.

What this all means is that all companies need to master the processes and techniques that will lead them to success. Choosing the right structure, as well as the tools and procedures to be productive, is essential. In the end, the best techniques are the ones the whole team is in agreement with and allow you to accomplish the goals you set out to achieve.

Don't just think that, once you set up your techniques, things won't change. They will and do all the time. That's why the belief of flexibility, which we will discuss later on, is such a vital one to have.

Jason Cohen, founder and CTO of WPEngine, explains why techniques change over time:

> The challenges are difficult and there are no silver bullets when you go from startup to scale to growth. Communications and our own scale are our own worst nightmares. We have to produce new stuff. We have to always be innovative. You will have to change the second you start to scale. You have to be innovative and scale so that you don't eat your own lunch. Sustaining growth and innovation requires a whole different set of skills and techniques.

Jason's comment on "from startup to scale to growth" is the fundamental challenge for techniques, since the skillset to start is different than it is to scale than it is to grow.

Techniques will change as your company grows, pivots, or runs into competitors. The challenge entrepreneurs face is when and how to change.

Change too fast and the company can slip into chaos.

Change too slow and competitors will eat you for breakfast.

The high wire act that the entrepreneur performs has little margin for error. Adopting and mastering the techniques you need will make success a little easier. This is why "seeking the truth will guide my decisions" is an important part of the Ethos.

So, the real question is what techniques should you focus on?

The simple answer is focus on those that will generate the most revenue with the least amount of cost. The reason I say it this way is that, more often than not, entrepreneurs want to focus on the next shiny new market or mega-feature at the expense of making what they have now profitable. Put another way, look at what you are spending the most time on to generate revenue and figure out if there is a better way to do it.

Salesforce did this really well when they moved a traditional on-premise service to a completely web-based service. They realized that all those customer installations were cumbersome and costly. Why not just have servers that your customers access via the web? That changed the whole software business model forever and Software as a Service (SaaS) was born.

In reality, the same team that started the business will either get replaced or augmented with "adult supervision" once the business starts to grow. That can be challenging for entrepreneurs to accept. It even has a name—the founder's dilemma.

Coined by Noam Wasserman in a February 2008 *Harvard Business Review* article of the same name, the founder's dilemma asks the simple question: When should a founder leave?

The data that Noam cites shows an interesting trend that, given our rock star worship of successful founder-CEOs, is not really talked about:

> Successful CEO-cum-founders are a very rare breed. When I analyzed 212 American startups that sprang up in the late 1990s and early 2000s, I discovered that most founders surrendered management control long before their companies went public. By the time the ventures were three years old, 50% of founders were no longer the CEO; in year four, only 40% were still in the corner office; and fewer than 25% led their companies' initial public offerings. Other researchers have subsequently found similar trends in various industries and in other time periods. We remember the handful of founder-CEOs in corporate America, but they're the exceptions to the rule.

Noam's observations are a cautionary tale for entrepreneurs who think that they and they alone can get the company they founded past the finish line. Of course, most founders will never say that they lack the skills to scale. In fact, most will fight tooth and nail to make sure they keep control of their company, even if it's not in their best interests, as Noam highlights further down:

> Many entrepreneurs are overconfident about their prospects and naive about the problems they will face. For instance, in 1988, Purdue University strategy scholar Arnold Cooper and two colleagues asked 3,000 entrepreneurs two simple questions: "What are the odds of your business succeeding?" and "What are the odds of any business like yours succeeding?" Founders claimed that there was an 81% chance, on average, that they would succeed but only a 59% probability of success for other ventures like their own. In fact, 80% of the respondents pegged their chances of success at least 70%—and one in three claimed their likelihood of success was 100%.

To put those numbers in perspective, the actual success rate for entrepreneurs (i.e., growing a business to one billion dollars) hovers around 1%, according to CBInsights. Clearly a disconnect, but confidence is certainly an important trait to have, which we will explore later on.

Techniques are all the processes, procedures, and standards that you and your company need to execute to get things done. It's a continuum that shifts over time and over the stages the company passes through. Be diligent in recognizing when you and your team might need to change techniques or change talent—both of which can and will happen.

The most important thing to remember about techniques is that it takes practice to pick and perfect the ones that will work. It's much better to try, fail, innovate, and iterate than to get stuck in the same old procedural rut wondering why you're not moving. This ability to remain nimble and flexible in learning how processes and techniques must evolve is how entrepreneurs can keep successfully bobbing and weaving in the shifting business landscape.

SIX

Timing – Missed It by That Much

"Better three hours too soon than a minute too late."
— William Shakespeare, poet

The magic elixir of talent, technology, and technique is hard to get right, yet it's essential when challenging the status quo to get your product to market. The next equally important "t" is timing, which is almost always out of your control. It's often timing that ultimately determines if your brilliant idea will get market traction, as we will soon see.

AltaVista, launched in 1994, was the first natural language search engine for web pages. Back then, less than 14% of U.S. adults used the internet. By the time Google came around in 1998, 36% of U.S. adults were on the internet and the growth was accelerating. What Google got right and AltaVista got wrong was, either by luck or design, the timing of a search tool that gave relevant results. Not surprisingly, it turns out that relevant results are the magic for search since those add the most value for the end user. And timing matters too, a lot. Have you heard from AltaVista lately?

No idea, no matter how good or innovative, will be successful if there is no market for it. Even more important than a market is market timing. Timing can make or break an idea or a company. Even well-established companies can fall victim to market timing if they don't respect how fast a market can evolve. Time is never on your side. A perfect example of not respecting timing, among other things, is Blockbuster.

Blockbuster was a powerhouse in the video industry. As a kid, I loved going to Blockbuster with my family to rent a couple of movies for the weekend. It was fun to browse all the new titles and fight with my two brothers about which movie we got to play first. The good old days of "be kind and rewind."

At its peak in 2004, Blockbuster had about 60,000 employees and over 9,000 stores yet, six years later, it filed for bankruptcy. What happened?

Netflix happened.

Started in 1998 by Reed Hastings, Netflix was created because Hastings was an unsatisfied Blockbuster customer. Back then, most did not take Netflix seriously, including Blockbuster, because who would not want to browse for videos with the family on a Friday night or, God forbid, wait for a movie to be shipped to you? It seemed like a niche that would never take off until you look a little deeper into how Blockbuster was making money.

It turns out that Blockbuster earned a tremendous amount of money from late fees, and that was its Achilles heel. Making money off of penalizing your customers will iritate them. A disgruntled customer will look for an alternative to solve their problem, and that's exactly what Netflix offered. Simply put, Blockbuster penalized a customer's lack of time to return a movie—Netflix did not.

Netflix offered several advantages for customers. The biggest one was that you could keep a movie as long as you wanted without any annoying late fees. Netflix even gave you pre-addressed return mailers to make it super easy. Compare that to Blockbuster that made over 20% of their profits on late fees, and the timing was ripe for Netflix to crush Blockbuster by giving customers back their time.

On top of no late fees, Netflix's selection was much larger and you ordered at home online and not out at some crowded store. The most important feature, though, was that movies were delivered right to your door. This was a precursor to today's on-demand economy that we now have all grown accustomed to.

The timing of these features was not popular at first. Waiting a couple of days to get your movies took some getting used to, but this was tempered by the realization that "gee, I can keep it forever with no late fees." As Netflix grew and word of mouth spread, people adopted it and left Blockbuster in the dust.

The story of Blockbuster's demise and Netflix's rise has to do with more than timing, but it's a classic example of how being too late to the new game, even when you get a heads up, can be fatal. In fact, Reed met with Blockbuster back in 2000 to pitch the idea of merging. He was laughed out of the room.

Timing is something that is hard to get right. There are so many confounding factors that contribute to being too early or too late with a product offering or service. Entrepreneurs need to constantly scan the marketplace for the best time to launch.

Timing has another aspect that's a little more personal and also conspires against us—when to actually take the jump and start a business.

Anand Sanwal, CEO of CBInsights, an entrepreneur in the SaaS data analytics space, sums it up this way:

> There is never really a perfect time. It's hard to get everything lined up. At the end of the day you have to leap and just get it done. Have enough money to survive. You can only prepare so much. You have to have the basics and get the prep work done. There is no perfect time to pull the trigger.

I share Anand's thoughts on this. When I started Lab Sensor Solutions, the timing was not ideal. I had a cushy corporate job that paid the bills, but also had a bunch of personal issues that made it not the best time to jump ship. However, my co-founders and I realized that we needed to get started since several factors were building up to a real need in the marketplace. The most important of those factors was the quality mandates of the Affordable Care Act (ACA). Still, we did not perfectly get the timing right.

At the time of this writing, Lab Sensor Solutions (LSS) is still early to a developing market (monitoring medical perishables) that's been stalled due to the new administration in the U.S. (more on governments later on). The implication was we had to make a decision—wait for the market to develop or pivot to something else. That's a tough call to make since one of the most important things a startup must do is to stay focused. Pivots can defocus a company and, if done at the wrong time, crater it as well. For LSS, we decided that the timing for market adoption was too soon and it was time to pivot to other perishables like fresh food.

Tim Yin, CEO of TN Technologies, an entrepreneur in the import/export business, knows that it can be frustrating waiting for things to happen:

> It's important to have a positive attitude and to see reality. Be persistent. The timing may be wrong and that will make you feel lousy. It can be a lonely time. Don't let small things bother you. The time will come. The question is: Will you be ready for it?

Tim brings up a good point that patience is different than procrastinating. It makes a lot of sense to plan out when you'll make a move, but not wait too long for the exact right time. The art of timing is knowing the difference between patience and procrastination.

The test I use to determine if it's patience or procrastination is simple—are the necessary building blocks available to me to make my idea happen? By building blocks I mean the fundamental components or technology. Things like cloud computing, 3D printing, offshore manufacturing, etc. If all the necessary building blocks exist and I'm not moving, then I'm procrastinating. Of course, factors like market need and business model are important too but, in order to vet those, you first need to create something to show people.

Each of us has personal constraints on our time. It seems like it's never the right time to take the plunge and start a new company. The challenges of time, with its never-ending parade of excuses, can make you the proverbial deer in the headlights. Excuses like: I'll do it next year when the kids go to school; when I have enough savings; when my idea is more solidified; after I get that bonus. These are all "valid" reasons to delay, yet if you think long and hard about it, you'll realize that there will always be an excuse to not start.

So what's stopping you?

Ankkit O. Aggarwal, CEO of HydeWest, an entrepreneur in the hospitality industry, puts it perfectly:

> It's important to dream big to achieve big. Sow the seed when you have the idea. There's no right time to start anything you have been dreaming or thinking of. Don't let the debate in your head about the right time stop you. Make your dreams happen.

That's the challenge of timing. It will always push you to err on the side of the comfortable, to wait until the time is "right," or to drag your feet until you're absolutely forced to make the move. Everyone goes through it, so don't beat yourself up too much. Just take action.

Timing is always something that entrepreneurs will have to worry about. When to look for another founder? Hire staff? Fire staff? Launch a product? Time will conspire against you, if you let it, and make it that much harder to succeed.

Again, time is never on your side.

RethinkDB is a classic example of a startup that had a great idea, yet the timing was off.

Databases are the lifeblood of any SaaS application. Without a good database backend, SaaS applications will be slow and prone to crash. RethinkDB did everything that they were supposed to do, including picking the right metrics to track their progress. The metrics they chose were things like response time, correctness, simplicity of the interface, and consistency of implementation. However, it turned out those were the wrong metrics—the right metric was "Does it work well enough?" It turned out that all those other metrics were only nice-to-haves, but were not critical.

Slava Akhmechet, founder of RethinkDB, did an excellent post-mortem on a January 2017 blog post on *defstartup* of the challenges he and his team faced. In it, he recounts several key challenges that made it hard for RethinkDB to beat out its main competitor, MongoDB. Slava's insights are hard-won and are a lesson in why even the best products might not win:

> A few people pointed out that we would have done better if we had built an experienced go-to-market team. That's 100% true, but the timing of our personal development didn't line up with the needs of the company. Initially, we didn't know we needed go-to-market expertise, so we didn't seek to include it on the founding team. By the time we built up a mental model that mapped well to reality, we found ourselves short on cash, in a difficult market filled with capable competitors, and a product that was three years behind. By then, the best go-to-market team in the world couldn't have saved us.

The last part is the most important and at the heart of getting the timing right. Your product cannot be years behind competitors' even if it's superior in every other way.

Customers will forgive a lot of sins if they see a responsive company that is improving their product regularly. That's what RethinkDB's competitor MongoDB did. When RethinkDB could not answer the question "How is RethinkDB different from MongoDB?", the timing deficit could not be overcome. What this meant was that all the features and functions that RethinkDB thought were important, were not important to customers. To top it off, RethinkDB was playing catch-up and that takes a lot more resources to pull off. It's always better to keep up than to catch up.

This is an all too common story when it comes to timing your product to the market. It also begs the question about what timing really is—a technology or product that does not fit the market, the wrong product at the right time, the right product at the wrong time, or the wrong product at the wrong time?

That's the dilemma of timing. When you "miss it by *that* much," it really does not matter what you call it—product market fit or timing. Every single entrepreneur will tell you "I wish I had more time." Time is a scarce commodity for entrepreneurs. It's the one thing that every entrepreneur has the same amount of - you can print money but you can't print time.

SEVEN

Customers - No Better Friend

"Customers don't know what they want until we've shown them."

— Steve Jobs, entrepreneur

Up until now, the challenges to the status quo we have discussed have been centered on the mostly internal struggles of starting a company and building a product. What that means is the things getting in the way are mostly of your own choosing. What we will discuss next are the external challenges that you have little control over. There is no better one to start off with than your customers and potential customers. Customers are also "the usual suspects" when a new idea is having trouble getting off the ground.

I don't know how many times I have heard a sales or marketing guy say, "Well, that's what the customers are telling us they need, so we need to build that." Customer feedback is essential for a company to gather and analyze, but it can be a slippery slope if all you do is track the customer needs needle. Taken in a vacuum, customer feedback will lead to wasted time and energy. Let me explain.

Customers and potential customers have many worries. To some, your new-fangled gadget will solve a real pain and for others it won't. Depending on how big a problem your gadget solves will dictate how interested and engaged customers will be. Put another way, if the pain isn't that great, your idea is just a nice-to-have. That's where the problems start.

Nice-to-have products will always be featured to death. It's inevitable because your trusty customer is trying to push you towards a product that's a must-have. This "feature creep" is not a good strategy. In the end, you often end up building something no one needs. It's like the design committee from hell or the five blind people trying to describe an elephant.

Basecamp (formally 37 Signals) is a not-so-old web startup that takes an interesting approach to customer feedback. For the most part, they actually ignore it. Well, not exactly.

Founded in 1999 by Jason Fried and David Heinemeier Hansson (inventor of Ruby on Rails, a website development platform), Basecamp is a simple project collaboration tool that helps people make progress together. Jason and David have had a profitable company, without taking any venture money, for the entire time they have been in business. It's quite a remarkable feat considering most Software as a Service (SaaS) companies want to grow fast and exit quickly. Part of their success is a manic, obsessive focus on what matters and what does not. Part of what does not matter is feature requests from customers.

I'm not talking about feedback in the sense that "the server's broken" or "I lost my email" or "my migration went bad." For those, they do a great job.

The type of feedback I'm talking about is all the features customers ask for. Those nasty little critters that burrow into your email support system and infest your customer support team with endless queries on "why can't you do this?"

Basecamp's feature feedback philosophy boils down to two simple concepts—birth and death.

Birth is when a new customer signs up or buys your service. At that point, this brand-spanking new customer is full of joy and promise. They are in the perfect spot to give some awesome and relevant feedback on "why did you buy?" This useful feedback will allow you to figure out what features and functions are closing sales.

Death is when a customer leaves you. Something went wrong when your paying customer decided to break up with you. Knowing why they left is critical to preventing other customers from leaving.

Feedback in between birth and death, while interesting, is not going to be as useful or as productive. It will only distract you from your vision that most of your customers won't see or know they need until you provide it for them.

What happens if you don't have any customers? Say you are starting off a new gig and need the feedback. Good point. I'm glad you asked.

It turns out that Jason has some advice on that as well—find your competitors' customers and ask them. This might seem hard to do at first but you would be surprised at how open customers are to giving feedback.

Look around at what others are doing to figure out what pain your competitors are not curing or, better yet, ask them the birth and death questions.

Think Netflix curing the late-fee pain and suffering that Blockbuster inflicted on their customers.

Think Uber making the painful experience of hailing a cab quick and easy.

Think Xero making accounting information simple to share.

Think Apple making it easy to carry 1,000 songs in your pocket.

Think UberConference making it simple to set up a conference.

These are a few examples of entrepreneurs finding a need and filling it by solving a problem that competitors either did not see, did not want to solve, or were too stubborn to look at what trends were emerging.

Customer feedback and input when you are first starting out is essential and critical to get. It is difficult to adhere to Steve Jobs' mantra above because the world is a dynamic and complex place. It's damn hard to predict—let alone please— the requests from a multitude of demanding customers. There will be trends that will emerge, and those trends need to be paid attention to or your company will go the way of taxicabs.

Be wary of tracking the customer needs needle. It will be erratic, distracting, and frustrating trying to be all things to all people. There is some truth in the words of John Lennon:

> Trying to please everybody is impossible—if you did that, you'd end up in the middle with nobody liking you. You've just got to make the decision about what you think is your best, and do it.

You are going to have to make decisions and see what happens. It will never be perfect and you will never know what you don't know. That's the beauty of entrepreneurship— be flexible enough to figure it out as you go along.

Eric Eggers, an entrepreneur in the healthcare space, thinks that you have to have a certain mindset to serve customers:

> I want to serve my clients the best I can and be of service. I sleep well at night knowing that I did whatever I could to make them successful. I don't beat

myself up if I do everything I can to help them. This does not mean I take on every project or not push back on something unreasonable. Sometimes, pushing back on a customer demand gives you what they really need.

It's hard to know what customers need even if you ask them or if they tell you. Many a company has failed when they ignored customer trends or market disruptions even when customers were clamoring for new products. Ask Blockbuster and Kodak how that feels.

Customer feedback will ebb and flow. It's important to keep a keen eye to trends that show a clear signal. Remember that, although two points do make a line, they don't make a trend, and there is an awful lot of noise out there.

That's why your customers are your best friends and your worst enemies. The challenge is making them happy while not chasing your tail while trying. You can do this by acting with integrity towards them and saying no when you need to say no. I know it sounds counterintuitive to reject a customer request but, in my experience, Steve Jobs is right on that—customers really don't know what they need until you show them.

EIGHT

Competitors – Makes the Pie Bigger

"Never compete with someone who has nothing to lose."
— Baltasar Gracián, prose writer

Congratulations! You made it past the internal struggles, convinced your family, assembled a team, launched a product, and now have some customers. Way to go. That's a major accomplishment. Now that you are in the marketplace and are making progress, you'll face the next big challenge— competitors. There is no better example of healthy competition than Avis vs. Hertz.

In 1946 Warren Avis invested $85,000 to create his first car rental operation located at Willow Run Airport in Detroit. This was the first rental car operation located at an airport. At the time, all rental car companies had offices in downtown locations. Warren's innovation created a new idea that expanded to other airports around the world. This created the market for airport rental cars and one of the most epic corporate rivalries of all time.

Capitalism creates markets where customers can buy goods and services. These markets are efficient when the free flow of information makes it easy for buyers and sellers to know what a particular good or service is worth. To make all that happen, markets need competitors.

Competition encourages the market to provide the best price for a good or service. It's the ultimate system of checks and balances. Without competitors, markets are inefficient and customers get little choice or poor-quality goods. Look at China or Russia as they start to realize that centralized control of an economy just does not work.

Avis is an interesting company because, even though it created the market for airport rental cars, it was not number one. It used that fact in one of the most successful and longest running marketing campaigns called "We Try Harder," which lasted over 50 years.

Created in 1962, the campaign's goal was to turn around Avis, who had never made a profit. The campaign highlighted Avis always being #2 to rival Hertz. Thus, the "We Try Harder" slogan was born.

The "We Try Harder" campaign was such a success that in 1963, Avis made a profit of $1.2M for the first time in its history. Their market share reflected that as well.

From 1963 to 1966, Avis's market share rose from 29% to 36% while rival Hertz shrunk from 61% to 49%. Not all of Hertz's market share went to Avis, but Avis did put a dent in it. In an ironic twist of fate, in 2015 Hertz dropped to #2, while Avis

Budget was #3, and Enterprise crushed them both at #1— always a bridesmaid but never a bride.

The rivalry between Hertz and Avis created innovations that made renting a car much more enjoyable. Computerized reservations, loyalty programs, quicker service, and pick-up services, to name a few. Those innovations would never have come about without healthy competition.

Competition is so important that governments have the power to block companies from buying other companies. These anti-trust laws prevent the creation of monopolies. Monopolies create markets that have little to no competition, which is not good for consumers.

Some argue that monopolies can't last. If a market is so inefficient, then a new entrant is bound to disrupt it. There is no better example of monopoly disruption than what Uber and Lyft did to the taxi industry.

Most cities regulate who can own and operate a taxi. There are strict regulations on fares, access to the airport, and only a certain number of taxi medallions are available. This creates a limited and monopolistic market since demand almost always outstrips supply.

Local government regulations create the taxi market and this factors in as well. To see why limits exist, we have to dig into the history of taxi medallions.

Taxi medallions are licenses issued by a city to allow the holder to drive a cab. The medallion system began in New York City in 1937, when then Mayor La Guardia signed the Haas Act. The law limited the total number of taxi medallions to 16,900 from an estimated 30,000 unlicensed cab drivers during the Great Depression. The primary motivation for cab licensing was growing public concern over proper car maintenance and who was driving.

Over the succeeding six decades, the number of medallions in NYC went from 11,787 in 1937 to 13,437 in 2014. During that same time, the population of New York went from 6.9M to 8.5M.

You would think that, if the taxicab market was more supply-and-demand based, this would sort itself out. Yet most cities limit the number of taxicabs due to the powerful taxicab lobby. This makes the medallions valuable.

For instance, consider that the value of a New York taxi medallion grew almost 7,000% between 1970 and 2010. The S&P index grew only 1,000% during that same time. As cities grew, demand for cabs increased, which made it harder and harder to hail a cab. Since only a few cab companies owned most medallions, there was little or no competition to improve the dismal cab experience until all those challenges we just discussed aligned in a magical way.

Uber and Lyft looked at this monopolistic market and decided that the market was inefficient and ripe for disruption. On top of that, hailing a cab was cumbersome. Uber and Lyft solved this problem with features like rides on demand, rating your driver, carpooling, and knowing exactly when your ride will arrive. This made the experience a lot more pleasant and efficient. All thanks to internet and mobile technology.

These innovations have made Uber worth \$62.5B and Lyft worth \$5.5B all within the last couple of years. Data from Certify (as reported by *TheStreet*) shows that, among business travelers, Uber surpassed taxis in terms of trips taken in April 2015.

It is true that local governments were responsible for creating the lack of competitiveness in the taxi market. This made the taxi companies not work as hard to please their customers or innovate on new ways to provide a better ride. This created a market with little to no competition and an attitude of "if it ain't broke, don't fix it." A market ripe for disruption.

Competition is not a zero-sum game. If a market is big enough and the demand is strong enough, then competition will be good for both consumers and companies. Competition drives innovation and creates different business models for different types of consumers. This makes the whole pie bigger.

Another example of a market that shows a dominant player that's ripe for disruption is web search.
Google is the dominant player in search. Google is so widespread that it's entered the dictionary as a verb.

Competitors like Yahoo and Bing are minor players in search, and some would say they will never catch up. This reality creates a search monopoly for Google. This puts Google in the driver's seat for any kind of search innovation.

Google's primary revenue generation engine, AdWords, is also one of its most annoying features. The reason is that Google tracks every single thing you search for and sells that data to advertisers. What this means is that Google knows a lot about your habits and behaviors. With this information, it can target ads to you across all sorts of social media platforms. It's uncanny how good it is.

To some, this is invasive and has led to a competitor in the search space that is making search anonymous. This competitor is DuckDuckGo, who I introduced briefly in Chapter Four.

Founded in 2008 by Gabriel Weinberg, DuckDuckGo is based in Paoli, Pennsylvania. Its slogan is "The search engine that doesn't track you"—which is exactly its competitive advantage against Google. They have seen a lot of growth among tech users who want to remain anonymous online. Before DuckDuckGo, people who wanted to be anonymous had to go through a proxy server that would cloak their IP address. That's hard to do and something that only technology-savvy people could pull off.

Now, Google Chrome does have incognito mode that prevents Chrome from saving the sites you visit. It's close to but not a true private browsing or searching experience. That's why DuckDuckGo is so unique. It does not store what you searched for by design.

Avis, Uber, Lyft, and DuckDuckGo all found a need and filled it. Their competitors either did not see the need or arrived too late. This is the hallmark of competition. This is what drives a lot of entrepreneurs to start businesses in crowded markets, against entrenched competitors. This "find a need and fill it" is what investors mean when they say to worry about your company's product market fit. It might seem counterintuitive, but competition is good for the following reasons:

- Competition keeps us on our toes.
- Competition creates innovative products.
- Competition makes the market pie bigger.

As entrepreneurs, we must embrace competition and use it to drive our ideas forward with a sense of purpose and urgency. Entrepreneurship is a competitive sport that needs players like DuckDuckGo, Uber, Lyft, and Avis to shake things up.

The challenge is to *get out of the zero-sum game mindset*. It's not a winner-take-all situation. As an entrepreneur, the Ethos that we follow must accept and respect competition. We must play by the rules and recognize that if we have no competition, then is there really a market for what we are creating? Chances are, no.

NINE

Investors - Those Who Makes the Rules

"Whoever has the gold makes the rules."
— Brant Parker and Johnny Hart, creators of *Wizard of Id*

You may find it a bit odd that investors factor in after customers, because don't you first need investors to build your product for customers? For some businesses, that is correct but nowadays most investors won't even take a meeting until you have shown some sort of market traction with your Minimum Viable Product (MVP). What this means is that before you get your first investor, outside of friends and family, you're going to have to get past the previous challenges and build something that a customer wants. Yes, I know, not intuitive at all.

Entrepreneurs have a love/hate relationship with investors. Entrepreneurs need investment to make and scale their idea, yet investors want traction before giving them any money. This tension makes finding the *right* investor as important as getting the investment itself.

Even after getting the investment, tensions could still flare up and issues could also arise: issues such as when to raise more money or when to sell the company. Both these issues can have negative outcomes for entrepreneurs. If they raise more money, they might lose control. If they sell too soon, they may not get anything.

Brett Fox, an entrepreneur in the semiconductor space and now a CEO coach, understands the challenges of raising money:

> Raising money is emotional. There are lots of things that can derail an investment. You have to remember that funding is a numbers game. When I was raising money for one of my companies, I got rejected 63 times before the 64th invested.
>
> Investors are not your friends. Just remember that they are looking after *their* best interests and not yours.
>
> Remember, don't give up if you hear things like "your idea sucks" or if you get rejected early on. Stick with it. Eventually, someone will want to invest in you.

The investor numbers game is the one thing I hear the most agony about from entrepreneurs. For those of you who have never raised money, let me explain.

Image you have to go on 100 blind dates in 100 days where your date gets to pick the restaurant, what food you eat, what you talk about, and the length of the date. On top of that, your dates don't really tell you if there was any chemistry. They just string you along until they find someone better. Sounds like as much fun as hearing fingernails scratching a blackboard or watching paint dry. For me, this is the worst part about being an entrepreneur—raising money and the "slow no." This is why I hope to meet Gil Dibner on day.

Gil Dibner is a venture capital investor focusing on companies in Europe and Israel. He penned a piece in 2014 titled "Towards a VC [Venture Capitalist] Code of Conduct." In it he outlines his thoughts on how a VC should conduct himself or herself. In the VC/entrepreneur relationship, the VC has both more knowledge and tolerance for some of their investments failing. The entrepreneur does not have the luxury of risk spreading since they only have one bet.

Gil's musing on this topic is informative and a balance between the VC's needs and the needs of the entrepreneur. An all too common problem with VCs is the "slow no," which to every entrepreneur I have ever talked to annoys them to no end. Gil's code encapsulates and takes care of that:

> **I will not string you along:** I will be straightforward and transparent about the likelihood of an investment. VCs can easily waste tons of entrepreneur time by not being honest about the likelihood of an investment, or by the all-too-common "it's interesting; let's talk again soon." The reality is, we don't invest in the vast majority of companies we see—and we should be honest about that. By not saying "no," VCs run the risk of an entrepreneur turning down another investor or jeopardizing a round by delaying it too long. It's better to give a quick "no" and then re-engage later than create a false sense of momentum.

Giving the quick no is a respectful way of not wasting an entrepreneur's time and aligns with having integrity to tell the truth, even if it's bad news. The more open and honest an investor is with an entrepreneur, the better it is for everyone. The challenge is finding those investors that will give you an honest no.

What this boils down to is what David Shen, an investor in Palo Alto, talks about in a piece "Qualities of an Awesome Investor" on his blog in August 2016. In it he lists 30 things that every awesome investor needs to do or be or know. It's a great list, but the one thing he puts above all things is trust:

> What kind of trust are we talking about? Trust that you won't run away or waste their money. Trust that you will not do stupid things. Trust that you will make them money. Trust that they can find you whenever they want. And so on.

We can all agree that being trustworthy is the most important trait to present to an investor. And on the other side of the table, trust starts with not stringing an entrepreneur along. Trust, and the many forms it takes, is an important cornerstone of *The Entrepreneur Ethos*.

All investors know that if they don't earn and maintain trust with their potential investments, no entrepreneur will come knocking. Entrepreneurs know that the whole investor dance is about having them trust you enough to put money into your idea. In the end, that's the most important factor—

independent of your talent, technology, technique, and timing.

All these investor challenges will weigh on an entrepreneur. It's tough to have to listen to an investor say no. It feels like a personal slam on what you have spent a lot of time working on, but it's part of the game. All entrepreneurs will face investor rejection more often than an investor will invest. That's just reality.

The number of companies looking for capital is much greater than the number of investors looking to invest. It's up to every entrepreneur to find the inner strength to marshal on, even when they hear the 50th or even 100th no. Like Brett Fox's quote above, the yes could be right around the corner. Just remember that rejection is part of the entrepreneur game and investor rejection is the worst part of that game.

Once you do find an investor, don't get seduced by the dollar signs.

Investors, like all groups, run along a distribution from bad to good. It's important to realize that the money you get from investors comes with strings that might not be apparent. That's why it's vital to seek out investors who are aligned to your vision, treat you with respect, and are honest in their assessments. It will take a lot of discipline (more on that later) to resist money from a shady investor with bad terms when you're desperate to keep your company's lights on. It's at these times where following *The Entrepreneur Ethos* will be the most challenging.

The general rule of thumb for determining if an investment deal is good or bad has a lot to do with comparable deals. If you get a deal that is too far away from what everyone else is getting, then that's a big red flag. How do you find this out? You ask your fellow entrepreneurs on a site like Founders Network, a peer-to-peer mentoring group for entrepreneurs. This type of peer feedback is critical to help determine if a deal is good or bad.

Investors have the money, so they make the rules. This reality can be a bitter pill to swallow. Entrepreneurs need to persevere through rejection after rejection since a yes might be right around the corner. It's the hustle, self-belief, and grit to raise money, tempered by the discipline to not take a bad deal, that living *The Entrepreneur Ethos* can help you through.

TEN

Government – Here to Help You

"Invention requires a long-term willingness to be misunderstood."
— Jeff Bezos, CEO of Amazon

The last challenge we'll discuss is one of the most frustrating, since it usually shows up late to the party or won't even let you start the party. Governments are and will always be a necessary evil simply because the rules of government are vastly different than the rules of business. Nothing demonstrates that better than Frank Capra's film *Mr. Smith Goes to Washington*.

In the film, Jimmy Stewart plays a new United States senator who has good intentions but who is naïve in the ways of how government works. His mentor, Senator Paine, wants to use Mr. Smith as a pawn in his political machine.

The big climactic ending scene is when Mr. Smith, on an epic filibuster to regain his good name, collapses. This sends Senator Paine out of the chamber riddled with guilt, bent on committing suicide, but his colleagues stop him. He returns to the chambers to confess to manipulating Mr. Smith and that he is not worthy of the Senate. This admission clears Mr. Smith's name.

Mr. Smith Goes to Washington was released in 1939. At the time, it was controversial in its portrayal of how government works. Unfortunately, fiction is not too far from fact, except for the guilt-ridded politician admitting wrongdoing—that's just pure fantasy today.

Entrepreneurs must exist within the confines of government rules and regulations. Without them, corporations would not exist, safety regulations would be left up to industries, and there would be no recourse for broken contracts. Like Mr. Smith, the naïve entrepreneur can get taken advantage of or derailed if they don't understand the complex nature of governments.

Yet, government does get in the way. Rules and regulations can make the burden so great that it's almost impossible to compete. These burdens are real, and every entrepreneur needs to take heed of the challenges they can create.

All countries are not the same when it comes to doing business. It may come as a surprise to most people that the United States is not the best place to do business.

According to a 2015 *Forbes* survey, Denmark ranks first while the United States ranks 22nd in ease of doing business. Seven of the top ten such countries are located in Europe. The criteria for this ranking takes into account 11 factors such as property rights, innovation, taxes, technology, corruption, freedom (personal, trade, and monetary), red tape, investor protection, and stock market performance. Even so, what's ironic and counterintuitive is that in 2014 the United States had about 60% of the world's venture capital investment.

Many speculate that the reason why so much VC money is in the U.S. is because Silicon Valley invented venture capital investing back in the 1970s. I'm sure many of those investors just figured *why leave?* The data also seems to bear that out.

It turns out that 43% of venture capital money (i.e., total investment dollars) and 38% of the deals (i.e., investments of any size) go to businesses located in and around Silicon Valley. This poses a big problem for governments who want to create the next Silicon Cape (South Africa), Silicon Alley (New York City), Silicon Slopes (Utah), Silicon Mountains (Colorado), Silicon Plateau (Bangalore, India), and Silicon Wadi (Israel). It's not that these areas are not creating companies or don't have investment dollars. Take Israel, for example.

According to the Organization for Economic Cooperation and Development (OECD), via *The Atlantic*, the U.S. ranks second in venture capital invested as a percentage of Gross Domestic Product (GDP). Israel is at number one and Sweden is at number three. What this means is that, while the U.S. may spend the most dollars on startups, it does not have a monopoly on entrepreneurship.

Governments try to create or grow an industry by passing laws. These laws either relax regulations (U.S. airline deregulation) or add requirements like the Affordable Care Act (ACA) in the U.S.

In 2013, the U.S. spent 17.1% of its GDP on healthcare, the most of any industrialized nation. Despite its high spending, the U.S. has poor overall population health compared to most other developed nations in life expectancy, infant mortality, and the obesity rate. These alarming statistics were one of the major drivers in the passing of the Affordable Care Act (ACA), also known as ObamaCare.

ObamaCare's goal was to give more Americans access to affordable, quality health insurance and to reduce the growth of healthcare spending in the U.S. There are several ways ObamaCare set out to achieve this.

The first was to sign up as many people as possible to achieve economies of scale. The second was paying for successful outcomes—what is known as paying for value (e.g., results) instead of volume (e.g., treatment after treatment that does not work). This value vs. volume shift is the opportunity opening that many digital health entrepreneurs are working on. Even though ObamaCare was a controversial program, it's one law that has driven a lot of investment and innovation, even though the current political climate wants to abolish or change it.

Laws like ObamaCare can kick-start an industry, while other laws or policies can make it easy to do business in a country. Take Estonia's e-Residency program.

The goal of Estonia's e-Residence program is:

> e-Residency offers to every world citizen a government-issued digital identity and the opportunity to run a trusted company online, unleashing the world's entrepreneurial potential.

e-Residency is not citizenship but rather a way to establish a company that can do secure transactions online from anywhere in the world. It's the first of its kind and has established Estonia as the place to start an online business. This is particularly helpful if your business deals in digital content like eBooks, audio courses, or videos where customers download the content. In reality, a business that provides that kind of product can also be based anywhere in the world with no real downside.

Estonia's e-Residency is a great example of a government trying to make it easy to start and run a business. There is little downside to anyone if these good intentions fail. This is not always the case.

Sometimes good intentions can backfire and lead to a global economic crisis. Case in point—the U.S. 2008 sub-prime mortgage meltdown.

What created this particular economic crisis seems to have been a mix of greed, government regulations, and a lack of oversight. Those government regulations started out with the noble cause of getting more people to own homes. This allowed greed to run unchecked and caused banks to be exposed to something that most people had never heard of—credit default swaps (CDS).

Both CDS and the drive for affordable housing started in the early 1990s from two very different types of needs. CDS were created to protect banks that made loans to corporations. Before CDS, banks had no way to hedge against a corporation defaulting. That was the power of a CDS, as the *JP Morgan Guide to Credit Derivatives* put it:

> Consider a corporate bond, which represents a bundle of risks, including perhaps duration, convexity, callability, and credit risk (constituting both the risk of default and the risk of volatility in credit spreads). If the only way to adjust credit risk is to buy or sell that bond, and consequently affect positioning across the entire bundle of risks, there is a clear inefficiency. Fixed income derivatives introduced the ability to manage duration, convexity, and callability independently of bond positions; credit derivatives complete the process by allowing the independent management of default or credit spread risk.

Pretty complex language that can be summed up as follows: I want to buy insurance against corporations defaulting on their bonds.

We'll see later that this gave all those smart Wall Street guys a way to make money, but also helped create the sub-prime mortgage crisis.

The final ingredient to the "perfect storm" was mortgages— the more the better.

In 1992, Fannie Mae and Freddie Mac (U.S. government loan companies) started to loosen their standards for mortgage buying. Before 1992, Fannie and Freddie could only buy mortgages that investors like Goldman Sachs or Citibank would buy—so-called prime mortgages. The requirements for such mortgages made it difficult for low-income (read high-risk) borrowers to buy a home.

Starting in 1992, the Community Reinvestment Act (CRA) of 1977 was amended to devote a percentage of Fannie and Freddie lending to support affordable housing. If sub-prime mortgages were an infectious disease, this would become Patient 0 for the epidemic that would happen over 15 years later.

As the years went on, CDS became more and more popular as the number of mortgages started to rise. Between 1992 and 2007, the quotas (number of loans) for affordable housing went from 30% to 50%. By 2008, that created 27 million sub-prime mortgages. Those mortgages accounted for 50% of all mortgages and Fannie and Freddie held 70% of them. Rating agencies even got into the mix by not properly rating the mortgage bundles that included high-risk mortgages in so-called "safe" high-grade bundles. Most people who deal with risk would say that having 50% of anything in high-risk positions is a recipe for disaster.

Disaster, meet the U.S. economy!

When default rates started to rise, the next domino fell—valuing all those CDS. The reason why this is important is because CDS were the hedge on risk of mortgage-backed securities. Yes, I know, this stuff can make your head spin, but bear with me.

So now the question is, how did CDS play into this? By the mid-2000s, banks and traders were using CDS to hedge against the failure of mortgage-backed securities. What this means is that when mortgage defaults started to rise, the value of these securities started to fall. That would trigger the CDS. Insurance companies were the ones that sold the CDS because, for them, it seemed like easy money. But when things went south, those same insurance companies were on the hook for hundreds of billions of dollars' worth of payouts to investors who had bought the CDS. Payouts they could not make.

This led the government to create the Troubled Asset Relief Program (TARP) to bail out the insurance companies. Yes, another government program to help fix the collateral damage caused by the good intentions of another government program.

The lesson in all this is that government policies are no substitute for common sense. All governments think they are here to help you but, in reality, most policymakers don't have a clue about what's good for entrepreneurs.

The Entrepreneur Ethos handles the government's wanting to help by instilling a sense of *what's-right* as opposed to *what's-legal*. The actions of all those banks and insurance companies were in clear violation of the Ethos of acting with integrity and earning the respect of the community. Unfortunately, millions in that community had no TARP program to help them and had to pay the price of foreclosures, bankruptcies, layoffs, and long-lasting economic ruin. Entrepreneurs, take heed whenever you hear that governments will come in to "help you."

PART TWO

Traits

As Part One showed us, there are many challenges in our way as entrepreneurs, as we battle against the status quo to move the world around to our point of view. The "status quo" may just be a statement of fact, but it is our biggest enemy, and we need to battle it daily.

To do this, entrepreneurs need to possess certain traits. These traits are listed first since they are the outwardly facing qualities and characteristics that outsiders first see.

These distinguishing qualities form the external manifestation of *The Entrepreneur Ethos* and are the traits of passion, discipline, problem-solving, confidence, focus, competitiveness, awkwardness, and grit that allow an entrepreneur to do the things that must be done on a day-to-day basis.

The first trait we will explore is passion, because all other traits are built on this. An entrepreneur without passion will not go far. Don't confuse the common advice of following your passion with having passion—the two are not the same, as you'll soon find out.

ELEVEN

Passion - Kick the Tires and Light the Fires

"The secret to successful hiring is this: look for the people who want to change the world."
— Marc Benioff, CEO of Salesforce

Annie Lawless would have had an ironic name for a lawyer. But Annie dropped out of law school to follow her lifetime love of nutrition and juicing to form Suja Juice. In hindsight, it seems obvious to follow your passion and build something that excites you, yet most people don't follow their gut and do what Annie did.

For Annie, the road to forming Suja Juice came about because she was fighting debilitating depression. Her depression started while attending law school and masked her inner dialog that kept telling her she should do something else. It's one thing to be drained because you're working 24/7 on something that excites you. It's quite another to feel the heavy weight of fatigue as you slog through a job or a lifestyle that you aren't passionate about.

Annie found out the hard way that law school was not her passion by enduring both physical and mental stress. This reluctance to change happens in all sorts of cultures because of social norms and community expectations. Entrepreneurs face this same challenge because venturing out on your own is not considered to be the safe, acceptable way to go.

To succeed at anything, each of us needs to have that inner drive or intrinsic motivation to know when something does not feel right. This gut feeling is how a passion projects like Annie's turns into a $300 million company.

Marvin Raab, an entrepreneur in the digital health space, puts passion another way:

> You've got to love what you're doing and the people with whom you're doing it. The money is important, but the enjoyment is significantly more important. Enjoyment, love, and passion allow you to get over the fears of the unknown that can be crippling.

Entrepreneurs have all sorts of motivations for starting a business. The ones who are successful also have a passion for what they are doing tempered with a pragmatic sense that this is actually a good idea. And as Marvin said, loving and enjoying what they do. Gary Erickson is a perfect example of that.

Back in 1990, Gary was an avid bicyclist who would go on 175-mile bicycle rides with his friends. At the time, his main source of fuel for these rides was energy bars. Halfway through one of these rides, Gary could not stomach eating another sticky, hard-to-digest, and unappetizing energy bar. At that moment, the idea for Clif Bar was born.

The road to success was not easy for Gary. Getting the right balance of taste and nutrition took countless trial batches. For a time, Gary was living in his parents' garage. That's dedication to following your passion. For Gary, it paid off.

Fast forward to the late 1990s and the energy bar food category was experiencing rapid growth. Many companies were seeing huge growth and the industry was hot. When an industry is rapidly growing, there are all sorts of new pressures on a business. One of those pressures supremely tested Gary's passion for his business. Gary recounts the story on NPR's podcast *How I Built This* on October 3, 2016:

> I left that morning for the office knowing that this was the day. I was waiting in the office and my partner was on the phone with the lawyers dotting the I's and crossing the T's on the contract ... within an hour we were waiting to get in the car to drive over and I said, "I need to take a walk around the block." I went out in the parking lot and started weeping ... I did not want to do it.

The "it" Gary was referring to was selling his company for $120M to Quaker Oats—something that his partner was pushing him to do. It got so far along that the paperwork was already done. All that was needed was for Gary to sign on the dotted line, but something inside Gary was nagging at him. Back to *How I Built This*:

For the three months we were working on selling the company I was not sleeping well. I was not riding my bike. I was probably not the best person to be around. I was fighting it internally.

I guess it's like walking off the field ... this was everything. This was my life. These are my employees. My family. It's named after my dad. It set me free to decide, no, I'm not selling ... I told my partner that I don't want to sell the company.

Even though this was a liberating experience for Gary, his partner wanted out. So Gary had to not only tell his employees they were not selling the company but he had to "dial for dollars" to find $60M to buy his partner out. That process would take seven months to negotiate and nine years to pay off.

Nine years to pay off a decision that Gary felt passionate about. Nine years of toil, hardship, communicating with his employees, and feeling passionate about building a business that he believed in, even when the temptation to take the easy way out was right in front of him. That's dedication. Today, Clif Bar is still going strong and has expanded from the original bar to drinks and a women-focused brand called Luna.

Gary did not settle for the big payoff; instead he thought about what his company and employees meant to him. Clif Bar was his passion, yet sometimes your passions might not be so obvious.

Steve Jobs, in his 2005 commencement address at Stanford, got a standing ovation when he told the eager young graduates:

> The only way to do great work is to love what you do. If you haven't found it yet, keep looking, and don't settle.

This seems like a call to follow your passion yet, starting out, computers didn't appear like Steve Jobs true passion. Cal Newport's September 2012 *Fast Company* article, "Do Like Steve Jobs Did: Don't Follow Your Passion," sums it up:

> If you had met a young Steve Jobs in the years leading up to his founding of Apple Computer, you wouldn't have pegged him as someone who was passionate about starting a technology company. Jobs had attended Reed College, a prestigious liberal arts enclave in Oregon, where he grew his hair long and took to walking barefoot. Unlike other technology visionaries of his era, Jobs wasn't particularly interested in either business or electronics as a student. He instead studied Western history and dance, and dabbled in Eastern mysticism.

Compare this to a guy like Apple's other co-founder, Steve Wozniak, who lived and breathed technology, and it's unclear that the young Steve Jobs had a passion for anything other than self-discovery. Even the first project that the two Steves worked on was Jobs basically outsourcing an Atari game to Wozniak. Jobs' passion was clearly not for doing the actual work. In fact, the birth of Apple Computer was quite by accident, as Cal's article continues to explain:

Steve arrived barefoot at the Byte Shop, Paul Terrell's pioneering Mountain View computer store, and offered Terrell the circuit boards for sale. Terrell didn't want to sell plain boards, but said he would buy assembled computers. He would pay $500 for each, and wanted fifty as soon as possible. Jobs jumped at the opportunity to make an even larger amount of money and began scrounging together startup capital. It was in this unexpected windfall that Apple Computer was born. As Young emphasizes, "Their plans were circumspect and small-time. They weren't dreaming of taking over the world."

If a young Steve Jobs had taken his own advice and decided to only pursue work he loved, we would find him today as one of the Los Altos Zen Center's most popular teachers. But he didn't follow this simple advice. Apple Computer was not born out of passion, but instead was the result of a lucky break—a "small-time" scheme that took off.

So is the moral of the Steve Jobs story, in regards to following your passions, that it leads to ruling the world or that it leads to becoming a Zen Buddhist monk? The lesson here is simple—following your passions has both risk and reward. If your passion happens to have a path to building a stellar company, then great. My guess is that most of our passions don't align perfectly to a profitable business. That's why you have to draw a hard line between the passions you'll follow for free and the ones you'll get paid for.

You don't have to be super-passionate about what you create to be successful. Sure, passion helps get you through the dark times when everything is crashing around you. So, in that sense, you only need enough passion to finish creating what you set out to build. I know this sounds crass, but if most of us followed our passions, would we be willing to toil night and day for years trying to build a company that has a low probability of success? The answer is no. However, all successful entrepreneurs are willing to follow their dreams and passions only if they feel supported and enriched along the way.

So, what's the magic balance?

In my mind, you need enough passion to keep you interested when the going gets tough, but not so much that you delude yourself into believing that you'll be successful no matter what. Mix in the anxiety of risk, fear of the unknown, and doubt in your abilities, and that delicate balance can be hard to find.

For me, my passion is to help people. I choose to do that by applying my skills in building businesses and understanding technology. I don't have as great a passion for technology as I do for helping people. Therefore, I need other founders who are more passionate about technology than I am. I still have passion for technology, but it's not something I strictly want to do day-in and day-out. What I do want to do every day is apply that technology and my skills in order to help people.

Once you do find that special something, it's time to use that passion to kick the tires and light the fires. By taking action, you'll tap into the motivation and energy reserves necessary to propel you toward your goals, and enable you to use that passion to help you overcome the challenges along the way toward a new status quo.

TWELVE

Discipline - The Wood Does Not Chop Itself

"Discipline = Freedom."
— Jocko Willink, author

I can bet that most of you have never heard of Jocko Willink. The ex-Navy SEAL and best-selling author of *Extreme Ownership* is an acquired taste. His podcast, *Jocko Podcast*, is part book club, part motivational speech, part kick in the ass, and all about getting after it. Jocko gets after it.

Awake most days at 4:43 a.m., Jocko puts a lot of effort into discipline, because discipline is one of the only factors that are within your control. When you are "up before the enemy," the world is a lot quieter. There are not many people awake to bug you. Now, I understand that 4:43 a.m. is pretty early to wake up, yet for Jocko it's the discipline of starting your day off on your own terms that really gets him going.

Discipline comes in many forms. Waking up early, staying focused on your Minimal Viable Product (MVP), grinding out all the un-fun grunt work of running a company, and working hard to release a product on time. Discipline is at the heart of making your company happen. Without discipline, nothing gets done.

It's discipline that pours the fuel of your passion into your company's engine to get you down the road.

However, the best stories of the importance of discipline come from failure. The biggest startup failure, by far, is lack of financial discipline. Translation: running out of money.

Every tech bubble has story after story of companies living large, spending big, and then fizzling out. The best one from the 2000 bubble was Pets.com.

At first, the premise of Pets.com sounded great—buy everything for your pet online. People love their pets and treat them like members of the family. What could go wrong? The only problem was that the whole craze of buying stuff online was not quite crazy enough to support shipping heavy dog food and cat litter direct to consumers.

To attract customers, Pets.com would sell at below costs—a common practice in the early days of the internet where the mantra was "we'll make it up on volume." After a while, that did not work. The lack of financial discipline forced them to close in late 2000, putting 320 employees out of business, along with one cute socket puppet mascot.

Financial discipline is the art of having enough money to keep your venture afloat until your walk through the "trough of sorrow" is complete. Paul Graham (Y Combinator) coined the phrase "trough of sorrow" as the point in a startup where growth has stalled. It's where founders usually quit. Funnily enough, the discipline to keep walking is often tested most when a company reaches a crossroad. Is it better to continue on the current path or pivot to something else?

The temptation to pivot always gets intense when the bank account is trending towards zero. It's only natural to feel that the grass will be greener on the other side of the pivot. Many times, a company has to pivot to survive, but not always. In some cases, having the discipline to stay the course is the best solution. Case in point, *Huffington Post*.

Founded in 2005 by Arianna Huffington, Kenneth Lerer, Andrew Breitbart, and Johan Perettion, the *Huffington Post*, or *Huff Post*, is a liberal-leaning site that was the answer to the conservative-leaning *Drudge Report* news aggregator. When it first launched, it got mixed reviews but they kept at it. It took until 2012, when reporter David Woods won the Pulitzer Prize for his ten-part series on wounded veterans, to solidify the importance of the *Huff Post*. Image that. Almost ten years to overnight success.

Discipline does have a dark side. Just because something worked before, that does not mean it will work again in all situations. This is the other side of discipline, where blindly sticking with an approach can run you off the rails. It was this dark side of discipline that led KiOR astray.

Founded in 2007, KiOR was the crown jewel of Khosla Ventures clean-energy technology play that created biofuel from wood chips. It was a bold move with the goal to replace oil with biomass in 25 years. With bold vision come bold problems. That was nothing new to Khosla Ventures.

Khosla Ventures had a unique method of hiring managers for a company. The process called "gene-pool engineering" is simple:

> The idea is that the initial team should know the industry well enough to be able to operate within it, but also be outside of the industry enough not to be constrained by its traditional thinking. The group should be able to thrive in "guided chaos."

This method served Khosla Ventures well for its software companies. It turns out that this method did not work so well for the slow-moving, heavily-regulated fuel market that was a lot more complex than writing software. As Paul O'Connor, one of the engineers, recounts in *Fortune*, the "gene-pool engineering" discipline was one of the main factors in KiOR's demise:

> Different parties disagree about which side was responsible—Khosla Ventures or O'Connor and the CEO [of KiOR]—but most agree that KiOR made poor hiring decisions as it staffed up. The result was a relative preponderance of lab researchers with Ph.Ds. and a dearth [lack] of people with technical, operational experience running energy facilities. The lack of people

with real operational experience "hurt KiOR a lot," says O'Connor.

Part of discipline is to know when your methods need to change, and KiOR failed at that. They did apply discipline to a known method that had worked in the past, but lacked the vision to abandon that discipline when things went south. This is the double-edged sword of discipline. Don't have blind allegiance to any course of action, especially one that is not working. If you grind along and get nowhere, it's time to change course.

The KiOR example also illustrates how tough the talent challenge can be to overcome, even if you have a proven technique and your timing is right.

It's imperative that part of your discipline must be the willingness to admit that your methods or tactics are not working and that it's time to ask some hard questions like:

- What are the metrics that matter?
- What milestones need to be hit and by when?
- Where and when do we need to shift gears?

Make a decision to try something new as an experiment. Always have the discipline to look for alternatives. The over-arching truth about discipline is summed up in the part of the Ethos that says:

These challenges do not deter me because I am self-aware enough to know that I don't always have all the answers.

Discipline is then the smart application of work to achieve meaningful results. If those results are constantly not being produced, then no amount of discipline is likely to help you succeed—that's that.

Entrepreneurs can sometimes lack discipline in the mundane matters of running their business because it's not always fun or exciting. However, this continued lack of discipline can ruin a company because the boring stuff, if left undone, will pile up and lead to poor results and, ultimately, chaos.

WebVan lacked the discipline to responsibly scale their business (technique challenge).

Blockbuster lacked the discipline to change their business model when it was clear that competitors like Netflix were gaining market share (competitor challenge). Even when Blockbuster did finally get rid of late fees, it was too late (timing challenge).

When I was at Cypress Semiconductor back in early 2000, we thought we were disciplined. We had specification after specification on how to run every single aspect of our business. The culture was one of "follow the specification or change it." While this made it easy to crank out chip after chip in a disciplined way, it was also a huge blind spot that prevented us from innovating.

This was before the internet bubble. For those of you who do not remember the crash of early-2000, it was a bloodbath. At Cypress we had a negative sales quarter—it was that bad. What our disciplined approach failed to uncover was that the world had changed. We were playing by pre-2000 internet rules, which were fueled by easy-to-get venture money that did not require making a profit or having a sustainable business. When the venture money dried up, our customers (said internet companies) could not get funding. That rippled down to our business, since they could no longer afford to buy our products.

These examples of lack of discipline would not have taken any great leap of creativity to fix. All that would have been required is some good old-fashioned hard work, a disciplined approach to problem solving, and being open to change. In the Cypress example, in hindsight, the leading indicator of pending doom—new product sales—was ignored because the money selling old products was so good. New product sales, or lack of them, are a leading indicator of a slowdown since technology is always changing and, if you don't change with it, customers won't keep buying your stuff. That's a hard discipline to adhere to when the old money was so easy to make.

It's clear that doing the right thing is often the hardest thing. That's why *The Entrepreneurs Ethos* is about seeking the truth about situations and, when the time has come, having the discipline to make the hard decisions and do the hard work to make a change.

Making the hard decisions requires both the discipline to recognize what the data is telling you and the willingness to take action to make something different happen. Following the Ethos helps make this easier since you understand that taking calculated risks comes with both rewards and downsides. It also helps to know exactly what success or failure looks like. That's half the battle.

Sometimes, that means letting go a bit.

Michael Clarke, CEO of Top Locker Media, knows a thing or two about how to do that:

> Get out of the business's way. The business will go further than you can personally go. You can't approach your life like a business. You can't outsource hanging out with your family. When you hold onto and wrap up your self-worth/validation, you get in the way of the business. You need to recognize that the discipline to step back and look at what's going on is just as valuable as building the business.

It's just like chopping a huge pile of wood. If you look at the pile, you'll just get overwhelmed with the task. It's only when you start chopping that you make progress, which allows you to make decisions about the process. No matter how much you think about chopping the wood, it won't chop itself.

THIRTEEN

Problem Solving - Houston,
We Have a Problem

"Hackers often describe what they do as playfully creative problem solving."
— Heather Brooke, American journalist

Richard Feynman was one of the most well respected physicists that ever lived. He was famous for playing the bongos, picking locks at Los Alamos, winning the Nobel Prize, and writing *Six Easy Pieces*, which explains the essentials of physics.

Dr. Feynman is also famous for taking part in the Rogers Commission which brought to light the reason for one of the most heartbreaking disasters of the twentieth century—the explosion of the Challenger space shuttle 73 seconds after liftoff on January 28, 1986.

Dr. Feynman, along with 13 other astronauts, pilots, physicists, and politicians, took on the task of determining the problems that had not been solved leading up to that fateful launch.

The reason I highlight Dr. Feynman is because of his 13-page "Personal Observations on the Reliability of the Shuttle" that strikes me as one of the best treatises ever written and which explained how he solved the problem of the shuttle explosion.

To see the brilliance in Dr. Feynman's problem-solving prowess, you need to look no further than the second paragraph of the "Solid Fuel Rockets (SFR)" section:

> It would appear that, for whatever purpose, be it for internal or external consumption, the management of NASA exaggerates the reliability of its product, to the point of fantasy.

That's a bold statement that shows his confidence and integrity, along with a little bit of chutzpah. It also highlights that even NASA, the king of checklists, Standard Operating Procedures (SOPs), and master levels of bureaucracy, could not get over the challenges of technology, talent, and technique.

The Challenger disaster also shows what can happen when you mix assumptions and shifting standards based on historical successes. Dr. Feynman likens it to:

> When playing Russian roulette the fact that the first shot got off safely is little comfort for the next.

This is at the heart of effective problem solving—never assume that past successes will predict future successes. For the Challenger, NASA failed to realize that the low temperature at launch was making the solid rocket booster seals brittle. A brittle seal cracks under stress and that led to fuel leaking out which caused the explosion.

Chris Klundt, CEO and founder of StudyBlue, and entrepreneur in the education space, knows all too well how a flaw in your assumptions can ruin your whole day:

> In 2012 our team was split between San Francisco and Wisconsin. We were working on an update and our entire database got deleted. Our backups were toast as well. At the time, we had 1M users and 50M pieces of content. We had no way to recover that. The whole team pulled together for 64 straight hours and we got innovative on how to solve the problem. Even an ex-employee came back to help out. We restored everything and not one person complained on the team. Everyone pitched in to fix the problem. We did not fire the guy that made the mistake because it was an honest mistake and a systematic one that should never have happened.

All startups can have similar situations to what Chris went through. The ones that make it figure out a way to solve problems quickly. This is at the core of what entrepreneurs do—find ways to solve a crisis without sinking the company.

Problems come in many forms. In some cases, your problem could be due to a procedure, or a scandal, or even of your own doing. Case in point, Zenefits.

Zenefits was one of the fastest growing companies ever. Its CEO, Parker Conrad, was touted and feared as a revolutionary in human resources. What Zenefits excelled at was health insurance brokering for lots and lots of small businesses. So it came as a shock that the golden boy of human resources resigned after it was revealed that he created a program to allow sales representatives to skirt requirements on a state insurance licensing course. Apparently, software was created to cheat the online exam so that more people could pass without studying—a big no-no in the regulated field of insurance. Not a good way at all to overcome the challenges of government.

With the ouster of Parker, the job of cleaning up Zenefits fell to David Sacks, the COO who was then promoted to CEO. What Zenefits did under Parker's tenure was potentially a complete company killer. David's approach to solving this problem was two-fold. First was "The Offer."

"The Offer" was that any employee hired before February 2016 could take a generous buyout if they didn't feel they could get behind his plan to save the company. That gamble, as many called it, paid off. Of the 1,100 employees at Zenefits, only 100 took The Offer. That's pretty interesting considering the corporate culture before and what David said about how he was going to turn things around.

The second was to solve the regulatory issues. For that, David implemented a simple strategy of admit, fix, settle, and repeat, which meant that all employees had to retake the certification tests. By admitting that past practices were not ethical, Zenefits got past the blame game. This allowed them to fix any problems and settle any fines or issues. Once this method got set in motion, then repeating it got a lot easier. The old saying that the cover-up is worse than the event holds true for not only scandals but when fixing internal problems as well.

David perfectly demonstrated following *The Entrepreneur Ethos* by demanding integrity from himself and his team, no matter how tough the situation may be. Only time will tell if Zenefits can right the ship but, as my grandmother used to say, "It's never too late to do the right thing."

My own experience with cover-ups is not as bad as either NASA or Zenefits. However, I can't even count the number of times a problem has come up and the person responsible tries to cover it up. This is especially bad at big companies where the political landscape is one of Cover Your Ass (CYA). Cypress had this problem in a big way.

Part of the Cypress culture, as we discussed before, was to "follow the specification or change it," which means that you follow all the procedures and policies to the letter unless you found a better way. Mostly, the better way was a change to a specification when you messed up. The typical mess-up was creating a bug in a product or missing your schedule. Everyone dreaded messing up.

We would have these trouble meetings called Root Cause Corrective Actions (RCCAs). These were so dreaded that everyone would wait until the last possible minute to declare a delay or tell someone they were in trouble. It reminded me a lot of the culture of NASA that led to the Shuttle exploding—hide problems and hope things work out somehow. These meetings were so common that every week the entire company's design leadership, upwards of 150 people, would spend hours in a meeting listening to the latest screw-ups from other divisions. It was miserable.

While capturing learning is important (which was the goal), the culture was so toxic when it came to admitting issues that no one ever wanted to 'fess up that things were bad. To put this in perspective, the trigger for an RCCA meeting was if you had missed a milestone. On average, 90% of projects missed milestones. Let's just say we spent a lot of time figuring out how to fix our scheduling problems without actually fixing our scheduling problems. The actual root cause of our scheduling issues was not that we didn't know how to schedule—it was that we always broke the project "prime directive."

The prime directive of projects says that management gets two and the team gets one of the project trinity—features, schedule, and budget. This means that if management wants a fast schedule on a budget, they have to give up features. The same goes for lots of features on a budget—then the team gets the schedule. At Cypress, management wanted all three and the results were predictable. Can you see how this type of attitude can make a team wait for a 'Hail Mary' to save a project?

It makes sense to delay letting your team know about a problem until the details are known, but that's not what I'm talking about here.

The problem is when a person or a team tries to sugarcoat an issue because they're afraid of looking bad or appearing out of control. I know you have seen this type of thing play out, and perhaps have even done it yourself out of fear. That was the tragedy of the Challenger explosion. It was the most glaring example of a culture of fear, which prevented reporting a problem. NASA management wanted all three of the trinity and that led to catastrophe. Cypress was the same way.

Your startup might not have the life and death consequences of launching a shuttle, but it could have the life and death of the company hanging in the balance. How you and your team embrace and solve the problems is what makes the difference.

Problem solving is what entrepreneurs do. It's how opportunities are created and how seemingly insurmountable challenges are overcome. Thankfully, the business world is full of problems to solve.

And all one has to do is surf the web to see the variety of challenges that the world faces today. From global warming, to food production, to transportation, to infrastructure, the problems are many yet they all share one common thread—

they are all solvable given enough time, money, commitment, and—most of all—an honest assessment of the challenges.

The lessons from the Challenger disaster and my time at Cypress demonstrate that open and honest problem assessments are the only way to solve them in a timely way. Without that, delays and tragedies will result.

FOURTEEN

Confidence - Not Cockiness

"You will never own the future if you care what other people think."
— Cindy Gallop, advertising executive

Most entrepreneurs don't have to wait four years after forming their company to actually get it launched. When I mean launched, I mean given permission to sell your services to a customer. This situation would distract most from even trying—let alone hang on for four long years. Yet that's exactly what happened with Herb Kelleher's company, Southwest Airlines. Herb's unwavering confidence pulled him through.

Herb had to fight for four years to make his dream a reality. The fight was not related to product market fit, financing, business model, or employees.

Herb's fight was against competitors. This is the ugly side of the challenge of competitors and not the beneficial "makes the pie bigger" side.

Herb's competitors filed all sorts of lawsuits to prevent him from starting his business. Each one, Herb and his team won. In fact, the very last fight was won mere hours before they were scheduled to offer their first flight. Can you image what confidence someone has to have to endure fight after fight after fight, and up to just hours before launch?

Southwest Airlines is today the envy of the airline industry, but that was not always the case. Back in the early 1970s, companies like Braniff, Trans Texas, and Continental were fighting tooth and nail to prevent Southwest from ever getting off the ground—literally. Their reasoning was that there were already "too many airlines serving Texas." For the chain-smoking, Wild Turkey-swilling Kelleher, it was a fight worth fighting.

A lawyer by trade, Herb Kelleher exudes a confidence and swagger that is part cheerleader and part Wild West cowboy. To think that before the first Southwest flight took off on June 18, 1971, it had been a knock-down drag-out brawl to start. Days before that first flight, a judge in Austin issued a restraining order preventing Southwest from operating. Undeterred, Herb pleaded the Southwest case to the Texas Supreme Court, which overruled the injunction hours before their maiden flight, and Southwest was born.

Entrepreneurs deal with all sorts of challenges to success. It can be downright frustrating to have to fight to bring your idea to reality. That's why all entrepreneurs need confidence in themselves and their teams to pull it off. In Herb's case, the competitor challenge hit him square in the jaw even before he launched. Most of the time, thankfully, that's not the case.

Herb is the perfect example that confidence does not mean being cocky or an asshole.

Bad behaviors are not productive nor desirable since that usually means you lack confidence or you're trying to hide something. Look at Theranos. Their cocky CEO was hiding some pretty damaging information about how well their technology worked—more on them later. The take-away from all this is:

> Be like Herb – confident not cocky, sans the chain smoking.

You can be confident in your direction even though you may not have an idea of how to get there. Plenty of startups have a great vision, yet find it challenging to detail exactly how they will make it work.

That's why a confident entrepreneur will also be willing to listen to others' ideas and be flexible in how they work at achieving the company's goals. This type of humility can be tricky since it's a fine line to balance. One has to look no further than Josh Pigford, founder of Baremetics.com, to see how being confident does not mean you can't also be humble as well.

Josh founded Baremetrics.com in 2013. Baremetrics.com is a SaaS platform for looking at your e-commerce transactions and optimizing them. Think QuickBooks meets Hubspot. Or, if you don't know what I'm talking about, read on.

The cool thing about Josh and Baremetrics.com is not their product, although it looks pretty awesome. What's brilliant about Josh is that he, along with 13 other companies, has embraced being an Open Startup. What that means is that they share, by posting up in real-time via Baremetrics.com for all to see, their Monthly Recurring Revenue (MRR) and how many customers they have. They do this to keep themselves honest and be transparent as to the real health of their business. To me, this is the pinnacle of confidence and humility, and here is why.

Most founders lie about how well things are going. Yes, I'm looking at you guys that say, "We're crushing it!" or "I'm super busy making it rain" or "Our MRR is growing at double digits." Usually, what's going on is far from that.

I get it.

Believe me, I do.

I have been in that same position and said the same exact things because, as an entrepreneur, I have to show the world that I'm confident in what I'm doing and projecting an aura of success. It's a trap we all fall into.

What's great about the Open Startup movement is there is no place to hide because, if you make public how your business is really doing, the numbers will speak for themselves. You have to have confidence in your business and also be humble enough to share reality. That's a bold act because it makes you vulnerable to criticism, yet it exactly aligns with the part of the Ethos that says, "I am self-aware enough to know that I don't always have all the answers."

How liberating it can be to not have to hide behind a fake facade of "It's always sunny in startup land." A lot of founders would be much happier if they practiced this.

If you're scared of putting your metrics on the web for the world to see, then why not try what Mihir Shah, CEO of Drobo does. Every week, he holds "Transparent Tuesday" where he sits with the whole company to review sales numbers, marketing strategies, and engineering updates. This not only encourages employees to share the truth, it also demonstrates Mihir's willingness to make changes when needed. It takes a lot of confidence to put yourself out there to hear the good, bad, and the ugly.

Compare the openness of Josh at Baremetrics.com and Mihir at Drobo to the overconfident and not so humble Martin Shkreli of Turing Pharmaceutical, who in 2013 raised drug prices on an HIV drug by 4,000 percent. The backlash was swift. The cocky Shkreli even maintained that he did "a great thing for society." Heck, even then-candidate Donald Trump thought the guy was a creep when he said in an interview:

> "He [Shkreli] looks like a spoiled brat to me. He's a hedge fund guy. I thought it was disgusting what he did."

All that overconfidence finally caught up with Shkreli. Shortly after the price increase, he was arrested on taking stock from a biotechnology firm he launched called Retrophin Inc., and using it to pay off unrelated business debts. The arrest was unrelated to the price increase but you gotta figure the Feds wanted to teach the young Mr. Shkreli a thing or two about humility and greed. On August 4, 2017, Mr. Shkreli was convicted of two counts of securities fraud and a single count of conspiracy. It's unclear how long Mr. Shkreli will spend in prison but it could be upwards of twenty years. Bad behavior has consequences.

Another cautionary tale about overconfidence comes from another drug company, Mylan, who owns 94% market share for EpiPens.

EpiPens are self-contained devices that allow a person to self-inject a life-saving drug called epinephrine, which treats serious allergic reactions to things like bee stings or peanut allergies.

In 2016 Mylan raised the price of its EpiPens by 500%. The resulting firestorm of criticism brought about comparisons of Mylan's CEO Heather Bresch to good old Mr. Shkreli. Kind of messed up on the news cycle a bit, did we, Ms. Bresch?

Ms. Bresch got dragged in front of Congress to explain herself. It did not go well. Rep. Tammy Duckworth called it a "monopoly" and seemed appalled that schools that entered the program had to sign a non-compete agreement, which meant they could not buy EpiPens from anyone else.

Having a near-monopoly on something should not give you the right to gouge people just because you can. The confounding problem with all this is that school districts have to buy large numbers of EpiPens and this much of a price increase could put kids at risk.

As we have seen, confidence is important. Having too much might make you think you feel untouchable and lead you down the path to certain doom. My hope is that you do not take the path that Shkreli or Bresch took.

Confidence is a fine line. It's important to be confident, but not so confident that you become cocky and start behaving badly.

What this boils down to is what author Jim Collins calls confident humility. Confident humility means keeping professional confidence and personal humility (self-awareness) in balance since these two traits are paradoxical—like many other of the traits, values, and beliefs of the Ethos can be. This also ties in with what is moral or right vs. what is legal. An entrepreneur who lives the Ethos will never hide behind the saying "well, it's legal" or "it's not *illegal*"—that kind of thinking is a slippery slope to unethical behavior.

FIFTEEN

Focus - Deadlines Focus the Mind

"Don't try to be original, just try to be good."
—Paul Rand, graphic designer

An OODA loop (Observe, Orient, Decide, Act) is a concept that most, if not all, military teams use to focus on the task at hand. John Boyd, who was a fighter pilot in the Korean War, described the OODA loop. He wrote such military masterpieces as *Aerial Attack Study* and *Energy-Maneuverability (E-M) Theory*. This may seem a bit off-track for a book on entrepreneurs, but the significance of the OODA loop is profound for all sorts of organizations.

OODA is simple in words but complex in meaning. Its application has often been misunderstood as only a tactic. It's actually a philosophy of managing the uncertainty of the world. In that context, the definition makes a lot of sense:

A learning system, a method for dealing with uncertainty, and a strategy for winning head-to-head contests and competitions. In war, business, or life, the OODA Loop can help you grapple with changing, challenging circumstances and come out the other side on top.

Sounds an awful lot like a startup. In fact, the whole concept of Minimum Viable Product (MVP) is the perfect example of an OODA loop in action.

MVP's sole purpose is to gauge the market potential of an idea. The first step is to **Observe** what is out in the world. The next step is to **Orient** your MVP to the market. After additional analysis you **Decide** if your MVP could be something useful. Then, the last step is to **Act** by putting your MVP out in the world. This cycle continues until you have a viable business or go figure out something else to do.

The thing to realize is that OODA adapts to the conditions it finds itself in. This may seem counterintuitive when talking about focus, yet adopting an OODA mindset allows you to focus on the right things, at the right times, and for the right reasons.

Focus prevents distraction from the goal, but you need to figure out if the goal is worth focusing on. Without a method to reassess your main focus, an entrepreneur can go off-track and end up down a path that cannot be undone.

Cathy Hughes, the founder of Radio One, a company that owns radio stations, credits focus as the main factor in her success. The amount of struggle that Cathy had to go through was tough given that she also had a young son to take care of:

> Focus. An elderly woman who provided childcare told
> me the secret to successful parenting was to keep your

attention focused on your children. And one of the key characteristics of an effective manager is to not have your attention distracted from your employees, goals, and objectives. You have to keep your eye on the prize, whether that's running a business or rearing a child.

Keeping your eyes on the prize.

Focus on what's important.

Don't let things distract you from the goal.

That kind of focus is how in 1999 Cathy became the first African American woman to run a public company.

A lot of the challenges we discussed in Part One can be successfully overcome with an OODA/focus mindset because small teams tend to get overwhelmed quickly with all the challenges that are thrown at them. With an OODA/focus mindset, the team can focus on the most pressing problems, solve them, and move on to the next ones. In some cases, a team's focus might be misplaced and need to be adjusted.

Daniel Kan, COO of Cruise Automation GM, knows the trick to maintaining focus when things might be distracting you:

> The company in the #1 spot does not think about the company in the #2 spot. They only focus on the most important thing to move the company forward—not

looking backward at what others are doing. The answer is never behind you. It's always ahead of you.

Focus is so important because it makes it crystal clear what's important and what's not. Too often, entrepreneurs get distracted by too many peripheral things. They spread themselves too thinly because they don't understand what's important to focus on. This is especially true when a company is going through the trough of sorrow. Recall that the trough of sorrow is the point where your product or service is struggling to find product market fit or customers to buy it.

The biggest trap an early stage entrepreneur can fall into is the shotgun approach to product and market development. This means that in the struggle to fit the product into the market, they look at way too many different markets or product variants.

Potential investors are notorious for filling an entrepreneur's head with new ideas. The classic "could your technology be used for this market? I understand it's unrelated to what you are doing." That question has wasted more time and caused more sleepless nights than maybe any other while people are trying to raise money.

My company, Lab Sensor Solutions, gets this all the time.

I can't even count the number of times a potential investor has wanted us to go into some different and tangential market that made no sense.

To give you some context, Lab Sensor Solutions makes a system that monitors the temperature and location of perishable medical items. These items include blood, urine, tissue samples, vaccines, drugs, organs, etc. Pretty specific stuff that requires a deep knowledge of how healthcare logistics works.

Sometimes, investors have a different idea about our business. We get asked questions all the time like: Can you track wine? What about produce? I hear that tracking whole milk is a real problem.

Can you see why this can make you go mental really quickly?

Danger, Will Robinson. Danger!

It's not that our technology can't do those things. It can, but it's a total distraction that we nevertheless have to carefully consider. It's hard enough to make a product for one market, let along several different ones. The only way to be successful is to focus on one and only one market to prove that your idea has product market fit, and then expand from there. That's exactly what we did when we went into tracking food. It turns out that tracking perishable food is close to tracking perishable medical supplies. I mean, the FDA does regulate both.

You don't have to be a young startup to fall into the lack of focus trap. In fact, it's when a startup starts to gain traction that vulnerability to lack of focus can be the most dangerous.

The world's favorite way to take notes, Evernote, found that out the hard way.

Evernote was a high-flying startup that raised $270M and in 2015 was valued at over $1B. Fast-forward to 2016 and the company known for its ease of use note-taking application that syncs across all platforms got into trouble. As an article in the August 2016 *New York Times* put it this way:

> After a stratospheric rise over the last few years, during which investors poured about $270 million into the company and valued it at $1 billion, Evernote hit hard times last year. Naysayers said the company had over-expanded, was spending too much money, and would be destroyed by competitors. The start-up soon became the poster child of a coming collapse in Silicon Valley.

Evernote is the classic case of meteoric growth followed by a slowdown when the original core idea sputters. Thankfully for Evernote, they have found their core again and are rebuilding. Early success can be intoxicating and, when a company tries to spread their magic to other things, they can lose their way. Prospects of a doom and gloom economy or having a hard time raising the next round will bring focus back to the core concept and how to get profitable. That's what Sean Behr, CEO of Zirx, a company providing on-demand valet services, had to do to survive:

> Mr. Behr said his goal was to make all of Zirx's consumers feel like stars.

But each customer was so expensive to acquire and serve that Zirx lost money and consumers in all six cities where it operated. By late last year [2015], Zirx, a San Francisco start-up that had raised $36 million, had only about a year's worth of cash left.

So in January, Mr. Behr, 41, walked his employees through nearly 40 PowerPoint slides detailing the company's precarious finances and explained that Zirx needed to take drastic actions. That month, he told customers that Zirx was shutting down its on-demand businesses where valets would park cars for any customer who asked, and would instead focus on more lucrative corporate clients.

"Investors used to say grow, grow, grow and don't worry about costs," Mr. Behr said. "Now you're encouraged to not run out of money and make sure you'll be around."

"Today, Zirx is profitable in eight of its nine markets," he said. The company has preserved $10 million from its last financing round to keep in the bank for a rainier day.

Sean's tale is all too common for startups that are financed by Venture Capital (VC) firms. VCs have a single focus—build billion-dollar companies, AKA "unicorns."

Unicorns are private companies that are worth $1B or more. Unicorns are important for investors because they help make up losses from the high failure rate of most startups.

To get acceptable returns, VCs bet on a lot of companies knowing that most will fail and a rare few will be worth over $1B (e.g., unicorns). However, this mentality favors growth/hype over building an ongoing concern (e.g., profitable, slow-growing business).

This focus on growth and hype can be counter to what an entrepreneur actually wants and has been the undoing of many a startup that lost focus while chasing unicorn status. Unicorn chasing is not entirely the entrepreneur's fault. It's baked into what a VC focuses on—big exits that pay back their entire fund.

Recall when we talked about investors in Part One, that there are contradictory goals between the entrepreneur and the investor. An investor is focused on hyper-growth so that they can exit the company and get a huge return. To put that in perspective, about 1% of VC investments are companies that are worth more than $1B.

To achieve these stellar returns, VCs and entrepreneurs focus on milestones and deadlines. These deadlines focus the mind on what's important and what's not. Picking these deadlines and milestones is a whole other book that I won't get into here. What I will say, is that part of following *the* Ethos is be aggressive with these milestones, but also be realistic. Focus is important, but focusing on crazy, unattainable goals is a recipe for disaster. Yet the dilemma all VC-backed startups face is that those who make the rules want the big returns—and that focus might not be the best thing to focus on.

SIXTEEN

Competitiveness - Where do I Sign up?

"Be undeniably good. No marketing effort or social media buzzword can be a substitute for that."
— Anthony Volodkin, Entrepreneur

A maniacal, passion-filled, disciplined focus on goals fuels another trait of entrepreneurs—competitiveness.

Entrepreneurs want to win. It's what drives them to take on all the challenges in Part One with a confidence that most people might feel is a fool's errand.

For me, the most unlikely yet perfect example of competitiveness is a simple cup of coffee.

To me, nothing says you're on the East Coast of the U.S. more than a cup of Joe and a Dunkin' donut. For whatever reason, Dunkin' Donuts, with its brightly colored stores and enticing donuts, says "grab a donut and let's get to work."

It's the same sort of feeling I get when I walk into a Starbucks, but the work is different. For Dunkin', the work feels manual. More blue-collar. More working with my hands. Starbucks feels more creative. More non-fat, no whip, double mocha soy latte so I can finish my latest code drop or meet my part-time literary agent, who moonlights as a copywriter for Amazon.

Both places have a certain feel.

Both places cater to a certain clientele.

Both compete with each other for customers.

I know it might seem like an odd competition, but Dunkin' Donuts is gunning for Starbucks. Not to be outdone, Starbucks wants to convert Dunkin' Donuts customers to latte-drinking regulars. Both want to win and both see each other as the enemy to defeat, or at least to dethrone from the top spot.

That's healthy and desirable.

Every business needs a competitor that keeps it honest with itself and its customers.

It's these competitive rivalries that breed innovation and disrupt the status quo, as we discussed in Part One.

Entrepreneurs love a good fight and are usually the ones who are disrupting the status quo to take on a big rival.

Netflix vs. Blockbuster.

Microsoft vs. IBM.

Microsoft vs. Apple.

McDonald's vs. Burger King.

Uber vs. Lyft.

These rivalries make the world better because each company wants to win.

Entrepreneurs are competitive with themselves and their teams. They want to win and to win big. It's that drive to compete that keeps entrepreneurs creating companies even against all the odds. Healthy competition is an important part of *The Entrepreneur Ethos* because, to improve, we have to compete against people who are at least equal to or better than us.

Iron sharpens iron.

During the early stages of a developing market, competitors vie for market share at the expense of profits. This move is to try and stave off competitors that have neither the stomach nor war chest to fight on. That's exactly what Uber is doing in the on-demand ride market against its biggest rival, Lyft.

Uber is the dominant player but it still has to contend with the capable Lyft, while also planning for the next big wave of competitors.

Tesla, who is creating a marketplace for Tesla owners to "rent" out their self-driving cars, will likely be Uber's next big challenge.

Competition breeds a better product and a better company. It also proves that a real market exists. Competition is also not a zero-sum game, as we discussed in Part One.

A big enough market will have plenty of room for competitors and many approaches to solving the same problem. That's what's happening in the new bot space.

Bots are programs that interact with people to do useful things. The twist with bots is that they apply Artificial Intelligence (AI) to interact like a real person.

Amazon Alexa is a bot.

Apple Siri is a bot.

Bots will slowly start to take over many of the mundane tasks that humans do now. Things like customer service, setting up meetings, and trading stock. It's a new, huge, and exciting market with the end game being that the customer will not be able to tell they are talking to a machine—the famous Turing Test.

The bot space is competitive, with hundreds of entrepreneurs competing to win over customers and market share. It's too early to tell who might come out on top or if bots are even the future. Competition will make bots better and also disrupt the traditional players that bots are trying to replace. It's the same type of thing that happened in ride sharing versus taxis.

Incumbents need to heed competitors—even unlikely ones.

As Clayton Christensen, author of *The Innovator's Dilemma*, puts it, competitors can be created when a company is not paying attention:

> Companies unwittingly open the door to "disruptive innovations" at the bottom of the market. An innovation that is disruptive allows a whole new population of consumers at the bottom of a market access to a product or service that was historically only accessible to consumers with a lot of money or a lot of skill.
>
> Characteristics of disruptive businesses, at least in their initial stages, can include: lower gross margins, smaller target markets, and simpler products and services that may not appear as attractive as existing solutions when compared against traditional performance metrics. Because these lower tiers of the market offer lower gross margins, they are unattractive to other firms moving upward in the market, creating space at the bottom of the market for new disruptive competitors to emerge.

These "disruptive competitors" are usually entrepreneurs who see an unmet need and attack it. This is exactly what Freshsales is doing to Salesforce.

Salesforce is a complex and powerful Customer Relationship Management (CRM) tool that grew out of a need that was not well-met—managing customers to maximize sales. As Salesforce grew, so did its offerings. Today, it's the largest SaaS-based CRM solution. It's also hard to use because it has been built over decades. It's a Frankenstein of features, configuration screens, importing contacts, and reports that will make your head spin. This dominance has created a big opportunity at the lower end of the market for upstart Freshsales.

Freshsales is a CRM offering from Freshdesk, a startup backed by Google Ventures (Google's investment arm) in the customer service space. Its single goal, from all of its bus ads around San Francisco, is to reduce the frustrations of companies that would have to spend a lot of time setting up Salesforce by getting them productive quickly with the things they need.

This is not the first time Freshdesk has taken on a dominant player. Before Salesforce, Freshdesk took on Zenefits (benefit packages to businesses). In response, Zenefits tried to continue its growth by breaking the law and fell from its top spot, as discussed earlier.

Competitive forces can sometimes make companies do bad things. The good news is that cheaters will get caught.

Reputable entrepreneurs want to compete and win above board. That's the best and most sustainable away to succeed.

The "winning at all costs" mantra is self-destructive. Business is not war and, although the consequences of losing are real, it's not life and death.

Mark McGuinness, an author and creative coach, has a good perspective on the competitiveness of being an entrepreneur:

> It's a game. You have to play the game and it can be unforgiving. The entrepreneur enjoys playing the game. You will not just go sit on a bench. You play because you love the game and, even though you want to win, playing is what gets you out of bed.

Good old-fashioned competition, where high-quality companies go up against each other based on their merits, hard work, and innovation is what all good entrepreneurs strive for.

Like in sports, sometimes you win and sometimes you lose, but the way you play the game is important. No two companies exemplify this more than bitter rivals Coca-Cola and Pepsi.

Several times over their multi-decade feud to be the best colored sugar water, thieves willing to sell Coca-Cola's famous secret formula have approached Pepsi. Every time, Pepsi cooperated with law enforcement to bring the thieves to justice. Pepsi could have taken the secret formula and used it to undermine Coca-Cola, but it chose to play fair.

This is what fair competition is all about. It's also an abundance mindset instead of a winner-take-all or scarcity mindset. When a company feels that it's in a winner-take-all market, illegal activities are prone to happen.

Part of following the Ethos is to recognize that competition is good and healthy for you. By playing fair and working hard, all those nightmares you have about some big competitor crushing you don't seem so far-fetched. Just remember, there are thousands of entrepreneurs willing to go against the biggest companies out there. It might seem like a horrible idea to those companies, but competitive entrepreneurs will always ask, "Where do I sign up?"

SEVENTEEN

Awkwardness - Waiting to be a Swan

"If you're not embarrassed by the first version of your product, you've launched too late."
— Reid Hoffman, entrepreneur

I'm sure by this point you're thinking to yourself—these entrepreneur people are a different breed fueled with passion, discipline, focus, and a competitiveness that seems borderline crazy. You could be 100% correct in that. All these traits lead to the one other thing that entrepreneurs do that can make it awkward to interact with the rest of society.

Entrepreneurs think different.

They have an uncanny ability to see trends that most others don't. This superpower feels a lot like Clark Kent hiding his Superman secret. This awkward feeling manifests itself in many ways. The most prevalent way is the "imposter syndrome."

Two American psychologists, Pauline Clance and Suzanne Imes, first named the imposter syndrome. They described it as:

> The feeling of phoniness in people who believe that they are not intelligent, capable, or creative despite evidence of high achievement. They are highly motivated to achieve, but also live in fear of being "found out" or exposed as frauds.

Imposter syndrome often comes from the fear that what we are good at does not add value to the world.

Upwards of 70% of people who are in the high-achiever realm have reported suffering from it. Those who set the bar low are rarely victims.

Nobel Laureate Maya Angelou once said about feeling like a phony:

> I have written eleven books, but each time I think, "Uh oh, they're going to find out now. I've run a game on everybody, and they're going to find me out."

Most high achievers do have the passion, confidence, and discipline to make their ideas happen, and the same goes for entrepreneurs. Part of the imposter syndrome stems from comparing our achievements to others and discounting them. This never-settled feeling is what drives overachievers to continue to push and push hard.

Too often we fall into the trap of our inner dialog taking over and putting thoughts into our heads that make us doubt ourselves.

I wish I could speak as well as Zig Ziglar.

I wish I could run numbers like Anand Sanwal.

I wish I could write as well as Steven Pressfield.

I wish I could articulate a point like Sam Harris.

These internal dialogs or self-doubts feed the paranoia that you, the imposter, will be found out.

Imposter syndrome can be crippling to a new entrepreneur. New entrepreneurs will want to play it safe and not risk being exposed as a fraud.

Margie Warrell, author of three books *Stop Playing Safe, Find Your Courage,* and *Brave*, has had her own struggles with imposter syndrome. She has some wise words about why playing it safe (e.g., not embracing your inner awkwardness) is not the best strategy:

> While playing safe removes the immediate risk of exposure, it opens up the greater risk of never knowing just how capable, deserving, and "more than" worthy you truly are.
>
> It's why, regardless of gender, we must all dare to lay our pride and vulnerability on the line, particularly when our fears are urging us to play safe.

It takes courage to declare that your idea is special and worth pursuing even when you feel so awkward inside. This awkwardness should be celebrated, even while you are working to overcome it.

There is also another awkwardness that most entrepreneurs have. It's an external awkwardness of having to explain what you do to others. Most people will have no idea what it's like to create something. Explaining what you do can feel like you're speaking a different language. Sure, some people will be impressed that you took a risk, but explaining your vision to a cocktail party guest can be excruciating.

This type of awkwardness can cause the entrepreneur to come across as arrogant, introverted, or aloof when you are really nothing like that. This can come about because it's challenging to explain to people why you do what you do.

Most people don't take the risks that entrepreneurs take. They sit in their nice "comfy" corporate job, waiting for their two-week vacation. These types of people are the first to criticize an entrepreneur's ideas. These naysayers aggravate the situation to the point where most entrepreneurs don't want to be around them and hear the negativity.

To be fair to the naysayers, it's hard for entrepreneurs to hear that what they have poured their blood, sweat, and tears into may not sound all that great to others.

Criticism is hard to hear, and harder to deal with.

Often those types of interactions cause both parties to feel and act even more awkward.

Eduardo Henrique, co-founder of Movile, sums up this awkwardness perfectly:

> Being an entrepreneur is not a normal thing. They are crazy people. They are insane. They do stupid and irrational things all the time. Rational and reasonable people don't follow this path. Entrepreneurs leave their comfort zone all the time.

The outward focus of entrepreneurs in being the cheerleader for their cause can make them look awkward, crazy, and self-serving. It's hard to separate yourself from your work, especially when that work is new, different, and all consuming. As Eduardo says, it really is not a normal thing to be an entrepreneur.

It can also be awkward to admit that we don't have all the answers. Those feelings can ruin your company if not dealt with.

In *Why Entrepreneurs Don't Scale*, John Hamm details four characteristics that prevent entrepreneurs from scaling. All four—loyalty to comrades, task orientation, single-mindedness, and working in isolation—are signs of being awkward. This is especially problematic when the entrepreneur runs a technology company.

John's data comes from working with over 100 entrepreneurs. He saw first-hand how they struggled to grow beyond a handful of employees or launch new products. In every case, a composite look at the four traits shed some light on how awkward being an entrepreneur can be.

Loyalty to your comrades is a noble trait. But blind loyalty can prevent those awkward but necessary discussions when people are not meeting expectations. This stubborn loyalty has its downsides, as John summarizes:

> Such stubborn loyalty, at the expense of an organization's success, is surprisingly common. But leaders, who scale, while not lacking in sympathy toward individuals, understand that the organization's success depends on every team member's strengths. These leaders understand that their first allegiance must be to a broad community of employees, customers, and investors, and to the fundamentals of the business—not to any single friend.

It's common to feel loyalty to those who helped you start your business. It makes it that much harder to have the awkward discussions if they are not meeting expectations. It's a tough position to be in, but essential for your success, if scaling up your company is the next goal.

Task-oriented entrepreneurs love to get stuff done. Early on in a startup, they are the lifeblood of building the initial product. They are the engineers who have a great idea and know exactly how to build it. The problem comes later when it's time to scale and they often can't or won't transition into a more strategic, hands-off role. Back to John's analysis:

> Leaders able to scale, by contrast, understand the importance of a streamlined strategy. They learn to extract three or four high-level goals from a longer list and focus their teams accordingly. And in the face of a new threat or opportunity, they release people from promises that were made at a different point in the development process, allowing them to delay or cancel goals they had committed to when they made sense.

The inability to make the awkward transition from task-oriented geek to corner-office strategist is the primary reason founder CEOs get replaced. It's a tough transition from contributor to executive when your whole self-worth to date has been wrapped up in your technical prowess.

Task-orientation can also lead to the next major factor in not scaling—single-mindedness. This trait is great when an idea is getting off the ground, but gets in the way when scaling. As John notes, at a certain point an entrepreneur needs to broaden their worldview:

> By contrast, executives who scale learn to listen to others and take their opinions into account. They grow with their companies because they realize that their passion is not the only one that matters, and they intentionally broaden their perspective to encompass a range of endeavors.

A fanatical focus on getting the idea rolling is necessary when a startup is first getting going. In fact, it's desirable to protect a new idea from competitors, and even potential investors, until it's ready. Working in isolation makes that possible, but there will come a time when you'll have to break out of the lab, as John continues to explain:

> An embryonic idea demands protection; in fact, the gestational development itself is excitingly secretive. But after the birth of the product or the idea, the internal focus must shift, lest it impede responsiveness to market demands for the finished product.

Introverted entrepreneurs are often brilliant, but that's not enough. Leaders who endure know that success requires more than brilliance. Leaders who scale know that they must present their product to the world in ways that it's understood. For most, it will be an awkward transition.

At times, you'll feel like an ugly duckling waiting for your swan suit. It's an awkward transition that most entrepreneurs endure, and all the while feeling isolated and lonely. Don't worry.

Once you recognize that growing as an entrepreneur is like this, your attitude can change. Remember, you are not alone. We, as a community, need to recognize the signs of isolation and awkwardness in others and ourselves in order to get help. If you know yourself and have a solid support network, the transition from awkwardness will be a kinder gentler journey of continued self-discovery.

EIGHTEEN

Grit - Hard is What Makes it Great

"Timing, perseverance, and ten years of trying will eventually make you look like an overnight success."
— Biz Stone, entrepreneur

I'm always curious why an entrepreneur who has already made billions upon billions of dollars would start another company. Clearly, they know how hard it is. They have conquered all the challenges and yet want to roll the dice again. You would think they would just want to buy an island and drink Mai Tais all day.

This feeling of having to be in the game is similar to the military veteran who misses war. I have read accounts of veterans coming back from a conflict and not being able to assimilate into civilian society because they had no mission.

No sense of purpose.

No greater good.

No struggle to overcome.

That last one is important and the main reason grit is an important part of being an entrepreneur.

True entrepreneurs miss the struggle and the fight to bring new ideas to life. It's this struggle to win that is fueled by the grit that successful entrepreneurs must have.

Marcus Aurelius, emperor of Rome from 161 to 180 AD and a follower of Stoicism best describes this concept as follows:

> The impediment to action advances action. What stands in the way becomes the way.

For entrepreneurs, author Ryan Holiday translated this concept perfectly in this best-selling book *The Obstacle is the Way: The Timeless Art of Turning Trials into Triumph*. If that title doesn't encapsulate entrepreneurship, them I don't know what does.

Nathan Rose, CEO of Assemble Advisory, and entrepreneur in the crowdfunding space, has some interesting insights into this type of behavior:

> An entrepreneur benefits from challenges and struggles. Setbacks make you stronger in the end, and learning what does not work. The best way to live a life is to do things that give you shocks. Subject yourself to randomness and shocks and benefit from it.

I agree with Nathan that overcoming challenges and struggles requires grit. Leading an easy life will atrophy your resolve and diminish your will to keep pushing your idea against the status quo. History has shown that when societies transition from hardship to comfort, their ability to defend their way of life diminishes. Genghis Khan and the Mongolian people are a good example.

The Mongolian people lived a hard life. The great Asian steppe is a brutal wasteland with few resources and little protection. From an early age, Mongolian boys learned to fight and live off the land. And that living was hard and unforgiving. Before a conquest, most Mongolian warriors would eat a mix of blood and milk from their horse.

As Genghis Khan started to conquer the Middle East and Europe, the spoils of conquest seeped into the Mongolian culture. Instead of wearing coats made of rats, the new Mongolian ruling class wore fine silks and pampered themselves with great banquets.

Their hard life had built Mongolian grit but, as the living got easier, that grit soon faded. Like all great empires the Mongols fell, not because of their lack of will or loss of desire to conquer or failure to maintain their empire, but rather due to their lack of grit.

Lack of grit is common among new entrepreneurs, but that doesn't mean it can't be acquired.

The allure of glory and the trappings of success lure new entrepreneurs into the game, but they often don't have a sense of the grind it will take to make payroll. Most don't realize that the "overnight" successes of Google, Microsoft, Apple, Facebook, or Twitter came about because the founders of those companies had the grit to grind it out for a decade even when success seemed unlikely.

So what exactly is grit?

Grit can be hard to define. All elite groups of people, from military special operations to professional sports teams, try to find the magic formula to figure out who will succeed and who will fail. What most have concluded is that it's not talent or determination or even hard work. Rather, it's this mysterious quality of "grit" that holds all those attributes together. The same can be applied to successful entrepreneurs.

For me, grit is being able to continue towards the goal when it's become uncomfortable or even painful to do so.

But as with all the other traits we have talked about so far, just because you have grit doesn't mean you will succeed.

Success comes about from the right balance and application of all the traits, values, and beliefs of the Ethos, with a bit of luck thrown in.

Pokémon Go creator John Hanke is a case study in grit. His company, Niantic, which makes games, is the accumulation of 20 years of work. John's journey is an interesting one and it's summed up in the name of his company:

The Niantic is the name of a whaling ship that came up during the gold rush and, through a variety of circumstances, got dragged on shore. This happened with other ships too. Over the years, San Francisco was basically just built over these ships. You could stand on top of them now, and you wouldn't know it.

It's safe to say that John's 20-year "overnight" success with Pokémon Go came about via grit, since you never know that what you are working on could be the next big thing. John's grit was more intellectual in that he knew his vision of the future was going to take time and technology to build. Grit helped John grind through all the struggles while waiting for the world to get ready for Augmented Reality (AR). For others, their grit is more "I will not quit until I'm done." That's how Cathy Hughes (from the Focus chapter) realized her dreams.

Cathy Hughes grew up in Omaha, Nebraska. She had a love of radio at an early age. Each morning she would perform her radio show in the family's only bathroom, to the objections of her four brothers and sisters. This dedication to self-improvement, under duress, would serve her well when, at 16, she became pregnant—not the usual way a media mogul starts out.

To most people, her life was over. Just another teenage statistic. But Cathy had other plans. She wanted to make a better life for herself and for her young son. Cathy was so determined that she would take her son to college classes with her. All this hard work paid off when she got the opportunity to buy her first radio station in 1979. At that point, you would think that life would get easier but, for Cathy, things got harder.

She separated from her husband within a year of buying that station and the business started to struggle. She lost her home, but refused to give up her company. She and her son slept on the floor of the radio station until she finally turned the business around after seven years of saving every penny, hustling up new business, working as a disc jockey, and building her brand. Seven years of day-in and day-out, cooking on a hot plate, washing up in the station's restroom, and working as a DJ to make it all work.

From those humble and hard beginnings, Cathy became the first African-American woman to be the CEO of a publicly traded company (May 1999).

Now, Radio One is run by her son Alfred and, as of October 2015, has 53 radio stations in 16 markets with TV (TV One) and online (Interactive One). Her rise from teenage mother to media mogul is a true testament to Cathy's grit and can-do attitude, with a lot of focus thrown in.

The stakes for Cathy were pretty high. She "burned the bridges" and had no alternative but to be successful.

Ravi Kurani, CEO of Sutro, sums up what grit really is:

Aggressively fight for what you believe in all the way to your core. When you get down to your raw core, push a little more. That's what it takes to be an entrepreneur.

This is at the heart of grit—no matter what happens, keep on driving to the goal until you can't drive anymore.

Grit is a multi-faceted metric that most high-achieving cultures—like entrepreneurs, professional athletes, and military special operations—attribute to being the one character trait to measure success, all else being equal.

Is this true? Can there be one trait that determines success, or is it just anecdotal evidence based on survivor bias? Survivor bias is the logical error of concentrating on the people who made it past some selection process, and overlooking those who did not.

Angela Duckworth, research psychologist and MacArthur Fellow at the University of Pennsylvania, aimed to find out.

Her research on grit and self-control set out to determine the traits that make people successful in stressful and competitive environments. What she learned and continues to pursue is in her lab's research statement, taken from a May 2016 *Slate* post:

> Our research has established the predictive power of grit and self-control, over and beyond measures of talent, for objectively measured success outcomes. For instance, in prospective longitudinal studies, grit

predicts surviving the arduous first summer of training at West Point, reaching the final rounds of the National Spelling Bee, retention in the U.S. Special Forces, retention and performance among novice teachers, and graduation from Chicago public high schools, over and beyond domain-relevant talent measures such as IQ, SAT, or standardized achievement test scores and physical fitness. In cross-sectional studies, grit correlates with lifetime educational attainment and, inversely, lifetime career changes and divorce.

That's a bold and compelling statement, given that all organizations that train elite groups of people want to know how to weed out the ones who won't be successful from the ones who will.

Dr. Duckworth is not without her detractors.

Several researchers have critiqued her research as having "range-restriction issues," which means that the cohorts that she is looking at have already met some standard for admittance (e.g., Survivor Bias). An example of this would be looking at the grit of Ivy Leaguers and saying that SAT scores are not as big a factor as grit when the criteria for admission into that cohort is determined by SAT scores. Although, it could be argued that comparisons of grit among only Ivy Leaguers should take out the SAT factor.

Still, her research is compelling and insightful in that it tries to define grit based on findings from her "Grit Scale" questionnaire:

Grit is passion and perseverance for very long-term goals.

Grit is having stamina.

Grit is sticking with your future, day in, day out, not just for the week, not just for the month, but also for years, and working really hard to make that future a reality.

Grit is living life like it's a marathon, not a sprint.

If you look at her definition, it combines several attributes of entrepreneurs that are necessary, but not sufficient, for success. It's clear that if you stick with a bad long-term goal, success will never happen.

Having grit, but not having the smarts to figure out the right goals, will be a poor predictor of success.

I know plenty of people with plenty of grit who will never be as successful as a Zuckerberg or a Duckworth. In fact, most entrepreneurs, with grit or not, won't be successful because that's the nature of the game. The numbers don't lie on that. Success in the entrepreneurial world is elusive. Most of us won't ever build a unicorn or even a centaur (a company worth > $100M). The vast majority of us will grind it out on idea after idea at company after company until we retire or switch back to a corporate job. But, that said, do you think that stops entrepreneurs from suiting up and getting out there on the field?

Grit is one of many traits that indicate whether an entrepreneur has the potential for success. Doing the hard things is what, as they say, builds character and makes achieving any kind of success that much sweeter. Entrepreneurs who adhere to the Ethos will have a leg up in the game and will use their grit (and every other trait, value, and belief) to move their ideas forward. That's just how the game is played.

PART THREE

Values

Part Two detailed the mostly outwardly facing Traits of entrepreneurs that others would first notice and identify as belonging to entrepreneurs.

Part Three will deal with Values. Values are the principles, ideals, and standards that form the "code of conduct" for entrepreneurs out in the greater community. The values listed in *The Entrepreneur Ethos* are the guide star for how we are to view and hold ourselves in the business world.

The values of integrity, scholarship, action, independence, risk-taking, tenacity, hustle, and collaboration are how entrepreneurs continually get beyond the daily grind and hold on to their vision to make the world, or at least their little corner of it, a better place.

The most important value is integrity. Without integrity, all the other values don't matter. Nothing an entrepreneur does will be worth anything if they don't maintain integrity while doing it. But it's this single value that can be hardest to follow when the world is collapsing around you. Integrity separates the true entrepreneurs from the casual opportunists who take the low road. Living the Ethos and maintaining your integrity will keep you on the high road – the only road you really want to travel.

NINETEEN

Integrity - When No One is Watching

"For a successful technology, reality must take precedence over public relations, for nature cannot be fooled."
— Richard Feynman, physicist

Elizabeth Holmes comes from a long line of innovators. Her great-great-great-grandfather founded Fleischmann's Yeast, which comes in those cute little red and yellow packets that no well-stocked 1960s kitchen could live without.

Like many before her, Elizabeth dropped out of Stanford to pursue a startup that would revolutionize the world. The hype and money that poured into her company rocketed her to the top at such a meteoric speed that in 2015 *Forbes* proclaimed her "America's Richest Self-Made Woman."

Holmes' company, Theranos, wanted to revolutionize blood testing by having one machine do lots of blood tests with micro-volumes of blood. The idea was that, if it worked, you could get real-time blood results right in a doctor's office, overcoming a huge technology challenge and positioning Theranos way ahead of competitors.

Yet to some, things seemed too good to be true. In October 2015, an investigative report by *The Wall Street Journal* hinted that the technology her company had developed might have exaggerated its capabilities. Other serious allegations about the accuracy of Theranos' technology continued to come to light in December 2015. *The Washington Post* revealed that in 2012 the U.S. military found test accuracy and consistency issues with Edison, the company's blood testing device, and that they had requested the FDA to investigate.

All throughout these allegations and reports, Elizabeth denied that anything was wrong with her company's technology. She assured everyone that any problems they'd encountered had been fixed. Then things started to get worse.

The Centers for Medicare and Medicaid Services (CMS) inspected the Theranos lab in Newark, CA, in November 2015 and noted in a letter that:

> It was determined that the deficient practices of the laboratory pose immediate jeopardy to patient health and safety.

When regulators question your operation and determine that it poses those kinds of problems, you have a serious integrity issue on your hands.

Entrepreneurs must have integrity beyond reproach. It is not enough to merely "follow the law" or claim, "we did nothing illegal" or engage in questionable activities, though not specifically forbidden. Those statements can put you on a slippery slope.

Integrity matters both outwardly-facing (to customers, investors, and regulatory bodies) but also inwardly-facing. Employees know what is going on more than you might think. If they see that your outward-facing story is different than your inward-facing story, that's a huge problem.

Integrity is a central value of the Ethos because it's through ironclad integrity that enables others to trust what you say and do.

Integrity is the glue that holds the Ethos together.

Too often, entrepreneurs have the "win by any means necessary" attitude and justify that it's okay to sometimes "break the rules for the greater good." Nothing can be farther from the truth.

History has shown that cheaters always get caught. It's now even easier to catch people in a lie since the internet and social media document every single aspect of our lives. It's hard to keep secrets, let alone concoct a web of lies to take advantage of circumstances. Ask Bernie Madoff, Kenneth Lay (Enron), or Dennis Kozlowski (Tyco) whom *Time* put in their Top Ten of Criminal Executive Officers, if you don't believe me.

Integrity is an important part of one's character that can't be minimized or taken for granted. It has to always be cultivated and protected. Nothing demonstrates the complete breakdown of integrity than the firestorm of sexual harassment scandals that came to light in the early part of 2017.

Sexual harassment is one of the most despicable kinds of integrity lapses because it assumes an entitlement attitude and thus the ability to dominate or intimidate another person. The list of offenders was a who's who of technology movers and shakers, all men in powerful positions, who used their position to exploit others and/or cover up their bad behavior.

Men like Dave McClure of 500 Startups. Justin Caldbeck, Matt Mazzeo, and Jonathan Teo of Binary Capital. Amit Singhal, Ed Baker, Emil Michael, and Travis Kalanick of Uber.

I was especially disappointed with Dave McClure. My company, Lab Sensor Solutions, was part of Dave's 500 startups accelerator (Batch 14). I personally looked up to Dave as someone who had the right attitude about inclusion and giving underrepresented groups (e.g. women and minorities) a shot at being entrepreneurs. I'm still proud to be #500Strong but these scandals have highlighted that those we hold in high regard can falter – all the more reason to follow the Ethos.

All of these high-level executives have either been fired or have resigned. The press, social media, and the internet provide immediate and lasting exposure of bad behavior—so it's best to simply maintain a high level of integrity at all times in all situations. Don't believe me? Research shows that high integrity is the way to go if you want to be successful.

In his book *Return on Character*, author Fred Kiel details his seven years of research on CEO character and performance. Based on his research, "character-driven" leaders who displayed the four cardinal virtues—integrity, compassion, the ability to forgive and forget, and accountability—returned five times larger Return on Assets (ROAs) than their "self-focused" peers.

Low integrity or "self-focused" leaders tend to drive their groups, division, or companies into the ground. The reason they fail is because when times get tough, they can't rally their people to get behind them. This bears out in Kiel's research as follows:

> A workforce that feels cared for is more productive than one that feels neglected, and that translates into bottom-line financial results. Employees have 26% higher engagement and enthusiasm among those that feel valued, respected, and fairly paid, which is what "character-driven" leaders do. They also work harder.

Nice guys and gals do finish first.

This does not shock me at all.

Countless times throughout my career, I have seen low-integrity leaders crater the performance of a group or company.

One time I had a boss who would never admit that his group was at fault. If any issue came up, he would aggressively defend his group to the detriment of the company. It got so bad once that his own group had to call him out on the lie, in front of everyone, insisting that bad things were about to happen. His response was the classic, "Let's take this offline."

Translation: "I'm going to yell at you for making me look bad."

If you cannot take criticism, you should not be leading people. Period. End of story.

For entrepreneurs, integrity is paramount when it comes to not only dealing with employees and customers, but also investors. The startup investor community is small and people talk. An entrepreneur who does not have stellar integrity will be found out. For example, take WrkRiot, whose CEO, "Michael X", was allegedly pulling all sorts crazy stuff like wire fraud that was not only unethical, but criminal.

Penny Kim broke the story on the blogging platform *Medium* and it was shocking to what level Michael X went to hide the truth about the company. She describes the outright lies the company told her and the red flags that she should have looked for in hindsight. Early on in her recounting, you feel that this is not going to end well:

> They seemed like veteran entrepreneurs, the kind I could trust, but one thing that would later haunt me was something Charlie said. When I asked him if hired employees were given a probationary period (it was standard for several of my past employers), he said, "No, because I hire fast and fire fast." I didn't know which part of that sentence gave me more pause.
>
> Red flag #1: When someone says they "hire fast and fire fast," believe them and walk away.

"Hire fast and fire fast" is what poor leaders do. It also is a big warning sign that the leader is a "blame it on other people" kind of person. Translation: low integrity.

A leader's job, especially the CEO's, is to hire the right people and make them successful. Being cavalier or even glib about how impulsive you are on the most important decision a company can make, reeks of low integrity.

Penny continues her recount with the depths that the CEO went to control the company and hide the problems it was facing. The most striking example was the company's hiring practices. Penny explains:

> We had eight young Chinese employees on H-1B visas [foreign worker permits for highly skilled workers] with us as developers, limited in experience but eager to please and learn. They ended up being the ones to

suffer the most. We also had three new business development team members. One of them befriended me quickly (I'll call him Bruce) and eventually told me that he and the other two were poached from another startup across the hallway by our CEO who wanted a group of friends. Essentially, they were hired bros with ambiguous titles. I quickly leaned on Bruce as a friend (less cautiously than usual) because he seemed like a genuine person who was interested in helping me adjust to the new area.

Red flag #5: When your leader hires people for reasons other than their professional experience or qualifications, you may have a bad leader.

At first blush, hiring friends and people who you can relate to is not a red flag. It's common for a group of friends to start a company since they already know each other and most likely have worked together before. It's actually a great way to overcome the early talent challenges.

The flaw in the plan is when you hire friends who have no business doing what they are assigned to do. This perpetuates a "bro" culture that is just an echo chamber repeating "party-line" doctrine and a platform for bad behavior. On top of that, hiring young and inexperienced foreign employees makes the management fantasy bubble even bigger, especially for employees on H-1B visas. Those employees are stuck in the muck because getting an H-1B visa requires a sponsoring company—something that's hard to get and hard to change.

Up until now, the integrity of that CEO was questionable, but it could have been just a communications problem. What Penny recounted next pushed Michael over the line:

> Thursday, August 4th was D-Day. This was the day that set the destructive snowball in motion. That afternoon in the office, Michael emailed each employee a personalized PDF receipt of a Wells Fargo wire transfer with the message:
>
> "Here is the receipt [for the wire transfer]. It has been calculated for the taxes on your semi-monthly salary and signing bonus. The money is arriving either today or tomorrow. I am sorry about the delay."

Sounds legit but Penny, being skeptical, decided to do some research. It turned out that the wire transfer was a fraud and the money was not coming. If you are dealing with someone with low integrity, you need to check everything.

Penny is still trying to get the money she is due from the company. Crazy as it sounds; the CEO rebranded the company under a new name and is still trying to make it work.

What's encouraging about this story is how the internet came to Penny's aid. *Hacker News* (a Y Combinator Site) started a thread to track and document the cover-up and the *New York Times* wrote a piece about Penny's experience. This happened within the span of a few months.

The WrkRiot example and the sexual harassment scandals previously discussed underscore the need for an Ethos that sets standards for the ways the entrepreneur community should act. These low-integrity incidents will only get worse if the community does not step up and condemn them. The good news is that organizations like the National Venture Capital Association are in the process of drafting a Code of Conduct to battle sexual harassment. That's a good first step, but it's not enough.

Startups are hard enough to run without trying to hide the dirty laundry. Entrepreneurs are judged, not only by their results, but also by their reputation. Tarnish your reputation and people will find out. The entrepreneur game is not about winning at all costs, or screwing over the people who trust you, or taking advantage of your position or power. Rather, it's a tough journey that requires a high level of integrity, at all times, even when no one is watching.

TWENTY

Scholarship - I'm a Wander

"The only way to win is to learn faster than anyone else."
— Eric Reis, entrepreneur

The importance of integrity cannot be emphasized enough. It's the foundation of the Ethos, and one of its most important applications is intellectual honesty related to scholarship. Scholarship, the vetting of new technologies and methods, is vital to ensure that snake oil salesmen don't fool you by false or exaggerated claims.

Scholarship drives innovation by asking the tough questions. Vetting an idea that might not have any immediate commercial application can ultimately lead to creating an entire industry. The pursuit and value of this kind of scholarship will serve an entrepreneur well.

Entrepreneurs must have the desire and drive to learn as much as they can. For most, like Yan Huang, CEO of Press Release Jet, it starts when they were young:

As a kid, I was obsessed with taking things apart and putting them back together. I loved figuring out how things worked. That curiosity led me to create a website with, like, 5,000 pictures from a popular TV show. During that time, I was learning a lot of skills in programming. I had a responsive website before that came about. My website got hacked so many times that I had to learn a lot of skills. I would get hacked all the time and I spent thousands of hours learning how to fix the holes. At my site's peak, it got 10,000 unique visitors a day. There was always something breaking.

Yan's scholarship allowed him to eventually use his skills to build his software company. Through another form of scholarship, others seek knowledge about how the world works by playing games like Go.

Go is a popular strategy game that's simple in concept yet more complex than chess. Players of Go, like players of chess, spend years mastering the strategies and tactics to become a world master.

Go is far more complex than chess, with the average game spanning 150 turns while the average chess game spans 80. IBM's Deep Blue computer was the first computer to beat a world chess champion in a six-game tournament match in 1997.

Fast-forward to 2016 when Google's DeepMind first defeated a world champion Go player with their AlphaGo program (a computer program that plays Go). This win was a major step forward in Artificial Intelligence (AI). Why, you ask?

Games are the first step in teaching machines to do rule-based jobs that humans do now. AI is at the frontier of a wide confluence of many different disciplines all working together to solve complex problems. It's often through cross-discipline problem solving that major advancements occur. Take automated DNA sequencing, for example.

The Human Genome Project (HGP) kicked off in 1990 to completely sequence the human genome. Twenty-three years later, it accomplished the task for $2.7B (in 1991 dollars). Today, the complete human genome, all three billion bases, can be sequenced in an afternoon for somewhere around $1,000 (2015 data). Why so fast?

Watson and Crick (Nobel prize winners for DNA discovery), meet Gordon Moore (of Moore's Law fame and an Intel cofounder).

Moore's Law states that computing power doubles every 18 months. Did this epic reduction in both time and money for DNA sequencing happen because of the power of computing?

Well, almost.

According to the National Human Genome Research Institute (NHGRI), the pace of sequencing improvement has beaten Moore's Law every year since 2003. This demonstrates that scholarship complements compute power in all sorts' ways in all sorts of fields.

Compute power in a vacuum does not get you much. You need to have a complex problem to solve and an effective methodology to make the best use of all that horsepower.

One such application of compute power solving a challenging problem is IBM's Watson, a supercomputer driven by AI that is helping oncologists cure cancer.

The IBM strategy was first to send Watson to medical school.

IBM had Watson read every single medical textbook and medical journal, and trained it on countless patients to see if Watson could diagnose as well as a human doctor. The initial results are encouraging and led the team to expand what Watson learns:

> The idea is to use Watson's sophisticated artificial intelligence to find personalized treatments for every cancer patient by comparing disease and treatment histories, genetic data, scans, and symptoms against the vast universe of medical knowledge.

The goal for Watson is to recommend a treatment plan based on all the data and research. This is problematic for doctors since it can take a team of human researchers weeks to find the same result.

Watson should be able to make a treatment recommendation in mere minutes. The important part of training Watson is that its diagnosis depends on analyzing quantitative data that can then render a treatment plan that's specific to the individual—something that human doctors are not good at.

This focus on bringing compute power to solve medical issues creates a vast ecosystem that startups can thrive in.

Companies in the digital health field seek ways to solve some of the most challenging, as well as mundane, problems. Even the government is getting involved. It has started the Cancer Moonshot as a way to rally efforts around a common cause, like the U.S. did in the 1960s to send a man to the moon.

The Cancer Moonshot will provide the funding necessary for researchers to speed up the development of new cancer detection methods and treatments. The U.S. government is proposing to invest $1B to make this a success. These types of big and bold scholarship efforts create a ripple effect that enable lots of startups to take participate.

CB Insights, a research firm focused on startups, did an excellent analysis on companies that are reinventing medicine in fifteen categories such as care planning, supply management, diagnostics, care coordination, patient experience, and hospital navigation. Those issues require many different skills and tools to help companies figure out how to make healthcare better and more efficient. None of this would be possible or successful without legions of curious entrepreneurs expanding knowledge through scholarship to solve the toughest health problems society faces.

Take, for instance, the Chan Zuckerberg Initiative (CZI).

Founded by the couple, Dr. Priscilla Chan and Mark Zuckerberg, CZI's goal is to advance human potential and promote equality. How will they do that? I'll let them explain (via their website):

We want every child to grow up in a better world. Our hopes for the future center on two ideas: advancing human potential and promoting equality. We'll focus first on personalized learning, curing disease, connecting people, and building strong communities. We will make long-term investments over 25, 50, or even 100 years because our greatest challenges need time to solve.

Not your typical rapid growth startup. What this means is that they're willing to play the long-term game to allow continuing scholarship to help advance humankind. It's part basic research and part startup, all to the tune of $3B.

CZI's first major undertaking is to build a BioHub that will bring together great minds and leading scientists and engineers from Stanford University, U.C. Berkeley, and U.C. San Francisco to understand and treat disease. Think of the BioHub as part of that basic research startup.

CZI is also making investments in other companies, such as Andela, that trains software developers in Africa. This investment is part of their aggressive plan to cure disease by the end of the century by using the same techniques that Zuckerberg used to build Facebook.

The Human Genome Project, Cancer Moonshot, the Bill and Melinda Gates Foundation, and the Chan Zuckerberg Initiative are examples of true scholarship for the greater good. At first, these don't seem like entrepreneurial endeavors, but they actually are. Recall that entrepreneurs want to change the world by building products or services that do not yet exist. Most of the time, those products or services are for profit, but that does not always have to be the case.

Before an industry develops, it needs a grounding in basic science. These foundations allow an industry to grow and thrive by providing knowledge and funding. Without researchers wandering through the proverbial woods of knowledge, industries like semiconductors, AI, biotech, and solar power would not exist.

Entrepreneurs need to devote time to scholarship because it gives them the edge to help create the next big markets. Without an appreciation of the rigors of science and research, the technological challenges to create those big markets will never be overcome. Staying up on scholarship will help guide every entrepreneur in whatever directions they wander.

TWENTY-ONE
Action-Oriented - Don't Wait
for an Invitation

"Do not wait to strike till the iron is hot; but make it hot by striking."
— William Butler Yeats, poet

I used to have a boss who was fond of saying, "Never let money get in the way of progress." This rings true for so many reasons.

Entrepreneurs have to be action-oriented to make progress. No one hands an entrepreneur a pile of money and says, "Here you go. Now make something happen."

No, the people who get funded have already built a prototype, have validated the market, and perhaps already have customers. They don't let the lack of money get in their way.

Even crowdfunding entrepreneurs have to lay out their idea, explain how they will make it happen, and convince strangers to part with their hard-earned money.

Taking action is essential to making an idea turn into reality—and the more aggressive the action, the better.

Now I know some of you will be a bit bent about this mention of aggression since the word is generally negative. Sure, I could have used adjectives like assertive, active, or proactive, but those don't capture what I'm talking about.

Aggression separates talkers from doers.

Aggression is action backed up by intent to make things happen.

Being aggressive is not a bad thing.

All entrepreneurs need to be aggressive in taking action because no one is going to encourage you to build your disruptive idea. Heck, most people don't care. I'm sure even your family, who are most likely your first investors, gave you money so they could stop hearing about how awesome your idea is. See, action and aggression pay off.

Part of taking action is to first know what action to take even if you don't know exactly what that is. In other words, be resolute and be decisive.

Jon Naster, CEO of Hack The Entrepreneur, thinks taking action is the most important trait of an entrepreneur:

You need to make decisions quickly and confidently. Take action with all the available info. No straight line to the end. Don't worry about three-to-six months, worry about the next step. It's always about making the decision. Being decisive is what makes things happen.

It's important that entrepreneurs take action even when not all the data is known or if the conditions are not ideal.

You don't need perfect information to take action.

What you do need is confidence to at least try something.

That's the advice Sam Parr, CEO of Hustle Time Media, has for making big things happen:

> When you start something, you have an idea what it will be but you have no idea what to do. I'm not sure how it will be. As you start to do it, you will see an opportunity. It's fine to start with 10% since the 90% will come later.
>
> Don't think about the end goal. You'll figure it out along the way. Just do it and start—even if it's a silly idea. It is important to just start something. It's a huge issue to overcomplicate things. I have a huge bias towards action. Just don't think about anything, just do it. It will be awful and it will fail, but keep doing it.

Being action-oriented is essential to getting off the mark and starting your run. You will never know the full path because the world is too complex, and the tyranny of too much information can confuse you. It's best to just start and then figure it out as you go along.

I do have one caution on starting, though.

Sam's advice notwithstanding, before you start, it's important to have *some* idea about where you are going. It does not have to be perfect, but have an idea and some belief that it's a reasonable next step.

This action without direction is a trap that some new entrepreneurs fall into. They are so eager to start something that they don't fully vet an idea or concept. Usually it's because they want to be the next "Uber of X." It's not bad to want that, but don't waste time spinning your wheels without at least a solid thesis that can be tested—that's one of the reasons scholarship is so important.

Once you have the need identified, then taking directed action is the natural next step. This is Anand's take when he started his company, CBInsights:

> There is never a perfect time to start. Don't worry if you get this or that lined up. It's hard to get everything lined up. At the end of the day, you have to leap and get it done. Take action. Have enough money to survive. You can only prepare so much. You have to have the basics and get the prep work done. There is no perfect time to pull the trigger.

Investors take the same approach when they evaluate a startup. It used to be that 14 PowerPoint slides would get you a $1M check back in 2000, so long as your deck had the word "internet" in it. Nowadays, investors want a Minimal Viable Product (MVP), some market traction (i.e., acceptance), and a pretty good idea on how to scale. This means that all those ideas that are rattling around in your head have to come out and amount to something before anyone will give you the time of day.

This vetting process is a good thing that most new entrepreneurs are afraid of, and here is why.

I can't count the number of times I have tried to talk with an aspiring entrepreneur about their brilliant idea. They won't give me any details or are so vague that it's impossible to understand what they want to do. They fear someone will steal their idea if they talk about it. That's crazy.

Ideas by themselves are worthless.

Action is what matters.

Your great idea is going to morph into something different as you build it. The only way to figure out what it will become is to get feedback and take appropriate action so that you learn. Learning and evolving are your best friends when it comes to new ideas, and the learning only comes about when you take action.

The actions you take must have purpose. As you build your idea, you want your action to translate into traction. As Joel Runyon, CEO of IMPOSSIBLE, says, a lot of your actions may create nothing, but even that's an important first step:

> First, throw everything against the wall until something sticks. Once you get traction, then start to focus. Don't quit your day job. Start on the side. Find something that works. If it's important to you, you'll find the time. You have to create a lot more delineations. Work on it as a side gig. When stuff works, narrow down and double down on it.

This is an important point when you feel you can't take action. As Joel mentioned, if it's important enough, you will find the time. That's also a good way to weed out activities that are not worth doing. If you are so jazzed about something that you constantly make time for it, then you might be onto something.

Entrepreneurs who follow the Ethos have a bias for action, which means that, given the choice between two things, they will always take the one that requires action. Usually that's the harder choice anyway. But that action will bring you to a place you haven't been before, along with some new knowledge, and the path to the future will look a little clearer.

TWENTY-TWO
Independence - Means Running Your Race

"There is only one success - to be able to spend your life in your own way."
— Christopher Morley, journalist

Most entrepreneurs would agree that following their chosen path is a lonely job. This loneliness, in part, comes about because entrepreneurs are independent types leading the charge and, as they say, it's lonely at the top.

Independence, by its very nature, is a requirement for being an entrepreneur. You, and often you alone, need to keep your vision alive despite all evidence to the contrary. There are others who have come before, and possibly others in the next cubicle, yet no amount of advice and coaching will be exactly what an entrepreneur needs at any particular moment.

Independent thinking is how an entrepreneur got here to begin with. First by figuring out the idea, then bringing it into existence, and then continuing to breathe life into it. Every idea or product is a leap of faith.

There is no roadmap.

There is no path through the valley.

There is no sage to impart cosmic wisdom.

With independence come responsibility, but also the flexibility to create and enhance your idea. That's a lot of power, and some entrepreneurs can't handle it. The freedom to chart their own course unrestricted can feel more like a cross they have to bear. This is the devil in the flip side of independence.

That's why the Ethos is set up not as a how-to guide, but as more of a framework to help entrepreneurs navigate uncharted territory. Without guidance, bad things can happen. This is exactly what happened to the Apollo Group, the company that runs University of Phoenix.

Founded in the 1970s, The University of Phoenix (UOP) was the poster child of for-profit education. Its market was specific and focused on students who were 23 or older, were working full-time, and had at least two years of workplace experience. This focus allowed UOP to offer a high-quality option to working adults that other colleges were reluctant to provide. That all changed in the 2000s when the Apollo Group went public and the demand to maximize profit for shareholders took over.

To fuel enrollment UOP relaxed its standards, and it worked. Enrollment went from 124,000 in the fall of 2001 to 470,800 in the fall of 2010. This growth drove it to be one of the largest institutions of higher education in the world. Sounds great. Where do I sign up for that kind of growth?

Be careful what you wish for.

It turns out that most of those new students were financing their education with student loans that were easy to get (another attempt by the government to "help out") and, since the standards had been relaxed, many of those students could not afford the loans.

In 2015, U.S. student loan debt topped out at $1.26 TRILLION. Over 44.2 million Americans have student loan debt. That's a lot of debt for a lot of people.

Unlike most debt, however, you can't go into bankruptcy to get rid of it, and the lenders can come after you and even garnish your wages to pay it down.

Talk about a huge burden.

Throw in the troubles of getting a job in a stalled economy and you end up with a situation that can hurt a lot of people. In fact, it did.

Default rates on student loans skyrocketed. All those students, hopeful that an education would land them a dream job, were stuck holding the bag. This bad press led to the stock in Apollo Education Group sliding from a high of over

$90 to just below $10 before getting acquired by a consortium of investors in February 2017.

How this relates to entrepreneurial independence centers around responsibility.

There will always be a conflict between unconstrained action and constrained growth for the greater good. It's a tough balance to strike. Competitors are breathing down your neck and will take your customers if you don't service them, yet you don't want to create a pending financial disaster either.

The Apollo Group fell into the trap of being too independent from regulations, and a lot of students suffered for it: with great power, comes great responsibility.

Another aspect of independence, though, is something most entrepreneurs can relate to. This type of independence is why most entrepreneurs get in the game to begin with.

Creating your own destiny is a fundamental driving force and personal belief that all entrepreneurs share. This ability to pursue an idea almost unencumbered is wildly attractive. It's the reason entrepreneurs risk a perceived "stability" for the freedom to build their own life.

Independence does not necessarily mean being alone. Almost all investors agree that startups with more than one founder fare much better than someone going it alone (see Part One).

For the ultra-independent, though, that shared reality will be a struggle to manage.

This is especially true when founders have disagreements or are so independent that communications break down. Unfortunately, this is all too common and a major source of entrepreneurial failure.

Recall that Parker Conrad was the founder and CEO of Zenefits before a fraud scandal forced him to resign. The scandal involved cheating at certification tests to sell insurance—Zenefits' core business. Investors who demand hyper-growth sometimes encourage this brash and blatant subversion of the rules. While bending the rules seems natural to an entrepreneur, breaking them crosses the line.

Rule bending is what independent thinkers do. They challenge the status quo by seeing how far they can push the limits before the status quo pushes back. This limit pushing gets even more hazardous when there are no checks and balances.

Entrepreneurs need to be reminded where the line is and why it should not be crossed. For some, the line is blurry and movable. For those who follow the Ethos, the line is bright, straight, and clear. To determine where the line is, one only has to look to the part of the Ethos that deals with integrity:

> I demand integrity from my team and myself, no matter how tough a situation may be. All under my leadership are given equal and unbiased opportunities

to succeed. I lead myself and my company so that everyone involved is safe from harassment, bullying, and exploitation. My word is my bond.

Put practically, don't do what you don't want plastered on the front page of the *New York Times*. If that's still not enough guidance, don't do anything that would embarrass your grandmother.

Crossing that line gets a lot easier to justify when there are large amounts of money at stake. The independent outlaw cohort of the entrepreneur culture strives to change the world, rules be damned. One only has to look at the scandals of the recent past to see how this can morph into outright fraud. Erin Griffith did that in a December 2016 article in *Forbes* titled "The Ugly Unethical Underside of Silicon Valley":

> Lending Club's loan doctoring? That's not what startups are about. Same for WrkRiot, the startup that abruptly shut down after an employee accused it of forging wire-transfer documents. Or Skully, the failed maker of smart motorcycle helmets, being sued for "fraudulent bookkeeping." Or ScoreBig, the struggling ticketing site being sued by brokers. Or Rothenberg Ventures, the firm under investigation after using investors' money to finance founder Mike Rothenberg's side startup. (The firm says it informed investors.) Or Faraday Future and Hyperloop One, ambitious, well-funded companies now tainted by lawsuits and accusations of, respectively, overhype and of mismanagement. (Faraday has not commented on its suits; Hyperloop denies the accusation and had settled its suit.) Or any of the

dozens of smaller shady accounting shortcuts, growth hacks gone awry, and other implosions too minor to make headlines.

The price of innovation can show up as exaggerated estimates, rose-colored outlooks, and half-truths. When selling the future, these are all part of the game that entrepreneurs play to set themselves apart from the rest of the flock. That does not make it right and, in this age of constant information, these transgressions will be noticed sooner than later.

True independence comes with a responsibility to self-regulate and to do what's best for your company, your shareholders, and your society. Spouting untruths and making numbers up because everyone else is doing it is a cop out.

A culture that tolerates that will eventually implode.

To stay truly independent, entrepreneurs need to act with integrity so that society will continue to allow them to roam free. Without trust, government will take that freedom away, as Erin summarizes later on in the same piece:

> The romantic lone-cowboy tales make it easy for founders to rationalize questionable decisions. 'The whole 'fake it till you make it,' 'move fast and break things' attitude—all those sorts of battle cries are misinterpreted by some folks into making things up," says Jakub Kostecki, founder of StartupFactCheck, a consultancy that helps investors conduct due diligence

on startups. Three-quarters of the 150 early-stage startups he has investigated have pitched investors with misleading or purposely incomplete information, like identifying as "customers" people who are merely using a free trial, or taking full credit for past projects they played only a small role in.

The lone cowboy taking on the world is the romantic ideal of independence, yet many of the westerns I have seen tend to end poorly with that cowboy either being killed, brutalized, or shunned by the town. It's not that an independent spirit hell-bent on changing the world is a bad thing. Rather, it's when the winner-take-all, win-at-all-costs, lone cowboys start to think that the rules don't apply to them.

The rules always apply—to everyone, all the time.

The sexual harassment scandals that we talked about in the Integrity chapter are a perfect example of rules always applying, all the time. The behavior of those men occurred in private, which in their minds gave them immunity since anything could later be dismissed as "she-said, he-said." More importantly, their alleged behavior was at first discounted by the public since they were the "good guys." Talk about shifting sands covering up that straight line of decent behavior.

As we said, independence can make you feel lonely. Building a company is a lot like running a marathon in that you're busy running your own race and not worrying about what the others are doing. Distance running is the perfect analogy to entrepreneurship because, even though the race is an individual effort, you're running in the company of many other contestants. There are rules of the road, a code of conduct, support staff nearby, and spectators cheering you on. You're running as an independent, but you're immersed in the overall flow of every other runner out there running their own race as well, each striving for a personal best or, at the very least, to cross the finish line. It's a beautiful thing to get swept up in that entire collective effort, to be inspired (and perspired), and to draw strength from that communal struggle.

The same goes for being an entrepreneur. You are in that race alone, but you're part of a larger group of independent thinkers and doers, each trying to get to their own finish lines, with the public, if not cheering everyone on, at least interested in the outcome. They want to see you win, realize your vision, and perhaps make their lives better in some way. But they want you to win fair and square. There are no shortcuts to the finish line.

TWENTY-THREE

Risk-taking - High Wire Act

"If you're not a risk taker, you should get the hell out of business."
— Ray Kroc, entrepreneur

Philippe Petit embodies the true spirit of an entrepreneur, even though his project made no money and got him arrested. Philippe risked his life to do what no other person in the world ever did or will ever do—walk on a high wire between the twin towers of the World Trade Center in New York City.

Philippe's project was something that, on the surface, seemed completely insane. Who would break into the World Trade Center while it was under construction, smuggle in high-wire rigging, work all night setting up, and finally walk between the two towers 1,362 feet about the ground?

Completely bonkers!

Philippe took several calculated risks that, given his extensive training and planning, made him successful. Like all entrepreneurial success, the walk did not happen overnight.

Philippe's walk took six years to plan. He planned it down to every little detail. Even with that, things went wrong and he had to adjust. Things like sneaking all that high-wire rigging into a building crawling with security guards. Philippe still managed to pull off one of the most stunning individual acts the world has ever seen.

Risk-taking is part of being an entrepreneur. Risk tolerance is one thing that defines those who walk the high wire between a safe and secure job and the scary void of freedom. What is interesting about risk is that it's not a yes-or-no proposition, but a continuum that can vary widely.

Anand Sanwal, CEO of CBInsights, has an interesting take on risk:

> All the entrepreneurs I know—granted, it's a small sample size of about ten—have resources to start a company. If it does not work out, they can go be a corporate slob. This is not a bet-the-farm kinda thing for most. Ego risk as opposed to "I'm going to go bankrupt if this does not work." It's a different kind of thing. Sure, we take risks but the results of failure are a bruised ego more than anything. At least for the people I know.

Anand is actually not too far off. A study named NYLS79 done by the Bureau of Labor Statistics tracked more than 12,000, 14 to 22-year-olds starting in 1979 to see how they did in life. The sample created three cohorts: non-institutionalized civilians; Hispanic, Latino, black, and economically disadvantaged; and military. These cohorts were meant to accurately represent the entire population of youth 14 to 22-

years-old as of December 31, 1978. As reported in *The Atlantic*:

> The people who eventually became entrepreneurs tended to be from wealthier families with more educated parents. They generally reported higher self-esteem, and, importantly, performed better than average on learning aptitude tests. The most successful entrepreneurs, measured by income, also tended to fare well in salaried jobs before making the leap to running their own business.

The study also found that the demographic of people who matched this profile were white males who were educated. This implies that most entrepreneurs have a safety net, unlike Philippe, who literally had no safety net.

In light of the NYLS79 study, the trait of risk-taking in entrepreneurs is not as bold or as "risky" as perceived. The risk that the majority of entrepreneurs take is more of a time and ego risk rather than all-out failure. Sure, some will risk it all by maxing out their credit cards, refinancing mortgages, taking out personal loans, and even working side jobs. Those entrepreneurs are rare. Even if most did max everything out, there is still the option to get a nice comfy corporate job— hardly a catastrophic failure.

Risk-taking is an aspect of entrepreneurs that allows them to attempt something that has never been done before. But it's not, as we will find out, the *defining* aspect of entrepreneurs that makes them different. Like any group, it's one of many aspects that, when taken together, form the traits, values, and beliefs that we recognize about that group.

Any new venture is going to involve some type of risk, be it personal-related or business-related. It's the job of the entrepreneur to mitigate risk as much as possible, yet not let risk avoidance get in the way of progress. Entrepreneurs need to weigh the risks and rewards of a particular course of action against inaction, since not all risks can be mitigated.

Most people tend to ask for advice when faced with a risky decision. Advice is a double-edged sword depending on where it comes from. Several of the entrepreneurs I interviewed had some sound advice on advice.

Geoff Zawolkow, CEO of Lab Sensor Solutions, thinks you should "pick the advice that makes sense and discard the rest."

Jason Cohen founder and CTO of WPEngine, says "not any piece of advice by itself is so magical that it makes a difference."

Eric Eggers, an entrepreneur in the health space, thinks, "You have to listen to people. You can learn a lot from anybody. Learn and synthesize what you learned to move things forward."

As this relates to advice on risk, it's clear that the ultimate decision is yours and yours alone.

That's why the best advice on risk-taking is from Andrea Barrica, CEO of O.school:

> Test your hypothesis. Get out of the building. Test, test, test.

When you boil down an unknown scenario to a hypothesis that can be tested, you immediately turn a mere risky decision into a data-driven decision. Sure, there might still be some exposure since you can't mitigate or test every single thing, but it's smart to reduce whatever risks you can by first testing some hypotheses.

In a sense, anything new will require a pragmatic approach. Risk is everywhere, and ignoring it will not make it go away. Following the crowd can sometimes amplify risk to unsafe levels. A great example of this is the book and movie *The Big Short*.

Recall that Credit Default Swaps (CDS) were the driving force behind the complete meltdown of the U.S. housing market in 2008 and the worldwide recession that followed. We talked about how the U.S. government created the environment that allowed this to happen in the "I'm Here to Help You" chapter. What we did not discuss is how Michael Burry, the head of Scion Asset Management, figured out that the whole real estate market was a house of cards. He took advantage of this insight and bet against the big banks and won.

Michael bought downside hedges (betting it will go down—a CDS in its own right) on all sorts of Real Estate Investment Trusts (REITs) because he understood the inherent risk of subprime mortgages and foresaw that the default rate was going to go through the roof. Since having shelter is a core need, rising default rates when people stop paying their mortgages is an early indication of serious economic problems.

This made him rich, but also a little sick in the head because borrowers were severely punished for their overindulgences. The defaulters lost their homes, their credit, and sometimes their lives, yet the lenders continued getting rich until it all finally collapsed.

Michael took a calculated risk and it paid off.

Lenders took risks and some of them failed.

A great many borrowers took risks and lost everything.

Risk tends to be "one side wins and one side loses" as there is always a downside. However, the downside needs to be evaluated, quantified, and put into a context. If the downside is small (e.g., losing a little money or wasting time), then taking the risk is acceptable. When the downside gets too big, you can get into trouble. That is precisely what happened to all those insurance companies that covered the CDS.

Taking calculated risks is what separates successful entrepreneurs from the unsuccessful ones. For most, the stakes are usually not make-or-break, but rather having to go back to a job where someone tells you what to do. In that case, the risk is having to convince your buddies that corporate coffee doesn't suck.

Your tolerance for risk is a high-wire act with the wire's height above ground as your metric—the closer to the ground, the less downside. As you ascend in height, your balance skills need to be sharp or the drop is going to hurt. This risk height tolerance is different for all of us. Following the Ethos will help you evaluate and take calculated risks, and discourage you from using risk as an excuse to do nothing. It's a fine line to balance on.

TWENTY-FOUR

Tenacity - Bulldog is my Middle Name

"Winners never quit and quitters never win."
— Vince Lombardi, American football coach

One does not usually link breakfast cereal, a presidential election, and Silicon Valley in the same sentence. Yet, one of the most inspirational stories about founders trying to save their company revolves around selling breakfast cereal.

The year was 2008 and Barack Obama was running for the presidency against John McCain. Silicon Valley was about to hit the next down cycle after the dot-com bust of 2000. Two design students from New England were trying to figure out how to save their struggling startup. As is often the case, inspiration came to them in their kitchen at two a.m. Why not sell breakfast cereal?

At first it does sound crazy, but this was not just any breakfast cereal. What Joe Gebbia and Brian Chesky created in their San Francisco apartment kitchen that fateful morning were Obama O's and Cap'n McCains. This would set in motion a series of events that would not only save their struggling company, Air Bed and Breakfast, but also create one of the most valuable private companies in recent memory.

The idea behind creating the breakfast cereal was to get the media to notice their company during the Democratic National Convention. The idea worked. Joe and Brian sent 100 boxes of Obama O's and Cap'n McCains to every major news outlet and got a tremendous amount of coverage. All told, the team sold 800 boxes at a price of $40 each. Not bad for a couple of design students with no breakfast cereal experience.

This gave the team some runway (cash to pay themselves) but not enough to save the company. After the convention, however, sales tanked. This stage of a startup, the flat sales, no-growth phase is referred to as the trough of sorrow. Something needed to change and change quick. Enter Y Combinator.

Y Combinator is a top accelerator (program to help grow your startup) in Silicon Valley. It has launched companies like Dropbox, Instacart, Stripe, and Twitch. When Joe and Brian pitched Airbnb to Paul Graham (head honcho at YC), he immediately did not get it. He told them there was no market for something like this. Breakfast cereal to the rescue.

But Joe and Brian, being the sort of guys who don't give up, had brought Paul a box of Obama O's to that first meeting. Impressed by the gift and by the $20K they had raised selling breakfast cereal, Paul decided to give them a shot. The rest is history.

Joe and Brian conquered the challenges of customers and investors by being tenacious and passionate enough to solve the problems of generating revenue and getting noticed.

Today Airbnb is in 191 countries, 34,000 cities, has had over 60 million guests, and is worth $31B as of its last funding round in March 2017.

The Airbnb story highlights the trait of tenacity and how successful entrepreneurs never give up until they have exhausted every possible idea. This worked for Airbnb, and it has worked for countless other companies who had to pivot their way from idea to idea until they achieved that most elusive of all early startup distinctions—product market fit.

Almost all startups never end up with the idea they started with. All had to pivot to find their niche in the market. In some cases, entrepreneurs need to do whatever it takes to stay alive—even if it means selling breakfast cereal.

Michelle Mazzara, founder and CEO of Luvafoodie, knows what it takes to be tenacious:

> You have to stick to it and find a way to make it work. If you are a quitter, it won't work out well for you. I had to pivot my company from online dating to heart-healthy food because I was not hitting my goals and the vision of where I wanted to be. I had to be tenacious as hell to make sure I got the right product mix to be successful.

Michelle is not alone.

Groupon started out as ThePoint.com, a platform that asked people to give money or do something as a group—but only once a "tipping point" of people agreed to take part. Now, it's a group-buying site.

Flickr started out as a multiplayer online role-playing game then pivoted to a photo-sharing site.

Facebook started out as Facemash, a site comparable to HotOrNot.com, which put two pictures of people side-by-side and asked the user which one is "hotter."

What all these companies have in common is that they had to figure out whether to stay the course or pivot. This decision is harder than it might appear since tenacity is all about staying the course until you figure it out.

Entrepreneurial tenacity is one part "bulldog dedication to your idea" and one part "realization that the pivot must happen." The art is figuring out *when* it's time to pivot—not *if* you will pivot. This gives new entrepreneurs heartburn since they're usually still in love with their original idea.

There is no hard and fast rule on how long you have to wait to pivot. Most companies spend years in the trough of sorrow trying to second-guess whether their product is right for the market. Still others might pivot too early and completely crater their company. This is exactly what happened to Pioneers of the Inevitable (POTI).

Founded in 2006, POTI's flagship product, Songbird, launched in 2007 as an open-source desktop replacement for iTunes. That's a bold move considering iTunes kinda invented the digital media player—or at least was the first that got wide adoption. One of the problems with Songbird was that it open-sourced its platform so that others could build upon the core technology.

It's the classic "build it and they will come" strategy coupled with "we'll figure out how to make money later." By itself, the open source model was not the problem, but rather how to monetize such a model.

The struggle to monetize led to the departure of founder Rob Lord in 2009 and POTI struggled through its first pivot to be more like Spotify (a music streaming service). Its next pivot came as songbird.me, an online social music service that was attracting over one million users a month. Not bad, but nothing like the numbers that Pandora and Spotify were getting (about 100 million monthly users).

The lesson from POTI (now defunct) is that their original idea put them into a hard fight against iTunes. It took development of the music streaming market to finally make their platform relevant. In this case, their tenacity was admirable but futile since their timing (covered in Part One) was off. We'll talk more about music streaming in Part Five, since the development of that market brings together some wonderful examples of the Ethos in action.

Tenacity is what gets entrepreneurs through the trough of sorrow and out into the sunshine at the other end. Often the other end is a pivot or, in the case of POTI, the end of the road. That does not mean you don't try or don't keep grinding away until you can't grind anymore. That ultimate decision to change tactics, direction, or product is what most entrepreneurs will have to make at some point. Being tenacious has its limits.

Like anything, common sense should dictate when to stay the course or when to turn the rudder. The main point is, when you have a well-formed idea and you're making progress, then being tenacious is what makes the difference between winning and losing. Most of the time entrepreneurs give up too early, because the difference between success and failure is a fine line and you can only see as far as the horizon.

It's like the bulldog that won't let go of the ball. You fight and fight to get the slimy ball out of his mouth. It's a fun game for the bulldog, although maybe not for you, until finally the ball is ripped to shreds. No more ball, game over.

Entrepreneurs who follow the Ethos know when to let go of the ball before it gets shredded. It's much better to keep the ball (product, market, company) intact than go down for the count because you resisted change too long or played too hard against the big dogs.

TWENTY-FIVE

Hustle - Don't Hate the Playa, Hate the Game

"Some people want it to happen, some people wish it would happen, others make it happen."
— Michael Jordan, former basketball player

One of my favorite email newsletters is by a former hotdog stand entrepreneur named Sam, who grew his email list from zero to 150,000 in less than six months. That's an amazing feat and, even more amazing is that he didn't start out doing this.

Hustle Time Media Inc. is the voice of the millennial generation that wants to make a difference. Founder Sam Parr's first hustle was Hustle Con, an event that brought together entrepreneurs to learn strategies for starting and growing their companies, and also a chance to mingle with a talented crowd of like-minded people.

The genius of Hustle Con was that it provided startup tactics for non-techies—a welcome perspective in the tech-heavy world of Silicon Valley.

The success of Hustle Con was due in large part to how Sam and his team communicated with prospective conference attendees. Those email communications got such a great response because they were well written and offered a unique perspective. From that, Sam created The Hustle—a daily newsletter with a millennial slant on the world.

For some people, hustle has a negative connotation since it's usually associated with somebody getting ripped off. For entrepreneurs who follow the Ethos, it's more about taking advantage of the opportunities in order to thrive and survive.

Hustle is aggressively going after your business goals in a way that you do whatever it takes to win, within the bounds of the Ethos, of course.

In Sam's case, growing Hustle Time Media Inc. is about hustling up enough interest and customers to continue the company's stellar growth. One thing that's counterintuitive about hustling up business is something Sam learned about building a successful company:

> I have a sense of urgency, but I also have a lot of patience. Anything big worth having will take time. Like ten years or more. What I care about the most is relative growth, not absolute growth. I know what progression we need to make. We have weekly numbers on growth. I pay attention to that per week. I'm a hawk with that.

Entrepreneurial hustle is not about making the quick win but more about building a sustainable business that grows. Sure, getting the quick wins to pay the bills is important, but don't let that dictate how the business is being built or allow it to distract you from planning for long-term success.

The best way to manage expectations is to have a sense of urgency but not panic. The second you panic is the second you lose control. With panic, no matter how much hustling you do, you'll go nowhere.

Panic is not your friend.

Panic will make you delay the hard decisions by distracting you with the minor ones.

Panic is the result of fear.

Panic will destroy your company if you let it.

The irony is that the panicky entrepreneurs are the ones who seem to have the most hustle. These are the people who are always too busy to take a phone call, too rushed to go to a meeting, or too distracted to look up from their phone. This is the classic case of hustling for hustling's sake. Not a good thing.

Hustling for hustling's sake will not move your business forward.

Hustling is not about who can work the hardest or who is the most persistent. Rather, hustling is about making and taking advantage of opportunities that show up for yourself and your company. It's about getting out of your own way, leaving your comfort zone, stepping out into the void, and making things happen. That's exactly what Google did.

Today everyone knows Google or, now, Google as part of Alphabet. What most people either don't know or forget is that Google was not the first to do web search. Companies like Alta Vista and Excite were much bigger and much better funded, but their results were only based on searching the actual text of a website. This led to all sorts of false or broken links that were supposedly "equal" but useless to the user because the returns were based on the number of links and not the quality of those links.

Google's idea was different. What founders Page and Brin figured out was that the important consideration was who was citing your webpage. In other words, who was linking back to it or, like academic papers often do, citing your work.

This was a revelation.

The problem with determining this is that, first, you had to "crawl" the web and find all the sites and, second, find which sites linked to those sites. That's a compute-intensive job that, back in 1999, would have been hard for a couple of Ramen eating grad students to afford. That's where true entrepreneurial hustle came in, beautifully explained in an August 2005 *Wired* article, "The Birth of Google":

> Among a small set of Stanford insiders, Google was a hit. Energized, Brin and Page began improving the service, adding full-text search and more and more pages to the index. They quickly discovered that search engines require an extraordinary amount of computing resources. They didn't have the money to buy new computers, so they begged and borrowed Google into existence—a hard drive from the network lab, an idle CPU from the computer science loading docks. Using Page's dorm room as a machine lab, they fashioned a computational Frankenstein from spare parts, then jacked the whole thing into Stanford's broadband campus network. After filling Page's room with equipment, they converted Brin's dorm room into an office and programming center.

Pretty impressive for a couple of grad students. That Frankenstein server was the physical manifestation of hustle, and you can see it for yourself at the Computer History Museum, in Mountain View, CA—just a few miles away from Google headquarters.

Hustle is all about making things happen even with no resources and, sometimes, no clue.

TWENTY-SIX
Collaboration - The Blind
Leading the Blind

"Alone we can do so little; together we can do so much."
— Helen Keller, author

Governments around the world are trying to reproduce the magic of Silicon Valley by giving tax breaks, investing money, and attracting talent. The hope is that, if you infuse enough time, talent, and treasure in an area, then magic will happen.

It's true that all those components are important, but what's more important seems to be something that all the money in the world can't buy—collaboration.

This unique value of collaboration is more cultural than intellectual and it has been the pre-verbal secret sauce that has propelled Silicon Valley to the dizzying heights of success. This value of collaboration is epitomized in the movement that has built most of the software in the world—open-source, or free, software.

The free software movement traces its roots to the 50s and 60s at the dawn of the computer age. Back then, computers would ship with compilers and source code so you could fix your own bugs. Most of the time, the software was provided with no extra fees.

Image that. Fixing problems in a product you bought.

Fast-forward to 1983 and this "fix it yourself" movement started to pick up steam. The start of the movement happened when a software programmer named Richard Stallman launched the GNU Project, which means "GNU's Not Unix!" a recursive acronym to separate itself from the mainstream Unix operating system that users had to pay for.

The GNU Project was created to write a complete operating system free from all constraints. The main motivation behind this was being able to fix annoying hardware compatibility problems and to fix other issues without having to go back to the original source, which was almost always a company. These companies had their own priorities so quite often your particular issue might not get fixed anytime soon.

Even though the GNU Project was the birth of free software, it was a small operating system project called Linux that kicked the movement into full force.

The first Linux kernel was released in 1991 by Linus Torvalds and would soon became the operating system of choice for the emerging World Wide Web. With Linux, developers from all over the world could write software and make it available to the community to use and improve. The reason this is important is because most software is so complex that all sorts of unforeseen "bugs" will keep popping up over time.

By 1997, the free software movement transformed into the open-source movement and has grown into the backbone of pretty much all software developed on the planet.

You may be asking yourself, what the heck does open-source software have to do with entrepreneurship?

Well, a lot.

Open-source is not only the foundation for all Software as a Service (SaaS) startups, but it's also a strong determinant that separates entrepreneurs from plain businesspeople.

The well-known secret of the success of Silicon Valley is that people here want to help out and open-source is one of the best ways they can do that. It is collaboration at its best.

J.F. Gauthier, a serial entrepreneur who is now CEO of Startup Genome and author of the *Global Startup Ecosystem Reports*, sums up this unique entrepreneurial belief:

> The culture of Silicon Valley is unique. People talk a lot about culture. Is it different here? Yes, it is. People really share knowledge in Silicon Valley. They don't keep many secrets. For instance, everyone screams what he or she is doing at the top of his or her lungs. When I was starting out, I used to say I was in stealth mode. Friends would laugh and I stopped. You realize there are thousands of good ideas, and everyone thinks their idea is better than yours, so no need to hide.

When you share your best ideas, you realize that people love to help, they give you advice, make valuable introductions, etc. Everyone here feels we are working for an industry that wants to improve things, do things better. Google is part of the culture, and they do a lot to help others, like Google for Entrepreneurs. They encourage their employees to leave and create startups. There are 14,000 startups and maybe one or two of those compete with you. Should you worry about that? The culture is we are all trying to help each other out. Pay it forward, so to speak. That's why it's hard to reproduce the Valley in other places. The collaborative mindset is not as strong. But that's starting to change.

To those who are not entrepreneurs, helping out a competitor seems crazy and downright bad for business. That attitude should only be reserved for businesses that are competing in stable or commodity markets where innovation, growth, and profits have stalled.

In the dynamic world of startups, you don't have the luxury of being an island. The pace of change is so rapid that today's competitor might be tomorrow's partner.

This openness to share revolves around the end product of innovation, which J.F. also summarizes:

Software is not the issue. Technology is not the issue. It's all about knowledge exchange and knowledge networks. Working with others. Where do you fit? It's a multi-cell organism like the rainforest. Everyone is dependent on each other and the more others thrive the more you do too.

That last part is the most important and something I have firsthand knowledge of.

When we founded Lab Sensor Solutions, we had to make a decision about the software platforms to use to build our website. We decided on open-source platforms like Django (web framework), Postgres (database), and Ubuntu (Linux operating system) because they were stable and free to use. This decision allowed us to focus on our application and not the foundation of underlying technology—a much better use of our time.

Dependence on others makes collaboration a must. Sometimes when companies get too big, they revert back to the old mindset of protecting what is theirs. Two examples come to mind that have cratered startups because those companies chose to put themselves above the entire multi-cell organism—Google's Panda update and LinkedIn, which restricted access to its API.

Search Engine Optimization (SEO) has had its fair share of people and companies that have tried to game the system by creating content that might not be the most useful or "above board." Think the SEO equivalent of email spam.

Companies get discovered in a Google search by using SEO. The more you're discovered, the higher chance someone will click on your link. More clicks means more ad revenues or product sales—what every business wants.

Google has tried to make the rules of the game more skewed toward content they feel is "legitimate" rather than being just a link farm (e.g., just pages of links). It's been a struggle for Google to try to separate the good content from the bad or suspect content. The problem is that only Google really knows or gets to decide what constitutes good, bad, or suspect content.

That's why when the Panda update (a new search algorithm) came out, it completely changed the value of links and that cratered companies like Mahalo, Wisegeek.com, Ezinearticles.com, and Superpages.com. Those companies relied on search rankings to drive ad revenue to survive.

I'm not going to pass judgment on whether Google's Panda change was good or bad. I will just describe how it hurt Jason Calcantis's company, Mahalo, and how depending on others can be a double-edged sword.

Mahalo was a web directory and internet-based knowledge exchange that used humans to curate links. It contracted editors to review curated sites and write SEO-optimized results pages. The goal was to rank high in Google's search to drive clicks, which in turn would drive ad revenue for Mahalo. The controversy about Mahalo and other so-called "link farms" is that they added no original content. A good example of what a link farm is would be if a webpage had a list of websites for a specific topic, say losing weight, and that's all (e.g., no content wrapped around those links—just a long list of links).

Matt Cutts, a Google software engineer, went as far as saying sites like Mahalo were of "no value" and had "no original content." Ouch!

The results of the Panda update dropped organic search traffic to Mahalo by 75% because Panda filtered out "link farm" content. This led Mahalo to lay off 80 people and pivot to doing *Inside.com*—a curated daily newsletter for all sorts of subjects. Its Launch Ticker, a daily email of interesting stories, is one of my top three newsletters to read because it keeps me in the know on what's going on in the technology world.

For my money, *Inside.com* is a lot better than Mahalo and has a much better sustainable ad/subscription business model. Their email is relevant, timely, and you have to opt in, which makes the connection to the customer a lot more powerful. This connection to the customer cannot be manipulated by the likes of Google.

Mahalo is the perfect example of a business getting cratered by a change in a supporting service. Since everyone performs Google searches every day, it's understandable the widespread impact a change in search mechanics can have.

Another way to collaborate across services is via an Application Program Interface or API. The best way to think of an API is that it's a direct connection to a stream of information. A simple analogy would be calling a restaurant to find out the special of the day and what other food they have.

The number to the restaurant is the API and the resulting information allows you to make a decision to go there or not.

APIs are everywhere and all your favorite websites like Yelp, Facebook, Twitter, and LinkedIn have an API that lets other companies use their data to build other products.

Caliber was such a product that allowed LinkedIn users to send private messages to each other. It was gaining traction and had some level of success. That is, until LinkedIn changed their API policy.

LinkedIn denied Caliber the use of their Connections API to look up these connections. Caliber then had to pivot to use Gmail connections instead. That's a similar story like Entro, which used LinkedIn's API to help make introductions to people.

Entro was denied the use of LinkedIn's Messaging API to send messages to potential connections and went the Caliber route of using Gmail instead. The CEO of Entro, Seth Gold, put it in a *Recode* piece titled "LinkedIn is Sharing Less with Developers":

> We had to completely change our strategy. It did mess up my plans a lot, but I'm an entrepreneur. Whose plans *aren't* getting messed up?

Right you are, Seth.

Google's search changes and LinkedIn's API restrictions are all part of the risk of relying on others. Yet even LinkedIn and Google rely on users to sign up or search for things. In that sense, it's by the good graces of users that both companies exist. I guess once you hit a certain scale, a company may feel they no longer have to be part of the community. In the case of LinkedIn and Google, my opinion is that they saw lots of money flowing away from them to these other companies. That made them act in their own best self-interests instead of being a good member of the entrepreneurial community.

Good members of any community support and collaborate with each other. Often there may not be any immediate benefit to you, but that's not the point.

Being an entrepreneur is one of the hardest jobs in the world. Without the support of the community, the load will be heavy and success will be hard to come by. It's by helping each other that we lighten the burden. Collaboration is the key to sharing the burden, since none of us is as bright as all of us.

PART FOUR
Beliefs

Part Two defined the Traits that are the external manifestation of entrepreneurs and Part Three listed the internal Values that entrepreneurs aspire to. Part Four is about the Beliefs of entrepreneurs, the glue that binds the Ethos together.

Beliefs are the trust, faith, and confidence we place in someone or something. For entrepreneurs, these beliefs are the accepted norms of the community. Along with the preceding traits and values, they make up the trifecta that defines *The Entrepreneur Ethos*.

Without our beliefs, the traits and values we hold dear will not have a framework in which to operate. These are beliefs like having a vision of the future, self-awareness, self-belief, optimism, flexibility, self-determination, and creativity. All these beliefs guide entrepreneurs to get beyond the short-term challenges they face. Rather, our beliefs have to sustain us for the long haul.

The first belief we'll tackle is being a visionary. Vision is the cornerstone of being able to have and keep the faith in our ideas as we look for ways to bring them to life. Ultimately, we want to enable and inspire our team, investors, community, and others to see what we see.

TWENTY-SEVEN

Visionary – The Forrest
Through the Trees

"The best way to predict the future is to create it."
— Peter Drucker, business educator

It's pretty bold to have a master plan. I'm sure most of us have some sort of life plan but, to publish your master plan, now that takes some chutzpah. What's even bolder is to then update it like Elon Musk did. That, my friends, is being a master level visionary.

All entrepreneurs must have a vision for what they want to build. It might not be at the Elon Musk level, but it has to be something that is well formed, bold, and maybe a little crazy.

If you look at Elon's original master plan, which he published in 2006 on the Tesla website, you see some bold and crazy goals. The preface is the best:

Background: My day job is running a space transportation company called SpaceX, but on the side I am the chairman of Tesla Motors and help formulate the business and product strategy with Martin [CEO of Tesla] and the rest of the team. I have also been Tesla

Motor's primary funding source from when the company was just three people and a business plan.

Now, the fun part. Tesla's master plan:

- Build a sports car.
- Use that money to build an affordable car.
- Use that money to build an even more affordable car.
- While doing the above, also provide zero-emission electric power generation options.

You have to remember that back in 2006 if someone said, "Hey, we're going to build a car company—on top of that, it's going to be an electric car company," people would think you were mad, and for good reason.

The car business is brutal, low margin, and stuck in a rut when it comes to alternative fuel sources. Arnold Schwarzenegger, a previous governor of California (AKA "The Goverinator") had proposed the "Hydrogen Highway" infrastructure, a grand plan to create a chain of hydrogen-equipped filling stations along highways in order to ultimately replace gasoline with hydrogen as the automobile fuel source.

The major criticism with Elon's vision was that the then battery technology was behind the times and there was grumbling that electric cars would produce more pollution than gas powered cars because the batteries took so much energy to make.

In an electric, car the batteries are a big problem since they are a toxic combination of lithium and either cobalt oxide, iron phosphate, or manganese oxide. If you make the battery wrong, you can get a two-ton Samsung Note 7 pyrotechnic experience. Not good.

To solve these issues and others, Elon did something that was unexpected and again visionary—he open-sourced (e.g., made free for others to use) all of Tesla's electric vehicle technology. This rationale was nothing short of revolutionary. I'll let Elon explain:

> Technology leadership is not defined by patents, which history has repeatedly shown to be small protection indeed against a determined competitor, but rather by the ability of a company to attract and motivate the world's most talented engineers. We believe that applying the open source philosophy to our patents will strengthen rather than diminish Tesla's position in this regard.

It's bold as hell to give away the secret sauce of your business. I don't know many entrepreneurs who would do that. Heck, I don't know of any company—period—that would do that.

His point is important because it's taking action that builds great things, not filing a bunch of patents. This is master level collaboration that enables all sorts of companies to help work on our shared technology challenges—just like the open-source software movement. This helps Tesla by getting the larger community up to speed and working on the challenges of making batteries.

Getting back to the other part of the master plan, zero-emission electric power generation is the other big problem with electric cars. Elon proposed a solution using a Solar City investment and employing another major gamble, the Tesla power wall, which is a bank of batteries to store all the solar power made during the day. Today this seems rational and reasonable. Back in 2006 this was crazy. Even Elon thought so:

> Starting a car company is idiotic and an electric car company is idiocy squared.

Sometimes being a visionary makes you look more like an emperor with no clothes.

Fast-forward ten years and his master plan part deux is just as bold:

- Create stunning solar roofs with seamlessly integrated battery storage.
- Expand the electric vehicle product line to address all major segments.
- Develop a self-driving capability that is ten-times safer than manual via massive fleet learning.
- Enable your car to make money for you when you aren't using it.

Looking at this list, it still seems rather crazy to "enable your car to make money," but consider that Google's self-driving cars traveled 1.5M miles in six years, while Tesla's auto-piloted cars traveled 47M miles in six months. That's an amazing accomplishment and is certainly going to shorten the time for a car to drive by itself.

Cruise Automation (bought by GM) is working on this type of technology right now. Where there are competitors, there is a market.

Entrepreneurial vision does not have to be as bold or innovative as Tesla's. What it does need is being out in the open so other people can act on it—even if the path to get there might not be clear. Having a vision is important, but it's ultimately the realization of it that's more important.

Jane Bolander, CEO of JSY PR & Marketing, knows a thing or two about messaging and getting the word out. Communicating your vision is job number one:

> If you are good at convincing people of your vision, you will be successful. It's all about how you connect with people. Your vision is what needs to resonate and connect with those who will make it happen. If you don't have that, you'll never attract enough people to make your idea happen.

Vision without communication is the same thing as an idea without execution.

That's exactly what Philip Thomas, CEO of StaffJoy, thinks as well:

> You have to be really good at writing and speaking. I have seen some very smart people who can't communicate and it did not work. An under-appreciated skill for an entrepreneur is awesome communication skills.

Communicating your vision is how you empower your team to make it happen. Most of the time it's hard to clearly communicate to the rest of the world all the ideas bouncing around in your head. It's only through this communication, though, that your vision will be realized.

Sometimes a company can be too visionary and not able to communicate that vision to those who must execute it. For example, take Google X or, in the new Alphabet ecosystem, X.

X has a grand vision to produce "moonshots," which are bold and experimental undertakings that might not pan out. Some examples of X projects include Google Glass, Project Loon (internet hot air balloons), and wind energy kites. These technical and speculative projects are meant to push forward technology and to open up markets so that Alphabet can monetize them. For their vision, X gets an "A" in scholarship. However, X has not yet produced anything that's been monetizable. Part of X's problem is that, without a concrete vision, endgame, or timeframe, progress takes too long and scope-creep can settle in.

Like all the other traits, values, and beliefs we will discuss, vision is a delicate balance between the bold and the practical. It's one thing to have a grand vision and quite another to have a rational path to achieving it.

Elon's master plans do a great job in achieving that balance.

The road to Elon's "promised land" is paved with many incremental goals that allow for course corrections. What might seem like a fool's errand can work if the vision, the implementation, and the markets all align. That's what happened with Casper.

Casper is a direct-to-consumer mattress company that hopes to reduce the hassle and confusion of buying a mattress. Their vision is that buying a high-quality mattress should be easy and affordable. It's a simple vision yet, like starting an electric car company, kinda crazy.

Casper's CEO Philip Krim articulates Casper's vision and why they have raised over $70M dollars in financing:

> Buying a mattress remains one of the worst consumer experiences. We've invested in a unique user experience: whether you order on your phone or computer, we then pack the bed into a box the size of a set of golf clubs and deliver it right to you. And our mattress is also super comfortable—we layer expensive latex foam over memory foam for a minimalist design.

Not the most radical, out-of-this-world vision, but a vision nonetheless. And it's working. It also helps that you have a hundred days to return the bed for a full refund.

Your vision does not have to be complex. The simpler the vision, the easier it is to explain, disseminate, and execute. That's why it's important that an entrepreneur follows the Ethos and communicates their vision so that others can see the forest through the trees by:

1. Taking a step back.
2. Detaching from the chaos.
3. Seeing the bigger picture.
4. Charting your course.

Remember, as they say, if you don't know where you're going, then any road will take you there.

TWENTY-EIGHT
Self-awareness - Know Thyself

"A leader is one who knows the way, goes the way, and shows the way."

— John C. Maxwell, author

Richard J. Harrington is executive chairman of Cue Ball, a Boston-based Venture Capital (VC) firm. His journey started out, of all places, in plumbing where he ran a $5M plumbing supply business before going back to school to get his degree. After receiving his degree, he started to consult with companies and one of them, Thomson, would lay the foundation for how he would think about growing a business.

Back then, Thomson was a holding company for oil and gas concerns (investments) out of the U.K. A far cry from the Thomson Reuters of today that touts itself as "the answer company."

Richard's 27-year journey at Thomson led him to become CEO. That experience led him to author a book titled *Heart, Smarts, Guts, and Luck: What It Takes to Be an Entrepreneur and Build a Great Business*. What prompted him and his coauthors, Anthony K. Tjan and Tsun-Yan Hsieh, to put their thoughts onto paper was the following realization:

We could help small business owners be aware of their own capabilities, we could help them understand how to balance their teams. Smaller businesses need to understand that most of them are heart-driven. They have a passion, and they want to do something, but they don't know how to run anything.

This is an all too common problem with startup founders—all heart but no idea how to make things happen. If you, as a founder, don't have enough self-awareness to admit this, your path will be rough and tumble. Richard explains that, while passion is important, it's not the full picture:

You want to have passion before purpose, and purpose before product. If you're going to start a company, at least be aware of what you're getting yourself into. The worst thing we find is people looking for a product because they want to start a business to make money. They don't have the passion, and they're not going to make it.

Finding your purpose, personal or professional, is not as easy as it sounds and has a lot to do with your level of self-awareness. The best thing entrepreneurs can do to improve their effectiveness is to become more aware of what motivates them and their decision-making—their *Why* as we discussed before.

Without self-awareness, you cannot discover and understand your strengths and weaknesses. It is self-awareness that allows the best entrepreneurs to walk the fine line of leadership that requires projecting conviction while remaining humble. It's vital to be open to new ideas and different opinions. However, the conviction and ego that entrepreneurs need makes them less likely to embrace their vulnerabilities. All this makes self-awareness a critical piece of the entrepreneur puzzle.

Richard's co-author Anthony K. Tjan sums up the trinity of self-awareness in his *Harvard Business Review* article "How Leaders Become Self-Aware":

> Know thyself, improve thyself, and complement thyself [is the trinity of self-awareness].
>
> These are common-sense principles but are not necessarily commonly followed. Why? Because people don't always commit to stand in the face of truth. Intellectual honesty, rigorous commitment, and active truth-seeking are sine qua non to any self-awareness process.

Honesty, commitment, and truth-seeking are the path to self-awareness.

There are no secrets.

There are no shortcuts.

There is no magic to it.

Self-awareness plays a critical role in all the other traits, values, and beliefs we have discussed. It's important to be reflective on where you are and where you need to go. The belief that self-awareness is fundamental to success is a vital part of the Ethos. It's also the basis of humility, which is the outward manifestation of self-awareness.

Self-awareness needs to be learned, nurtured, and practiced like anything perishable. You can't neglect it or take it for granted. There have been countless times when an entrepreneur who lacks self-awareness has led their company down the path to destruction.

CB Insights, the leading provider of startup analysis, took a look at 178 startup failures post-mortem. The results of their analysis drips with founders not realizing that the company was going off the rails:

> The reasons for failure are varied but a few common threads do emerge, such as running out of money, inability to generate sustainable revenue, bad product-market fit, and losing to competitors.

All those problems directly relate to self-awareness and being able to admit that your strategy might not be the best way to go.

Unfortunately, the CB Insights data is nothing new.

Paul Graham, co-founder of Y Combinator (a top startup accelerator), identified the 18 mistakes that kill startups. Paul concedes that his list is not complete but does stress that the items in his list are all within the entrepreneur's control. Although he did not rank the list, you can see that entrepreneurs are generally not students of history. The most telling egress failure from his list is founders putting out a half-hearted effort:

> The failed startups you hear most about are the spectacular flameouts. Those are actually the elite of failures. The most common type is not the one that makes spectacular mistakes, but the one that doesn't do much of anything—the one we never even hear about, because it was some project a couple guys started on the side while working on their day jobs, but which never got anywhere and was gradually abandoned.
>
> Statistically, if you want to avoid failure, it would seem like the most important thing is to quit your day job. Most founders of failed startups don't quit their day jobs, and most founders of successful ones do. If startup failure were a disease, the CDC would be issuing bulletins warning people to avoid day jobs.
>
> Does that mean you should quit your day job? Not necessarily. I'm guessing here, but I'd guess that many of these would-be founders may not have the kind of determination it takes to start a company, and that in the back of their minds, they know it. The reason they don't invest more time in their startup is that they know it's a bad investment.
>
> Most startups fail because they don't make something people want. The reason most don't find a need and fill it is that they don't try hard enough.

That last part is the most important. Finding a need and filling it is fundamental to a successful business. If you don't fill a need, then no amount of passion, hustle, tenacity, or focus will make you successful. That's why being self-aware enough to say, "You know what? This might not be a good idea," can be paramount to success.

There are no easy answers to the challenges that entrepreneurs face, but one thing is crystal clear—you need to know how you'll react to any and all of them that show up.

In my case, I know that I have a problem finishing projects. For me, it's the hardest part of getting things done. I can start plenty of things and I usually have several projects I'm working on in various states of completeness. Knowing that I have this challenge, I surround myself with people who can finish strong. This inspires me to work on finishing because I don't want to let them down.

Developing your self-awareness will help you with your issues. You develop self-awareness by getting to know who you are, constantly trying to improve yourself, and finding people who complement you.

Those who discover how to "know thyself, improve thyself, and complement thyself" will be able to develop a higher level of self-awareness, so that self-belief will be easier to come by. The trick is not to be fooled by your passion or get distracted by the myriad things that will get in the way of your knowing, improving, and complementing of yourself.

TWENTY-NINE

Self-belief - I'm Good Enough

"Do not be embarrassed by your failures, learn from them and start again."
— Richard Branson, business magnate

When you think revolution, I'm pretty sure beer does not come to mind, even though some say that beer saved the world—but that's for another book.

Saving the world aside, the craft beer revolution in the United States can teach us many lessons. To me, the most important one is how a reluctant sixth-generation brewer sparked a movement that saw the number of U.S. breweries go from a mere 284 in 1990 to over 4,000 by 2015. That reluctant brewer is Jim Koch of the Boston Beer Company, maker of Samuel Adams Boston Lager. Jim is the poster boy for self-belief.

Jim's story involves social conformity, soul searching, and family legacy. It's a perfect example of belief in yourself when others don't get your idea, or even think it's the dumbest thing you have ever done.

Jim's family heritage is steeped in brewing. Six generations of Koch firstborn men were brewers, and when it was time for

Jim to follow in the family business, his dad told him three simple words.

Don't do it.

Jim took his father's advice and enrolled in college. After graduating (the first in his family to do so), he decided to get his MBA/JD, but dropped out to do some soul-searching, via rock climbing with Outbound. This three-year rock climbing experience was great but, when push came to shove, he went back to finish his MBA/JD. That landed him a nice corporate job at the biggest consulting firm in Boston, The Boston Consulting Group (BCG).

For the better part of seven years, Jim flew first-class around the country to work with all sorts of businesses. It was a pretty sweet gig, yet something was missing. What prompted Jim to reconsider brewing was an article he read about one of the only successful craft beer makers in the U.S.—Fritz Maytag over at San Francisco's Anchor Steam Brewery.

At this point in history, American beer was water with foam on it. Nothing encapsulated that more than the popular "Tastes Great. Less Filling" ad campaign that Miller Lite so fondly used with big burly football players debating during TV timeouts in the late 1980s. If you wanted a complex, tasty beer you had to buy an import from Europe. This gap in the market for American-made craft beer is what prompted Jim to take a trip to the family attic to retrieve an old Koch family recipe.

In a 2016 interview on NPR's *How I Built This,* Jim recounts the moment he told his dad that he was going to go from BCG hotshot back to brewer:

> When I told him, I was kinda hoping that he would put his arm around me, because this 150-year-old family tradition was going to be carried on. No, he looked at me and said, "Jim, you have done some really stupid things in your life. This is the stupidest."
>
> "Thanks, dad. I love you too."

You have to have a tremendous amount of self-belief to start a brewery in a market where most mainstream consumers don't want anything to do with a craft beer. For an entrepreneur, that's what it's all about—having enough belief in yourself to find your passion and then make it happen.

Of course, for Jim it helped a whole hell of a lot that he had both a family history of brewing and the business smarts to make it work. However, even though he'd consulted with many Fortune 500 companies while at BCG, he still was a bit naive on running his own business, as he recounts during that same NPR interview:

> I was hoping to get a distributor. Well, there were five beer distributors in Boston. I went to each one of them. They all turned me down, because to them it looked like a stupid idea. This was a beer that had a lot of color and it had a lot of flavor and a lot of taste. This was in the heyday of lite beer.

They would ask me, "What's your marketing plan?" I don't really have a marketing plan. "What's your advertising budget?" I don't have any money for advertising. "Well, tell me about the company." Ah, it's me and my 23-year-old ex-secretary. The only way I could get my beer out there was I would put cold beer in my briefcase every morning. I could fit seven beers and I had these two blue cool packs and a sleeve of cups and I went from bar to bar. Cold calling. Just walking in.

Even though he didn't have a marketing budget, an advertising budget, or sales experience, Jim did what he had to do to sell his beer. His original business plan had him hitting $1M in sales in five years but, because of his hustle and self-belief, it only took him five months to hit that goal. Amazing.

Jim's steadfast belief in himself echoed the part of the Ethos that says "failure is an option, but not the final result." He did a lot of things right, and he exemplified so many of the traits, values, and beliefs it takes to make a successful entrepreneur.

Fast-forward ten years and the Boston Beer Company is a successful company and is looking to go public. Being the ever innovator, Jim did not want to go public in the traditional way. His approach is another break-the-mold, create-a-revolution, power-to-the-people moment:

I wanted to reward my investors, so I went to a couple of investment bankers to have them describe the IPO process. But when they described it, you realize that there is nothing public about the process. It is all for their buddies at the big institutions to buy the stock and make a bunch of money, and that bothered me.

I thought that I have to find a way around that. So I started thinking about it and I came up with this idea.

So we put coupons on the six-packs that allowed you to buy 33 shares of Boston Beer Company at $15 per share. So it was $495 dollars. You just had to send in a check. The investment banks freaked out about it. They told me you couldn't do it. It will never work. They gave me all these reasons not to, but I stood my ground. I was insistent and I knew that the investment banks were going to make money on this, so I refused to compromise on this.

Eventually, they all came around and we got 130,000 or so people to send it the check. We got $65M dollars. That was the first time something like that had been done and other people have continued to do it and followed up on it.

It takes an amazing amount of self-belief to put an offer to buy into your company on six-packs of beer and hope that people take you up on it. You need to believe that you are good enough, smart enough, and likeable enough for people to support you. Making a tasty beer sure helps. Jim's leap of faith in generating revenue for his company is what, some twenty years later, made crowdfunding possible. More on that later.

Jim's tremendous amount of self-belief melded with good old-fashioned hard work is what made the Boston Beer Company a huge success. So the next time you want a great beer, grab a Samuel Adams and raise a toast to Jim Koch.

THIRTY

Optimism - Why Not Me? Why Not Now?

"Be the hero of your own movie."
— Joe Rogan, comedian

The English poet William Ernest Henley's famous poem *Invictus* was inspired by his impoverished childhood and the amputation of his leg due to tuberculosis. Many world leaders and stoics quote the poem as a testament to grit, resilience, and endurance in the face of overwhelming obstacles. It is true that *Invictus* is all those things, but it's also something else.

In my mind *Invictus* encapsulates the optimism that a successful entrepreneur has to have. Specifically, it's the last two lines of the last stanza that sum it up nicely:

> It matters not how strait the gate,
> How charged with punishments the scroll,
> I am the master of my fate,
> I am the captain of my soul.

To me, those last two lines are the most optimistic in literature.

Optimism is more than vital to being an entrepreneur. In fact, I would say that all entrepreneurs have to be optimistic about the future, since the odds of making it are literally dismal—yet thousands of companies get started by optimistic founders each year trying to be one of "the ones."

Optimism is a powerful belief for an entrepreneur, and helps get them past all the negative emotions that will come up in the normal course of business. Science backs this up.

Laura Entris, a writer for *Entrepreneur Magazine*, wrote a February 2014 piece titled "Entrepreneurs: Your Irrational Optimism Is Necessary" to explore why optimism is so important for an entrepreneur:

> Negative emotions diminish the brain's capacity to think broadly and find creative solutions. The vise grip of fear and stress and the emotions they generate—anger, blame, panic, resentment, shame—limit thought to a narrow field that obscures options.
>
> "Positive emotions help speed recovery from negative emotions," says Barbara Fredrickson, author of *Positivity* and a professor of psychology at the University of North Carolina, Chapel Hill. "When people are able to self-generate a positive emotion or perspective, that enables them to bounce back. It's not just that you bounce back and then you feel good—feeling good drives the process."

Bouncing back from setbacks and failures is what entrepreneurs must do to continue moving forward. There is so much that could go wrong that any less of a mindset could paralyze them into inaction. Sharks must keep swimming or they die.

Optimism is the fuel that drives entrepreneurs to take risk after risk on the path to success. In many respects, optimism is also why entrepreneurs are able to enjoy the journey.

Famous entrepreneur and adventurer Sir Richard Branson has not always been successful. Some of his failures include Virgin Cola and Virgin Ware (fashion), but that does not deter him from being both adventurous and optimistic:

> Virgin is an adventurous company because I am an adventurer as well as an entrepreneur. We were the first to cross the Atlantic in a balloon, and we've broken lots of other world records. That's been part of the spirit of building the brand and building the company, and that is what sets us apart from the more staid companies we compete with.

That adventurous spirit can only be achieved with a healthy dose of optimism since, like being an entrepreneur, being an adventurer means facing more failure than success, more pain than pleasure, and more challenge than ease.

It's all about the proverbial journey, not the reward.

Gary Vaynerchuk of *Wine Library TV* fame and founder of VaynerMedia put optimism in a classic Gary kinda way. His piece "There's No 'Undefeated' in Entrepreneurship," bleeds optimism:

Being an entrepreneur is a lot like being a fighter in the UFC. In the UFC, everybody's going to get smashed in the face. It's just part of the sport. Entrepreneurship is the same—there's going to be hard blows you'll have to take along the way. Shake it off and get back up. You may lose the round, but there's still the whole fight left. I may have shut down two divisions at VaynerMedia, but in four years, VaynerMedia has gone from $4-million to $100-million in revenue.

There is no "undefeated" in entrepreneurship.

The biggest truth in entrepreneurship is that losing is a part of the game and, the quicker you realize this, the sooner you won't be paralyzed by the thought of making a mistake in business. By default, you need to be able to respect your losses.

What I like about Gary's view is that he expects to get punched in the face like a UFC fighter. That's not only healthy and realistic, but the best part is that he also expects to get back up and continue to fight.

Brandon Foo, CEO of Polymail, talks about why optimism is such a powerful entrepreneur belief:

I think that the biggest core belief is optimism. A lot of people will see problems and entrepreneurs will see opportunities. Entrepreneurs always see the opportunity. They are excited to see problems and solve them. Be aggressive and persistent. They never give up. They are always motived with a sense of optimism.

See the opportunity in problems.

Never give up.

Optimism is a core belief of the Ethos.

But being optimistic all the time can be tough. There will always be those times when you've plopped down in your corner, battered and bruised, trying to catch your breath. You know the odds are against you and you fear your defeat is assured. You also know there is a fine line between optimistic and delusional thinking, but you realize you're still in the fight. It ain't over till it's over.

Two of the best examples of this kind of fight come from sports. Two particular teams with two spectacular players come to mind—Joe Montana, legendary quarterback for the San Francisco 49ers, and Steph Curry, stellar point guard of the Golden State Warriors.

Joe Montana is one of the best quarterbacks of all time. During the 1980s he led the San Francisco 49ers to four Super Bowl victories and was a legend when it came to the hurry-up offense. Joe's drive to win and his optimism that he could pull it off were deadly in the last minutes of a close game. More often than not, a trailing 49er team would pull off a victory in the final minutes of the game. The 1982 NFC conference championship is the best example of how skill, tenacity, and optimism came together to produce "The Catch."

Down 27-21 against the Dallas Cowboys, it seemed that the 49ers were going to lose. With only 4:54 left in the game, the 49ers got the ball back deep in their own territory. With masterful skill, the 49er offense drove downfield to the six-yard line with 58 seconds left.

I saw this game as a kid, and I remember it like it was yesterday. The excitement and drama were almost too much to bear. That final play was magic, when Dwight Clark leaped in the air and caught a touchdown pass to tie the score on what would have been the last play of the game. The extra point afterward sealed the deal and the 49ers won by one point, and "The Catch" went down in sports history.

Although it took a tremendous amount of skill to pull off the win, optimism was at the heart of it. Joe Montana knew in his heart that they could win if and when he got down to business. That's the same feeling I get watching Steph Curry play.

It's become reasonable to expect unreasonable things from Steph Curry.

The Golden State Warriors' star guard has a knack for making half-court shots to win close games. Of course, Steph is multi-talented and dedicated to his craft. Still, it takes a tremendous amount of optimism to even attempt a 60-footer at the buzzer.

Of course, both of these players are highly skilled and have the drive, determination, and work ethic to succeed. What binds it all together is their optimism that, when they play their best, victory will be theirs. That's also what all entrepreneurs need to realize when they enter the arena.

Success requires pushing hard, when pushing hard can seem like a waste of time. You have to reignite your optimism and let it carry you along. Always have that optimistic mindset close at hand and ready to give you an added boost.

It's at those critical moments when the more optimistic entrepreneur will hear the bell and step back into the ring while the other less optimistic ones will throw in the towel.

Entrepreneurs who follow the Ethos know that they'll need every advantage to succeed. Being optimistic is doable, gets results, and doesn't cost you anything.

This optimistic mindset comes down to the mantra—Why not me? Why not now?

THIRTY-ONE
Flexibility - Be Comfortable Being Uncomfortable

"Bullshit entrepreneurs cry about the way they want it to be."
— Gary Vaynerchuk, entrepreneur

If there is one saying, one single thing, that all entrepreneurs need to live by, it's this:

Be comfortable with being uncomfortable.

That's at the heart of flexibility and without being flexible, the zigs and zags of the entrepreneur lifestyle will whipsaw you between anger and panic—two emotions you want to minimize at all costs.

Flexibility is the primary reason startups crush big companies. A big company will have procedures and processes to follow, a "we have always done it this way" mindset, and a political system resistant to change. A big company has to fight the same challenges that an entrepreneur must fight, but the key difference is that big companies also need to fight themselves—there is no bigger status quo battle than that.

Entrepreneurs do not and cannot have the baggage of "we have always done it this way."

This makes the entrepreneur a deadly foe to an entrenched company, even though that company has more resources, more people, and more money. The simple fact is that being flexible makes a startup much more nimble and much more dangerous, even when it's late to the market or technology.

Amazon did not invent selling books online. It was actually Barnes & Noble who started to sell books online back in 1997.

The reason Amazon beat out Barnes & Noble in the online book game has a lot to do with flexibility. Amazon had no other business but to sell books online while Barnes & Noble had to also deal with its brick and mortar stores. That created constraints that the upstart did not have.

Constraints like a large brick and mortar footprint, a 100-year-old bureaucracy, and fat profits all contributed to Barnes & Noble's inflexibility.

Recall that Blockbuster had the same challenges against upstart Netflix. Locked into brick and mortar stores, it had to contend with large and complex supply chains. Throw in its big ugly Achilles heel, late fees, and you can start to see that Blockbuster did not have the flexibility to compete, unlike Netflix who could adjust its strategy as it saw fit.

Flexibility is especially important during times of hyper growth when a company is changing so fast that it's hard to recognize it from week to week. That's the lesson Alexis Maybank of Project September learned while at eBay and Gilt Group. Both companies saw meteoric growth in both sales and staff. As Alexis recounts in an interview on *33 voices*, flexibility was critical to success:

> Flexibility is one of the most important core values you can establish as a part of the ethos at your company. No matter what people say, your business will evolve from the get-go. There will be highs, lows, left turns, and right turns. It will never be a straight line.

Startups must zig and zag as they grow. Add in a pivot or two and you realize that a flexible mindset is the only way to avoid going crazy.

You must always remember that change is inevitable.

The way you handle change will go a long way to making your idea a reality. You do need to be careful, however.

Too much flexibility can be counterproductive, especially when it comes to direction. Being too flexible can lead to a defocus from the goal or product. A product that is too flexible can try to be all things to all people and yet find no traction whatsoever. This is what happens when an entrepreneur has raised a lot of money and starts to build too much too soon or, like RewardMe (a customer loyalty platform for brands), scale too fast.

RewardMe is the classic case of not only too much money too soon, but too much flexibility. Jun Loayza, one of RewardMe's founders, gives an excellent analysis in his piece "Premature Scaling Killed Us":

> We were funded, had a working product, clients, and revenue. On the surface, it seemed like we were growing fast and moving toward the right trajectory.
>
> Within two years we had grown tremendously, but that growth ultimately killed us.
>
> Our demise happened because we tried to scale prematurely at RewardMe. We attended expensive conferences and trade shows, booked flights to meet with clients, added several people to the growth team, bought tons of hardware before we sold it to clients (so we had to hold inventory), and delegated customer support before finding product market fit.
>
> Though on paper we had tremendous progress, we brute forced our growth and never established a stable product or a scalable customer acquisition channel.

RewardMe's demise was part lack of discipline, part too much independence, and part too much flexibility. With money, customers, and the mantra to grow (and grow fast), you can get caught up in a "spray and pray" growth mentality. Too much flexibility can be a bad thing without the discipline to temper that flexibility wisely.

Flexibility is something even established companies need in order to survive. We have talked about how Blockbuster could not get out of its own way when it came to late fees and the failure to go digital. That inflexibility killed them. For the counter example, one only has to look as far as Dick's Sporting Goods to see that being flexible might actually save them.

Dick's Sporting Goods is like the Barnes & Noble of sporting goods. Founded in 1948 Dick's, like most brick and mortar retailers, had been struggling to stay relevant in the Amazon era. What's different about Dick's is that it chose to branch out, pivot if you will, to adjacent services related to sports—something its now-bankrupt competitor, Sports Authority, failed to do.

Sporting goods superstores like Big 5, Sports Basement, et al., are seeing a decline in sales because of, one, Amazon and, two, manufacturers selling more of their own products online. Couple that with the rise of computer gaming, and it's pretty clear that looking outside of selling baseballs and tennis rackets is vital to survival.

That's why Dick's is taking its business digital via its Dick's Team Sports HQ. The site provides for online registration websites, customized uniforms, fan-wear, donations, and sponsorship. It's a classic on-demand, digital platform growth approach as opposed to relying on foot traffic to their traditional brick and mortar stores. Pretty slick move.

Along with Dick's Team Sports HQ, they have also acquired Blue Sombrero (youth sports league gear), Affinity Sports (league registration software), and GameChanger (youth sports scores and statistics). These will strengthen the move to where the sports world is going—direct to consumer, content-rich experiences so that little Timmy's T-ball stats can be shared, compared, and critiqued against his archrival cousin Jimmy.

Dick's is an established company, but its flexibility to pivot to new services and markets demonstrates a core belief of the Ethos. Pivots are the ultimate in flexibility and almost mandatory for startups. Some famous startups even pivoted into completely different businesses.

Slack started out as an online video game, but now is a team communications tool.

Vimeo was a way to communicate with your favorite bands, and now it's a place for all sorts of videos.

Twitch started out as a live webcasting platform, and now is a place to watch online gamers playing video games.

The list goes on and on and on.

Allison Martin, CEO of UDoTest, captures the nature of why flexibility is so important for an entrepreneur:

> All entrepreneurs are busy with the chaos of building a company. It's exciting, stressful, and a whole lot of fun, but the chaos makes it hard to take a linear path to success. That's why you have to be flexible in your approach or the zigs and zags of your startup will drive you crazy.

Entrepreneurs who don't have the flexibility mindset won't be able to pivot when they need to and could face their eventual demise. The data proves that out.

Data compiled by CB Insights shows that not having the flexibility to change can lead to startup failure. Looking at their report, the top three reasons that startups failed were: No Market Need (42%), Ran out of Cash (29%), and Not the Right Team (23%), while the bottom three were: Didn't Use Network/Advisors (8%), Burn Out (8%), and Failure to Pivot When Necessary (7%).

For my money, No Market Need seems awfully close to Failure to Pivot When Necessary since, once you figured out the market didn't exist, you should have pivoted.

Pivoting is all about realizing that you don't have product market fit and aren't being flexible enough to adjust.

Not filling a market need is a classic symptom of being inflexible to change. Back to the CB Insights list, if you look at #13, Pivot Gone Bad (10%) along with #9, Being Inflexible and Not Seeking or Using Customer Feedback (14%), it's obvious that flexibility is a key ingredient in many failures. So being flexible will not necessarily mean success, but being inflexible is not the right approach either. So, what is?

Perhaps the best way to look at flexibility is by doing thought experiments.

Albert Einstein made thought experiments famous by using them to prove his theory of relativity, since it's pretty hard to travel at the speed of light to prove your point. Entrepreneurship is hardly quantum mechanics, but the thought experiment technique is a good framework to do all the "what if's" for your business.

The technique takes some hypothesis and then considers possible actions, which leads to certain consequences. Given the hypothesis and the structure of the experiment, it may not be possible to actually perform the actions. Even if certain actions could be performed, there may not be a need to perform them in real life. That's the value of the thought experiment process. So for a business, a thought experiment could be trying to envision the best way to scale and grow. A thought experiment could help determine the guardrails to operate within and prevent you from getting too carried away.

It's good practice to put some constraints on your startup so that you can observe and manage progress. These guardrails could allow you to be as flexible as possible within those boundaries while preventing you from driving off a cliff. For example, a guardrail might be a strict budget on attending or displaying at conferences until certain sales milestones are met.

Just like the value of scholarship, flexibility is about always looking for a better way even when things are going well. Use thought experiments to test hypotheses and keep your creativity from getting out of hand. Use the traits, values, and beliefs of the Ethos and all the other tools at your disposal to help you enjoy the entrepreneur experience.

At the end of the day, it's all about being comfortable with being uncomfortable.

THIRTY-TWO

Self-Determination – Fall Seven Times, Stand up Eight

"People don't buy what you do; they buy why you do it."
— Simon Sinek, author

Cliff Young could be the most famous person you've never heard of. Of course, fame is subjective, but if you are in the ultra-endurance game, then most likely you do know Cliff.

Cliff completely smashed the mold when it came to what you would consider an ultra-endurance athlete. I'm sure the vision that comes to mind is an ultra-thin, ultra-fast, ultra-Spandexed physical specimen with single-digit body fat and six-pack abs framing their Adonis belt. Do you have that picture in your mind? Now let me describe Cliff Young.

Cliff Young was a sheep farmer in Australia. He showed up to his first race in work boots and overalls yet he CRUSHED everyone who entered the Westfield, which is an 875 km (544 miles) running race from Sydney to Melbourne. Most athletes at the time would finish the race in eight days. Cliff finished in five days, fifteen hours, and four minutes, smashing the course record by *two days*.

Let me repeat that.

He beat the record by *two days* in work boots and overalls.

What was Cliff's secret?

He never slept.

Cliff ran the entire five days, fifteen hours, and four minutes with no sleep. No one had ever done that before. Most athletes would run seventeen hours and then sleep seven.

While they slept, Cliff continued to run.

Cliff did not go fast. In fact, he kinda shuffled along at a speed-walking pace. This self-determination to keep going and not stop is the best real-life tortoise and hare analogy that I can think of.

This level of self-determination is what entrepreneurs must possess to have a chance at success. The interesting thing about self-determination is that it has much to do with your personal motivations for being an entrepreneur. We discussed this concept earlier in Chapter 1 and, since it's at the heart of self-determination, it bears repeating—what is your *Why*?

For Cliff, his *Why* was simple. He did not do it to win the awards or the prize money. He would routinely give those away. He did it to test himself and to see if he could do it. That's it. That's all.

Entrepreneurs can learn a lot from Cliff.

Lots and lots of startups now entice hotshot employees by providing a ridiculous variety of perks like free food, on-site medical/dental, car washing, apartment cleaning, and laundry. These are just a few of the offerings to attract talent, keep them productive, and keep them, period. Any startup that's venture funded will have some version of these.

Dropbox is one such company that led the perks arms race to the point where they were spending over $25,000 per employee per year on perks alone. That's about $38 million dollars a year in perks for the 1,500 Dropbox employees. Their opulence was so perverse that they had a silver panda commissioned for their front lobby at a cost of $100,000. What's even better is the note under the Panda:

> We're keeping the panda as a company-wide reminder of the importance of both our past and future in thoughtful spending—but it's one example. If you spot other ways we can help Dropbox save, please share them.

As of May 2016, many of the Dropbox perks are going away because the company is losing money. One only hopes that the corporate culture is stronger than the disappearing perks. So far, that seems to be the case.

Nathan Rose, CEO of Assemble Advisory, has some practical advice on reasons to decrease these extrinsic motivators:

Keep your costs low. Both personal costs and business costs. When you can live on very little, you have a lot more freedom to pursue things. When I started my business, I did something called base-lining. I went to Thailand and lived on $500 a month. Anyone can scrape together $5k-$10k to go figure it out for a year or so. It's hard to make money right away so getting your burn rate low will reduce your anxiety about money.

We cannot all trek off to Thailand to figure it out, but what Nathan says is important. Look at your life and figure out what you need. Reduce your burn rate to lessen your dependence on external factors so that when times are lean, you can get through them. This is also a good way to level set your expectations since being an entrepreneur is all about prioritizing what's important.

The Hustle (September 2010) wrote an excellent piece about why fancy job perks won't make you happy. It's a perfect example of how your expectations can cloud your judgment and weaken your self-determination when things get tough. Take a look at these perks that some of the hottest Valley companies were giving out in 2015:

- Expensify takes employees on an annual month-long trip to an exotic destination.
- Apple offers the opportunity for women to freeze their eggs.
- Netflix gives unlimited maternity and paternity leaves for the first year.

- Asana gives each employee a $10K allowance to spend on computers and desk décor.
- Full-time workers at Evernote get to have their house cleaned twice a month for free.
- Zillow gives all employees Fitbits and has a communal treadmill desk in every office.

All those perks sound great and I'm sure they are appreciated, but are they really necessary? Besides, once perks start going away, you're going to see a lot of people get upset and question why they're working at this "loser" company.

Fancy perks won't make you happy because they are fleeting and not required to get your job done. This is exactly why it's important that your *Why* be grounded inside you and not hooked to external stuff like month-long trips to an exotic destination.

The magic of the *Why* is that it anchors your self-determination. When you can circle back to the whole reason you are doing something, it refocuses your motivation to get the job done. Your *Why* is your guide star through good times and bad.

The easy way is not likely to lead to success. Your *Why* will help you traverse the hard path. Your *Why* is also the reason your team will follow you even when the challenges are overwhelming. Your *Why* will help them find their own *Why* and their own self-determination.

Invention requires iteration. To iterate over and over again, one has to have a firm resolve that all that effort will pay off. It's not easy to try and try only to fail and fail again. Your *Why* will have to be strong enough to suffer all the slings and arrows that will keep coming at you. Outrageous fortune, too.

The lesson in all those tries and trials is that you just keep standing up, no matter what. You make it a conditioned response that you will stand up. When you fall down seven times, you stand up eight. Or maybe it's eighty-eight. No matter. There is no other way.

THIRTY-THREE

Creativity - Have No Fear of Perfection

"Logic will get you from A to B. Imagination will take you everywhere."
— Albert Einstein, theoretical physicist

The lifeblood of an entrepreneur is creativity. Out of all the beliefs we have discussed, creativity is, without a doubt, something every entrepreneur believes in unconditionally.

Without creativity, an entrepreneur cannot solve complex problems or be able to zig and zag when the bad stuff hits the fan. All the values, traits, and beliefs an entrepreneur can muster will help him or her along the way, but it's through creativity that entrepreneurs invent the next big thing. That next big thing can be in any industry or any product—even ones that at first seem trivial or boring.

It's hard to image how you can innovate pizza, but Mountain View-based Zume Pizza did just that in 2016. Zume's innovation: robot-made pizzas cooked to order en route to your house.

Using robots to automate manual tasks is nothing new. The auto industry in Japan uses robots on their assembly lines and it's often joked that when demand subsides, the only layoffs are the robots. Automation does make a product more reliable and consistent since humans get tired and, when tired, they make mistakes. So why did Zume apply robotic technology to the artisan craft of making pizzas?

It turns out that the biggest cost of making pizza is—no surprise—the labor. A robot will be more consistent and not waste as many ingredients—thus also being more efficient. The big idea for Zume is not only robots but also the whole pizza experience. Alex Garden, co-founder and executive chairman of Zume, sums it up best:

> The robots will load all these individual ovens with different menu items. Then the truck will circle the neighborhood. At precisely three minutes and fifteen seconds before arriving at the customer's location, the cloud commands the oven to turn on and—Garden made the symbol of a large explosion emanating from his brain—BOOM, the customer gets a fresh, just-out-of-the-oven pizza delivered to their door.

Can you image a fleet of pizza trucks circling your neighborhood waiting for you to order? You can imagine this model applying to more than pizza as Alex envisions Zume to become "the Amazon of food." It's this kind of creativity that drives entrepreneurs to find a better way to transform an apparent innovation-less industry. Robots making pizza is all fine and good but, for my money, the most creative thing Zume did was reinventing the pizza box.

The pizza box is so twentieth-century. It's a square, slippery cardboard thing that leaks grease. The only innovation in the pizza box ecosystem was the invention of the pizza saver—a plastic mini three-legged stool that prevented the top of the box from squishing your delicious pizza toppings. Hardly blazing the innovation trail, if you ask me.

That's why the Zume pizza box is so cool. It's built with a dome that protects the pizza — so no need for the pizza saver. It also has eight slices embedded in the base with channels to move the grease to the center grease-capture reservoir. If that were not enough, it even has molded feet to prevent the warmth from making that ugly white condensation smear on your new dining room table. Those feet also double as a method to stack several pizzas together so they don't slide off your front seat as you turn a corner.

This kind of "reinvention of outdated things" creativity is everywhere. Look at how Uber transformed hailing a ride, Airbnb for finding a place to stay, and Etsy for helping creative people sell their crafts. These companies all took a new look at an old problem—a much different look—and thus created something entirely new.

Legacy ways of doing things are always ripe for creative disruptions that, at first, may seem silly or even stupid. It's when you look at an old thing with new eyes that true creativity happens. Just like what DocuSign did for signing documents.

I hate signing reams and reams of paper and getting a "copy" of some document that I will file away and never look at again. This is especially problematic when you buy a house and they "paper" the deal. Translation: let's kill trees, ruin the environment, and suffer paper cuts. That's why DocuSign is such an eloquent solution for a mundane task.

DocuSign allows you to legally sign any document, including scanned and online ones, without having to print them out and physically write your signature. This is brilliant if you are a lawyer or real estate agent because of the mountains of paperwork to sign to get your job done. No more printing out, faxing, and filing away paper copies of documents—yes, I said faxing.

With DocuSign it's all online and super simple. This creative approach to signing everyday documents has put DocuSign in the unicorn club with an evaluation of $3B based on its last round of financing.

At first blush DocuSign looks like a pretty boring business and signing documents is, well, boring. But creativity does not need to be some magical interesting thing that captivates the entire world and wins design awards. What creativity embodies in the entrepreneurial world is just the ability to solve real problems in a clever way. Take, for instance, the revolutionary Squatty Potty.

The Squatty Potty is a simple device that allows your body to maintain the proper physical alignment for a bowel movement. The design is simple—it's a step stool that you put your feet on to raise your legs while you do your business. At first glance, the Squatty Potty is not creative at all—it's just a molded plastic step stool. Squatty Potty's creativity comes into play in how they marketed it. Instead of having some dull actor in a white coat come out and intone something like, "Nine out of ten doctors agree that this will...blah, blah, blah," they got really creative.

They created a video called "This Unicorn Changed the Way I Poop" with a cute cartoon unicorn (a "real" one, not a $1B dollar company) that pooped magic rainbow soft serve when she used the Squatty Potty. The video went viral and was viewed over 28M times. It was so good that it moved my wife (pun intended) to order a three-pack.

Squatty Potty is a perfect example of being creative about something that most people might not admit having a problem with, or even realizing there was a problem that needed fixing. Finding a need and filling it is the first step. Getting the word out in such a way to generate interest is another step, and then getting customers to buy it is yet another. But sometimes you don't even need to solve a problem at all. All you have to do is provide an alternative to what others are already providing, like Chubbies does.

Chubbies started out as a line of short shorts for men. Founded by four guys who realized that most clothing companies were all about "fashion" and, to them, fashion is all about exclusivity and status. What they wanted was to be about inclusivity and not taking things too seriously. Chubbies realized that most 9-to-5 jobs suck and everyone looks forward to the weekend. This fact started the Chubbies Weekend Revolution (Exhibit A of their Manifesto):

> We exist to bring you the best weekend clothing that has ever been conceived. To us, the weekend represents everything Chubbies represents. From a product perspective, we started the company on two fundamental premises. First, that pants represented the workweek, cubicles, TPS [Testing Procedure Specification] reports and pointless spreadsheets. And second, the state of today's shorts-wear was dire. Cargos. Capris. Men everywhere [were] hiding their legs.

At first look, Chubbies was not that creative. Sure, designing some cool shorts for the weekend is fun but lots of people do that. What's the big idea? For Chubbies, it's how the weekend makes you feel and that's where they unleashed their creativity. For Chubbies, this has led to a $13M investment and some of the most popular videos on YouTube.

Chubbies creates videos that show what the weekend means to them. These videos are so creative that most go viral. My favorite is *Mario Cart on Lombard Street* where they have a bunch of people on big wheels, dressed up as Mario Bros. The video is so funny and so culturally relevant to the Chubbies demographic.

On last count, six of their videos had over a 1M views with two having over 25M views. This might not seem like a big deal, but consider that the average YouTube video gets between 3K to 10K views. Can you start to see how the power of being creative could affect your brand?

Creativity is something that an entrepreneur must apply to solve problems because, without it, the solution would be just a "me-too" or would not garner enough "wow" factors to make it. This does not mean that you have to be as uber-creative as the examples above.

There is no magic formula for being creative. Most of the time it's a lot of practicing your craft and looking for inspiration, often in completely different markets or industries than the one you are in. This can result in "borrowing" ideas from odd places. For example, scientists have created an adhesive that was inspired by the feet of geckos, those cute little lizards that can walk up walls. By studying the biology of the geckos' feet, they figured out how the gecko "sticks" to objects. That's definitely looking at things in a unique and novel way.

If you don't know exactly where to start, don't worry. Just start trying new things. Don't fret about finding the "perfect" solution—they don't exist. Rather, accept the fact that in order to create something new, you just need to think outside the (pizza) box.

PART FIVE

Dents in the Universe

The last three parts laid out the Traits, Values, and Beliefs that make up the core of the Ethos. By cultivating these, an entrepreneur creates a framework to fully and ethically engage in his or her challenge to the status quo. And what is the nature of that challenge?

As Steve Jobs famously said about why we are here:

> We're here to put a dent in the universe. Otherwise why else even be here?

Part Five is all about those Dents in the Universe.

Our lives are very different today than they were just a few short years ago, and there is every indication that the rate of change will continue to increase. Entrepreneurs will be in the vanguard of innovators that will bring myriad changes to life in the twenty-first century. The status will not remain "quo" for long.

There are so many industries that have already been impacted by entrepreneurs—it's hard to pick a few. The ones I have chosen to explore here are markets, technologies, and movements that are end-user focused. This means that your mom, dad, brother, sister, and nana will know about them.

THIRTY-FOUR

Cloud Computing - Software Eats the World

"Every kid coming out of school now thinks he can be the next Mark Zuckerberg, and with these new technologies like cloud computing, he actually has a shot."

– Marc Andreessen, investor

Back in the 1960s, mainframe users would type on a "terminal" to access the central server. These terminals were expensive, since you paid by the minute. And since they were time-shared, you had to wait until your terminal got serviced to see your results. Mainframes started to lose favor when Personal Computers (PCs) showed up around 1974. These new PCs could run their own programs and did not have to be connected to a mainframe. As PCs got cheaper and cheaper, the mainframe slowly lost influence, although most companies still run large batch update processes on mainframes.

When computers started to get networked together, information could be updated locally and shared regionally. That sharing made email and files much easier to send and collaborate on, at least within your Local Area Network (LAN). But sharing information outside your connected computers was still challenging until an affordable and interoperable internet came into being in the early 1990s.

Once the internet arrived, everything changed. Companies could now buy dedicated servers to "serve" up software for remote users to execute at will. This marked the shift to Software as a Service (SaaS), which started in the mid-2000s.

As this new model scaled, it became obvious that the servers these services were running on could themselves be services. Say that ten times fast. This new model ushered in the shift from dedicated server farms to the cloud.

The cloud now enables you to rent time on the likes of Amazon Web Services (AWS), Google, or IBM servers. The model looks an awful lot like the old days of terminals and mainframes where you paid by the minute, or by your bandwidth, or by the storage used, or all three. Cloud-computing has commoditized compute power and network access and thus revolutionized the way entrepreneurs bring their products and services to market.

The rise of the internet, SaaS, and cloud computing are examples of the visionary and collaborative aspects of the Ethos in action. This brave new world of computing could not have come about without dramatic advances in technology, vision, and collaboration.

Nowadays, the majority of startups are based on some sort of cloud service. This is the easiest and most capital-efficient way to determine if you have an MVP, the previously discussed Minimal Viable Product, which is the smallest set of features and functions a product needs for a customer to buy it. This

MVP requirement is now so pervasive that investors won't even look at a startup unless it has a proven MVP and is generating revenue—as we discussed in the Investors chapter in Part One.

As mentioned before, this is a world away from the gold-rush days of the late 1990's when your "internet" PowerPoint deck would create a feeding frenzy of investors throwing money at you.

I jest but not too much.

The advent of the web and the ubiquity of cloud-based services has made the entrepreneur's life much easier, but also much harder in some ways. There are so many new services out there to compete against, that it's difficult to differentiate yourself from the pack. Still, sometimes all it takes is a great idea and a whole lot of luck. Like what Canva did for design.

Founded in 2012 by Melanie Perkins, Cliff Obrecht, and Cameron Adams, Canva started out as Fusion Books, an online platform to allow students and teachers to create their own yearbooks. What the trio realized was that what they had built for yearbooks, could also be applied to other design projects, both printed and electronic. This creativity and flexibility allowed the Canva team to provide customers with a compelling product that no Canva competitor had.

By 2015 Canva had launched a marketplace and released Canva for Work to a user base of four million strong.

You would think that a process so complicated and as complex as design would not lend itself to the web. Moving images around is bandwidth-, storage-, and compute-intensive. Even more amazing is that Canva is based in Australia, which dispels the myth that you absolutely need to be in Silicon Valley. Unlike real estate, cloud computing is not about location, location, location.

The power of the cloud has inspired another idea first coined by Marc Andreessen, founder of Netscape and co-founder of VC firm Andreessen-Horowitz (a16z), that "Software is Eating the World."

Back in 2011 when a16z raised its first venture fund, the emerging technologies of the day were mobile, social, and cloud. The internet had been a fact of life for two decades and over two billion people had access by then. Riding high on that connectivity and technology, companies like Uber and Airbnb were disrupting established industries and enabling consumers to better utilize and profit from resources they already owned.

These companies and a multitude of others were made possible by the tremendous growth of infrastructure, connectivity, and compute power. The costs to run companies on the cloud got cheaper and cheaper, as we discussed in the Technology chapter in Part One.

For example, in 2000, a basic internet application like an Oracle database would cost you $150,000 a month. Ten years later that same application would cost $1,500 a month. This drastic cost reduction not only made creating an idea much easier, but also made it cheaper to offer to a larger and more dispersed set of customers.

Imagine an application like Canva back in 2000. It would have cost over ten times more to host. Their preferred user acquisition method called Freemium, which has both a limited free version and one that customers pay for, would have been prohibitively expensive.

Andreessen captured this phenomenon in "Why Software is Eating the World" with examples in a 2011 *Wall Street Journal* piece of the same title:

> With lower start-up costs and a vastly expanded market for online services, the result is a global economy that for the first time will be fully digitally wired—the dream of every cyber-visionary of the early 1990s, finally delivered, a full generation later.
>
> Perhaps the single most dramatic example of this phenomenon of software eating a traditional business is the suicide of Borders and corresponding rise of Amazon. In 2001, Borders agreed to hand over its online business to Amazon under the theory that online book sales were non-strategic and unimportant.
>
> Today, the world's largest bookseller, Amazon, is a software company—its core capability is its amazing software engine for selling virtually everything online,

no retail stores necessary ... Amazon rearranged its website to promote its Kindle digital books over physical books for the first time. Now even the books themselves are software.

Andreessen goes on to list companies like Netflix, Spotify, Pandora, Zynga (at least at that time), Rovio, Pixar, Shutterfly, Flickr, Google, Skype, LinkedIn, PayPal, et al., who all took a traditional market and applied cloud technology to make it better, faster, and cheaper. The internet enabled all consumer mobile and desktop devices to connect to a veritable sky-full of cloud computing services.

You'll see examples like these this time and again as we explore other dents in the universe. You'll also see how utilizing the internet infrastructure to access the cloud makes entrepreneurs much more collaborative, creative, and competitive, and in ways never imagined before. This serendipitous confluence of software, hardware, and people will continue to create even more dents in the universe.

THIRTY-FIVE

Audio Streaming – Pretty Fly
for a White Guy

"I think that's what happened to the record business when
'Napster' came around. The industry rejected what was
happening instead of accepting it as change."
— Jay-Z, rapper

When you think of music streaming, I'm sure that the last person who comes to mind is iconic musician Frank Zappa. Zappa's music career spanned more than 30 years and he released over 60 albums as a solo artist and with his band, the Mothers of Invention.

What many people don't know is that Frank also invented the music file sharing business model back in 1983.

Yes, you heard me right.

The father of Moon, Dweezil, Ahmet, and Diva Zappa came up with the idea that would be the basis for the $1.6B dollar (in 2016) music streaming business. His idea launched iconic music streaming brands such as iTunes, Spotify, Pandora, and Amazon.

Zappa's idea was a response to a problem that many artists and industry insiders hated—customers taping albums and giving them to friends. His idea, documented in his book, *The Real Frank Zappa*, outlines how he was going to solve this problem with technology:

> We [Zappa and Company] propose to acquire the rights to digitally duplicate and store THE BEST of every record company's difficult-to-move Quality Catalog Items [Q.C.I.], store them in a central processing location, and have them accessible by phone or cable TV, directly patchable into the user's home taping appliances, with the option of direct digital-to-digital transfer to F-1 (SONY consumer level digital tape encoder), Beta Hi-Fi, or ordinary analog cassette (requiring the installation of a rentable D-A converter in the phone itself ... the main chip is about $12).

> All accounting for royalty payments, billing to the customer, etc., would be automatic, built into the initial software for the system.

> The consumer has the option of subscribing to one or more Interest Categories, charged at a monthly rate, without regard for the quantity of music he or she decides to tape.

That's a pretty amazing description of music streaming, and streaming in general. Frank was ahead of his time and laid the foundation of what was to come. Unfortunately, his idea would sit on the shelf until technology caught up years later. No amount of vision or creativity could overcome the then challenges of technology and market timing.

Fast-forward to 1999 when Frank's idea would finally come about, but would cause more problems than anyone could have imagined. This new technology would have some unlikely opponents, and the drama it created would set back the music streaming industry for at least a decade.

This "public enemy #1" technology was created by a bunch of shy hackers who would create the fastest-growing business ever. That company was Napster.

Founded by Shawn Fanning, Shawn's uncle John Fanning, and Sean Parker, Napster was created to find a better way to share files. The led to a better, though problematic, way to download and share music on the internet.

Right from the start, some on the team worried about the legality of the service. But Shawn felt pretty strongly that if they built something cool, the rest would work itself out. This naiveté was due to Shawn's young age. He was 19 when he founded Napster. He was also so in love with his idea that he was blind to the consequences—a clear violation of the Ethos. How wrong he turned out to be.

Napster became the enemy that both artists and labels rallied against. It drove the adoption of Digital Rights Management (DRM), as well as perpetuating the stigma that anyone who downloads music was a criminal. DRM made file sharing much harder because it used encryption to protect the digital media files. If you don't have the key, you can't get access. DRM was a direct response to piracy and it has spread past audio to include movies and books.

Napster never recovered from all the bad press and lawsuits, and had to file for bankruptcy. However, it is now part of Rhapsody, where the same app is marketed legally because Rhapsody has distribution deals with the record labels.

Napster is one company that filled a need that the entrenched music industry did not want to fill. Had it persisted, this new method of music sharing would have seriously cut into profits. For record labels, the worry was real.

The guys at Napster were following parts of the Ethos—namely they had the vision, self-belief, and creativity to solve a problem in music distribution. But they failed at the integrity part of the Ethos by not realizing that their actions would negatively impact artists and record companies. Ultimately Napster's innovation became toxic, and kicked off a huge disruption in the music industry.

In the race to the bottom (e.g., low prices) to gain market share and audience, music has been reduced to a commodity. Revenue from music downloads is lower for both record companies and artists. Throw into the mix that it's now so much easier to create and distribute music. The music market has expanded, but the revenue generated for artists and labels has decreased. That's good for consumers, but clearly bad for the music industry as a whole.

It's gotten so bad that record labels now want a piece of a band's touring revenue and merchandise sales. That type of deal was taboo only a handful of years ago, but you can see why a label would want a cut to make up for their shortfall— it's a lot harder to pirate attending a live concert.

Any new technology trying to break into a stalled market can force competitors to fight so hard that unintended consequences can occur, like government stepping in and competitors filing lawsuits—both recipes for disaster.

Don't write off streaming or the music industry yet. After a long decline, things are starting to look up as *Bloomberg* reports in "The Music Industry is Finally Making Money on Streaming" on September 19, 2016:

> After almost two decades of relentless decline caused by piracy and falling prices, the music business is enjoying a fragile recovery thanks to the growth of paid streaming services like Spotify Ltd. and Apple Music.
>
> The U.S. industry is on pace to expand for the second straight year—the first time that's happened since the CD sales peaked in 1998 and 1999. Retail spending on recorded music grew 8.1 percent to $3.4 billion in the first half of 2016, according to a midyear report from the Recording Industry Association of America.

And to think that it took almost two decades to recover from a declining and dead business model that had been sparked by a couple of college kids in a dorm room.

A change in music streaming and downloading disrupted the entire creation and distribution of music. The way the industry and artists handled it is a cautionary tale of how a new technology can and will find a way to make a market more efficient and accessible. In its wake, downloading music has forever changed the relationship of fan, artist, and label. It has also ushered in a whole new movement that, while not as lucrative now, has the potential to be even bigger. That next big thing owes its start to an MTV VJ (video jockey) who was best known for his awesome permed hair and golden voice.

That next big thing is podcasting.

While record companies and artists were struggling to figure out how to make money in the new world of digital downloads, a movement was afoot to make the traditional radio talk show accessible to anyone with a microphone and something to say.

Adam Curry, the longhaired, blond MTV VJ, was not the first person to record a podcast, but his show, Daily Source Code (DSC), was a pivotal movement in podcasting history.

The reason was that the technology had yet to be perfected to record and distribute an MP3 file from anyone, anywhere. Curry's code, which would later become iPodder, was the first real proof of concept that could take a file off an RSS (Rich Site Summary) feed and sync it to iTunes, which, at the time, was the most popular way to listen to MP3 files on your iPod. Thus "pod" casting was born.

Podcasting is the exact opposite of music streaming in that the podcasters control everything from creation, promotion, distribution, and even sponsorship. Today podcasting has exploded into a medium that garners over one billion subscribers with over 180,000 active podcasts.

Even Facebook is getting into the audio and video-streaming world. Its offering appears to be a direct response to the sometimes low quality of connection that would make a live video experience as bad as a skipping VHS tape. This only proves the point that the next big thing might be broadcasting yourself in 4K video; if so, you'd better hope Grandma's internet connection is as strong as her Chanel No. 5.

The emerging audio and video streaming markets show us a nice interplay in how the Ethos is really an all-or-nothing kind of deal. The guys at Napster were creative, visionary, and optimistic hustlers, but they lacked the Ethos aspects of collaboration, integrity, and respect for an entrenched market. Once other companies like Apple and Spotify engaged with the record labels, the tide started to turn. This created a legitimate market for a legitimate technology where everyone benefitted—consumers, creators, and companies—exactly the way it's supposed to be.

Podcasting, on the other hand, grew organically with creators themselves controlling the content and distribution, and not third parties. The podcasting model is also more advertising based instead of pay-for-content, which makes pirating a lot less likely. It also makes distribution easier with services like iTunes, Sound Cloud, and Stitcher. More on video streaming in the next chapter.

THIRTY-SIX

Video Streaming – See What's Next

"Neither Redbox nor Netflix are even on the radar screen in terms of competition."
— Jim Keyes, CEO of Blockbuster in 2008

Video has come a long way from the battles of Beta vs. VHS or even the short-lived laser disk craze. I remember the first VHS tape we ever bought. It was the original *Star Wars* and we watched it so many times that we wore out the tape. Good times.

Unlike music streaming, video steaming has had a harder time being widely adopted. This was originally due to the limited bandwidth of most internet connections and the technical challenges of streaming high-quality video content on-demand—a feat that can still be a wonky proposition to this day.

One differentiation about video is that it takes a lot more money, time, and effort to create than audio. Another is that TV shows, the vast majority of video content, was, for the most part, free. Or at least used to be.

Of course, movies were something you paid for, but the distribution of movies was better controlled and, even though movies do get pirated, the impact of such piracy is hard to measure.

Ironically, the pioneer of pay-per-view movies, HBO, does not seem to care too much about piracy. One of its shows, *Game of Thrones* Season 4, Episode 2, set a piracy world record back in 2014. HBO's response was fascinating. Jeff Bewkes, the CEO of Time Warner who owns HBO, explains:

> Basically, we've been dealing with this issue for years with HBO, literally 20, 30 years, where people have always been running wires down on the back of apartment buildings and sharing with their neighbors.

> Our experience is, it all leads to more penetration, more paying subs [subscriptions], more health for HBO, less reliance on having to do paid advertising ... If you go around the world, I think you're right, *Game of Thrones* is the most pirated show in the world. Well, you know, that's better than an Emmy.

That attitude is not completely authentic in that HBO does pursue pirates and flags their shows on popular video platforms like YouTube and Torrent servers. What it does say is that piracy is everywhere and dealing with it is both a blessing and a curse. Even Amazon had the same problem with *The Grand Tour*.

The Grand Tour is a reboot of the popular BBC show *Top Gear* (a show focused on automobiles) starring the Three Musketeers of presenting: Jeremy Clarkson, Richard Hammond, and Captain Slow—James May. When it debuted in

November 2016, it was the most pirated British TV program, as well as the most pirated first-year series in history. That would suggest that Amazon lost 3.2 million pounds sterling (based on the cost to view a single episode) on that first episode. Ouch. I'm sure the publicity alone was well worth the price, though, since every single tech and Hollywood news outlet reported it.

Piracy is always going to be around. Each side will be innovating to stay ahead of the other. Content creators, who have seen their business models eroding, first with audio and now with video, don't want pirates stealing their content yet new distribution models are making easier than ever to view content. This is the classic challenge that force entrenched businesses (the status quo) to fight hard to stay alive against new paradigms, emerging technologies, and talented entrepreneurs who are not shackled by the mindsets of the past.

Paul Tassi, a contributor over at *Forbes*, called it back in 2012 when he published a popular piece entitled "You Will Never Kill Piracy, and Piracy Will Never Kill You." His argument is that piracy will always exist:

> The primary problem movie studios have to realize is that everything they charge for is massively overpriced. The fact that movie ticket prices keep going up is astonishing. How can they possibly think charging $10-15 per ticket for a new feature is going to increase the amount of people coming to theaters rather than renting the movie later or downloading it online for

free? Rather than lower prices, they double down, saying that gimmicks like 3D and IMAX are worth adding another $5 to your ticket.

Paul just described the fight that the status quo (movie studios) is waging against the better, faster, and cheaper world of video streaming. There is an opportunity here for a resourceful company to come up with a different way to access and pay for content that's easy, convenient, and fair. Ever the visionary, Paul has an idea that was spawned by the gaming industry that also gets pirated, but managed to figure out a better way:

> More or less, it's Steam (the online PC game distribution client) for movies. It allows you to rent or download your favorite films with ease, build a library, watch across devices, and share with your friends. The service would effectively allow you to beat the seven-step piracy process easily:
>
> 1. Open "Movie Steam"
>
> 2. Search for *The Hangover 2*
>
> 3. Click button to rent for $2 for 24 hours
>
> 4. Play movie

Look familiar? It's now what Netflix, Hulu, Google Play, and Amazon do with their online movie streaming and it seems to be working.

The revenues from streaming services are growing much faster than cable. According to *Business Insider* in April 2016:

> In 2015 the U.S. revenue for video streaming services like Netflix and Hulu grew by 29% to $5.1 billion. And while the U.S. streaming industry in 2015 was a fraction of its cable, satellite, and telco TV counterpart (with revenues of $105 billion), that sector grew by just 3% in 2015.

It's clear that video streaming is the future.

Cable companies are now waking up to the fact that the traditional model of "prime time" is going away.

Binge watching will be the new norm, along with off-hour and ad hoc watching. Convenience rules.

In fact, the future of movie theaters is also in jeopardy.

Sean Parker of Napster fame has a new venture, The Screening Room, which would allow first-run movies to be streamed to an in-home set-top box for $50. That's an interesting idea. It's already making Hollywood nervous, yet some heavyweights like Steven Spielberg, Ron Howard, Brian Grazer, Peter Jackson, and J.J. Abrams seem to be backing the idea. Even AMC Theaters has expressed interest.

It's great to see that Sean learned from his time at Napster and is now more aligned with the Ethos by playing nice and collaborating with the entrenched players to get buy-in.

Alex Winter, of "Bill and Ted's Excellent Adventure" fame (he played Bill), said it best about Sean's new venture that all entrepreneurs need to take notice of, in a June 2016 *Forbes* article by Mike Montgomery:

> Where I really credit The Screening Room is in [Parker's] willingness to innovate within the preexisting industries.
>
> Somebody really needs to be doing that. It doesn't mean The Screening Room is the be-all, end-all, but somebody needs to innovate. ... [With Parker,] you're talking about one of the most successful entrepreneurs in current history. He scaled Napster. He helped scale Facebook. He helped scale Spotify. He was able to make deals with the labels to make Spotify work. Whether you like Sean or not, he's an incredibly smart individual.

Pretty sound reasoning for someone known mostly for playing a mean air guitar. By starting The Screening Room, Sean is also a brilliant example of someone learning from his experience, acting with integrity, earning the respect of his team and community, and trying to make a positive impact.

There is an additional lesson here that is simple yet so often overlooked. It's captured best in the same Mike Montgomery *Forbes* piece that quoted Alex Winter:

> Entrepreneurs can take a lesson from the newly mature Sean Parker [of Napster fame]. Even when it looks like an industry can't be disrupted (no one thought theaters would actually ever get on board with first-run movies

in the home), sometimes it can. The key is creating the right relationships and finding ways for all parties to benefit. By tapping into the market of people who want to watch first-run movies but don't want to go to the theater, Parker can potentially expand the amount of revenue flowing to studios. Having AMC on his side might help convince the holdouts that this is a good idea.

Clayton Christensen, author of *The Innovator's Dilemma*, would be proud since it's this kind of disruption that his book is all about. It was Christensen who first introduced the concept that disruption happens when an incumbent's product performance exceeds the demand of most customers, and they lose their "edge" because the customers' needs have changed. This allows the disruptors to gain a foothold in the market since they provide a better fit or performance for the needs of the first movers. The Screening Room is doing just that, and AMC is trying hard to not get disrupted by it. Of course, AMC needs to be careful they don't destroy their existing product in order to build their next big thing, all before The Screening Room gains traction.

What's even more interesting is that video streaming is going mobile with live event streaming, and it's now possible to stream yourself, which could be yet another next big thing.

Facebook, Twitter, and Snapchat are all moving into the video domain and securing deals for content and building upon their already massive audience. Players like HBO and Amazon are also looking toward mobile as their next big wave.

It's amazing to see the innovation in video streaming and how creative entrepreneurs are challenging the status quo in big ways. These innovations come down to solving problems that other companies did not want to solve.

Netflix solving late fees and making streaming easy.

Hulu putting cable content on demand.

Amazon leveraging their Prime subscription to get people to try streaming video.

The biggest and most consistent movement across all of this is that these companies are all investing in original content. For my money, that's far and away the best way to create success and expand the market.

Original content is the most compelling and defendable force in the streaming puzzle. While interesting and innovative in its own right, the infrastructure to deliver content, being only bandwidth and delivery platforms, soon becomes just a commodity itself.

We all know that you buy commodities by the pound.

That's why original content is king, and that fact is not lost on social media companies who are rushing to jump on the video streaming bandwagon. It's the innovative, interesting, and creative content that keeps people coming back for more. Sure, selection, convenience, and ease of use are important, but compelling content is the major driver of the video streaming bus.

Without compelling content, the whole thing falls apart.

That's why visionary companies like Facebook, Amazon, Netflix, and Snap (formally SnapChat) will most likely win. They are disrupting the entrenched old guard who, like the record industry, grew fat and lazy on the old methods that allowed them to just continue printing money.

Even Apple is starting to explore original content because they realize that, without it, their AppleTV platform is just another pipe to content.

Content is what moves us.

Content makes an impact.

Content is king.

Entrepreneurs see this time and time again. Whole industries shift away from renting videos at a store or hailing a cab on the street because the old entrenched companies don't see the threat until it's too late.

The challenge for entrepreneurs always comes back to seeing a potential for disruption that most people either don't see or don't want to see.

This is why entrepreneurs make dents in the universe.

This is why entrepreneurs will crush big companies.

This ability to see an alternate universe when everyone else thinks you're crazy is what sets entrepreneurs apart from the rest of the world. Sometimes it's also their main source of the awkwardness we touched on earlier.

You can see that entrepreneurs in the video streaming market will have an advantage by adhering to the Ethos to find creative solutions to the new challenges of video streaming. They have the discipline, vision, and integrity to collaborate with the entrenched players to put forth an equitable vision of the future. I can't wait to see what's next.

THIRTY-SEVEN

Do-It-Yourself - You Can Do It

"It takes half your life before you discover life is a do-it-yourself project."

— Napoleon Hill, author

My family has always been of the attitude that, given enough time and yelling, we can fix anything. This stems from my dad's upbringing on a farm where you had to fix everything yourself. It's the primary reason why our family outings usually involved going to Sears (more on that later) to check out the latest tools and gadgets. We must have had a thousand tools, some I don't think we ever even used.

Home Depot was another place we often visited. At least once, if not twice, during a weekend we would pile into our tan station wagon to go get some 2x4s, 16-penny nails, and the ever-present contractor 12-pack of DAP caulking. For some reason, we never had enough caulking.

Lots of people have the urge to create or fix or build something with their hands. For some, this is just a hobby or a way to save money. For others, it is how they make a living.

This desire to Do It Yourself (DIY) is getting easier to implement. With the advent of the internet, you can now take your DIY skills and either displays them via YouTube videos or parlay them into side hustles that net you extra scratch. That's exactly what Etsy has figured out with its platform for DIYers.

Back in 2005, Rob Kalin, Chris Maguire, and Haim Schoppik created Etsy out of their Brooklyn apartment to give the makers (hipster name for DIYers) of the world an online platform to sell their handmade goods. Kinda like eBay meets Christmas Faire, or insert your favorite arts and crafts meet-up where you can buy those oh so cute knitted beer cozies.

By 2007 Etsy had 450,000 registered sellers (mostly by word of mouth) and generated $26 million in annual sales. That same year they secured over $3 million in investments. That is impressive for a niche e-commerce company started by three guys in an apartment.

As most startups go, the team that got you liftoff is not always the best team to continue to pilot the rocket ship. Etsy soon discovered the part of the Ethos that says, "I am self-aware enough to know that I don't always have all the answers."

CEO Rob Kalin is a maker and a dreamer at heart. These types of entrepreneurs have the vision and drive to create new and exciting products, but they are not always the best ones to execute on a VC-backed growth plan. Unfortunately, this disparity caused Maguire and Schoppik to exit in 2008, leaving Rob with the task of figuring the how to keep the rocket ship on course. Ruth Reader at *VentureBeat* explained in March 2015 how this type of event is make-or-break for a growing company:

> What should have been a dire moment for Etsy manifested as a key turning point. Deeply in need of leadership, Kalin hired Chad Dickerson, senior director of product at Yahoo. Dickerson was brought on as Etsy's Chief Technology Officer (CTO) and ultimately its saving grace. The exec took to the role quickly and built out Etsy's engineering team.
>
> Dickerson proved so effective that three years after he was hired as CTO, he made the leap into the role of CEO, replacing Kalin. This had not been Kalin's first step away from the company. In 2008, he also removed himself from day-to-day operations for a time. However, this time, Kalin would not be making a return. The executive shuffle marked a major change for the Etsy, both in its company culture and its corporate goals.

Rob Kalin is a great example of an entrepreneur who had enough self-awareness to make the tough decision to bring in someone else. Having self-awareness is one of the hardest parts of the Ethos to follow since that can run counter to its visionary, optimistic, and self-determination parts.

As happens so often with VC-backed companies, new management brings new ideas. The corporate culture shift at Etsy turned out to be a gamble that paid off. The big shift was to allow vendors to also sell manufactured products as well as the handcrafted products Etsy was known for. This move was met with an initial outcry, but as things settled down, the sellers realized that the power of the Etsy platform still continued to enable them to make more money than they could on their own sites.

This realization turned the new policy into a growth engine for the company. In 2015 revenue ended the year at $2.3B (23.6% growth Y/Y), with 1.5M active sellers (15.5% Y/Y growth) and 24M active buyers (21.4% Y/Y growth).

As Etsy shows, sometimes you have to pivot away from your core business and figure out a way to continue to grow. If you can do this successfully, then the rewards are huge. If you can't, then the results can be catastrophic, which is what happened to one of my favorite stores, Radio Shack.

Founded in 1921 by brothers Theodore and Milton Deutschmann, Radio Shack started out providing radio and audio hardware to naval officers stationed in Boston Harbor who liked to tinker. Though Radio Shack would survive the Great Depression, it was not an easy ride. Not until the 1960s would Radio Shack reemerge to become the de facto place for electronics hobbyists to get their parts.

Before we look into how Radio Shack became the center for hobbyists, it warrants a little closer look at Radio Shack before its transformation in the 1960s.

During the 1940s and early 1950s, Radio Shack saw its first decline. It decided to sell several hundred specialized products to highly specific professional and amateur radio enthusiasts—a diversion from its core hobbyist base. This led to the chain peddling an inventory of almost 25,000 items to anyone who would buy them.

This dilution of their value proposition (i.e., selling to hobbyists) created the situation where Radio Shack started losing money. This brought in Charles Tandy, who had built his family's leather business big enough to be listed on the New York Stock Exchange. Then he wanted to diversify.

Tandy realized that Radio Shack's model would work if they got back to their roots—hobbyists who wanted to buy cheaper gear and improve them through modifications and accessorizing over time.

Tandy had experience in super-serving (exceeding customer expectations) the hobbyist who loved to build leather crafts via his hobby kits. This knowledge would serve Radio Shack well when Tandy purchased the struggling nine-store chain in 1963. This set in motion the Radio Shack that the likes of Steve Jobs, Bill Gates, and Steve Wozniak would frequent to tinker with whatever new invention they were working on.

As a kid, I would go to Radio Shack all the time to browse the latest electronics and get parts to build computers, radios, and a telephone system to call between the basement and the upstairs. Like the founders of Apple and Microsoft, our family was an ideal customer for Radio Shack. So what went wrong?

Unlike Etsy, who pivoted to include manufactured products, Radio Shack started to wander again from its core base. By 1984, instead of supplying the general hobbyist with one-of-a-kind components, it moved to supplying the next big wave of technology—computers.

The TRS-80 was Radio Shack's entry into the computer market. By all performance measures, it was far superior to IBM's similar machine with one exception—software.

While IBM ran on DOS (Microsoft DOS, to be exact), the TRS-80 had its own propriety Operating System (OS) and few programs could run on it. This was their fatal flaw and marked the decline of their core value proposition to super-serve their hobbyist customers. Radio Shack Computer Centers started to pop up all over the country. The initial margins were high, but competition from Best Buy, Dell, and Fry's Electronics reduced those margins to the point where something had to happen.

In the inevitable move to follow the latest trends, Radio Shack started selling mobile phones to compete with rival Best Buy. This again proved to be a fool's errand. Their small footprint stores could not hold as much inventory as Best Buy where you could get your computer, cell phone, and matching washer and dryer all in one trip. This series of missteps and divergence from its core value proposition sped up Radio Shack's decline to the point where they filed bankruptcy in 2015.

During Radio Shack's decline, the Maker Movement saw a tremendous amount of growth with not only Etsy but Maker Faire, 3D printing, on-demand publishing, and—the most impactful—crowdfunding.

I'm sure many of you have uttered these exact words: "I've got this great idea for a product to make my life easier. Now if I only had some money to build a prototype..."

It's part of the maker and entrepreneur makeup to solve problems that they themselves have, and then see if others have those same problems. The rub is that even though the cost of designing, prototyping, and producing products is now low, building a business out of your hobby is not so simple. That's why crowdfunding sites like Kickstarter and Indiegogo have grown over the years.

Founded on April 28, 2009, Kickstarter has allowed 12 million people to back over 188,000 projects that have raised $2.8 billion dollars. The Kickstarter model is simple. A maker posts up a project and gets her friends, family, and strangers to invest by pledging a level of support. If the campaign meets its fundraising goal, then the maker gets the money. If they fall short of their funding goal, then no dinero.

This does two things. First, it provides a ready set of customers who want the product and, second, it provides the needed capital to build said product. This method of entrepreneurship has less risk than a venture-backed business, but can be just as successful. Katherine Krug, CEO of Better Back, is a perfect example of that.

Katherine suffered from chronic back pain while she was working at a technology company. She tried everything she could to relieve her sciatica pain. No luck, until she met up with an industrial designer to come up with her Better Back product.

Better Back is a posture strap that allows you to have perfect posture in any kind of situation. After using the Better Back prototype, her sciatica pain went away and people started to ask, "What's that thing?"

This prompted Katherine to start a Kickstarter campaign to see if others might also want her invention.

The response was amazing.

Katherine's goal was to raise a modest $12.5K, but her story and her campaign were so compelling that it took off.

By the end, Katherine had raised almost $1.2M from 16,459 backers. Her success led her to do a second campaign on Indiegogo that raised almost $2M more from 8,474 backers and landed her a spot on *SharkTank*.

Katherine's vision, grit, problem solving, creativity, hustle, and willingness to make the world a better place, are great examples of how she followed the Ethos to great success.

The great thing about crowdfunding is that you can put forth your idea or vision of the future and ask the crowd to fund you—all without personal financial risk. Now, this even extends to buying stock in a startup.

Equity crowdfunding is starting to take off because of a loosening of U.S. equity laws. My favorite newsletter, *The Hustle*, used SeedInvest.com to offer its readers the ability to buy an equity share in the company. Within 60 hours, the $300K they wanted to raise was sold out. That's not typical, but it does show how a great idea can get traction with a dedicated fan base that's willing to invest in that vision.

Full disclosure, I'm not only a big fan of *The Hustle*, I'm also an investor.

The equity crowdfunding trend will only speed up now that the regulatory framework (laws that allow anyone to invest in a startup) has been put in place. Even traditional crowdfunding companies like Indiegogo are getting into the act by allowing their campaigners the ability to offer an equity piece of their company along with a product.

Equity in a company is just like stock except, for a private company, you can't yet sell it. For people who want to take the risk, investing in an early equity round of financing can return a huge return if the company succeeds.

DIY has come a long way from the days of ordering tube radio kits from Radio Shack or an Indian Guides leather token badge kit from Tandy.

Nowadays, it's easy to parlay a hobby into a real business if you have the drive and determination to make it happen. The DIY culture has several aspects of the Ethos embedded in it—creativity, self-determination, problem solving, and scholarship, to name a few. It's these traits, values, and beliefs that enable many makers, like Katherine Krug, to make the jump to becoming entrepreneurs.

THIRTY-EIGHT
Gaming – Ready Player One

"Video games are bad for you? That's what they said about
rock-n-roll."
— Shigeru Miyamoto, creator of Donkey Kong

Blackjack and nuclear bombs might not seem related, but it
turns out those genius scientists at Los Alamos laboratories did
more than just calculate nuclear blast radii on their IBM-701
mainframes. They also figured out how to program blackjack
during those long, boring nights of waiting for test results.
Back then in 1954, the "games" were text-based and were
more of an intellectual exercise than the full-immersion
experience that we see in gaming today.

It was not until 1972 that video games made it out of the lab
and into our world. That year Nolan Bushnell and Al Alcorn of
Atari developed the first video game, Pong, which would
launch a leisure revolution that has seen games, well, explode
and get more complex, more realistic, and more addictive.

Now, gaming is big business.

In fact, so big that sites like Twitch, a video platform for
gamers, allows fans to watch others play games both on-
demand and in real time. Yes, Twitch now broadcasts people

playing games so other people can watch. Players can also get tips from fans. Real, cold, hard cash tips. I'll let that sink in for a second.

In 2016 video gaming revenue approached $100B and it's only going to get bigger given the ongoing move from desktops to mobile devices and the popularity of Augmented Reality (AR) games like Pokémon Go.

Pokémon Go is a great example of the power of mobile gaming. It's a game that overlays AR in the real world. You score points by physically going to places and collecting Pokémon's. Kinda like an online scavenger hunt—pretty darn cool.

Before we explore modern gaming, let's take a step back and look at its origins. It turns out that the gamification of our lives has its origins with stamps—green stamps, to be precise.

Sperry & Hutchinson, S&H for short, was founded in 1896. Its main product was S&H Green Stamps, which it sold to retailers so that the latter could give rewards as their customers filled up their "books" with green stamps. This was the first such rewards program in the U.S. S&H Green Stamps launched what would become the basis for loyalty programs that have popped up over the intervening century to stuff my wallet with card after card after card—so annoying.

Loyalty programs shine a spotlight on why gaming is so popular. The accumulation of points or rewards to receive both physical rewards and peer recognition makes us happy.

That's why games can be so addictive. Players are always pushing to win more points, attain greater powers, and acquire bigger ion cannons to blast away the Zorkx—but I'm getting ahead of myself.

Before Pong, players had to go to an arcade to drop rolls and rolls of quarters to play their favorite game. It was not until 1975 when Pong was released that you could play at home. Unfortunately for Atari, Pong was released to unenthusiastic retailers who could not figure out where it belonged.

In fact, Atari founder Nolan Bushnell had such a hard time finding retailers that he ended up selling it in the sports section of the Sears catalog. Back then, they considered the self-contained Pong hardware a sport. Talk about a market pivot.

It's important to consider how Bushnell lived the Ethos during this time. As with all visionaries, it can be lonely when no one gets your product. It's equally frustrating when you take a risk and hustle up an innovative product only to be shut out of the marketplace. Thankfully, Bushnell had enough self-belief and optimism to keep going.

Although Pong was only one game, it demonstrated that you did not need to go to the arcade to play video games. It would take a couple more years before the home gaming movement really took off, when Atari released another first—a multi-game console called the Atari 2600.

The Atari 2600 was a revolution and it paved the way for millions of people to play games at home. All you had to do was buy a new game cartridge and you were off and running. This touchtone would start the video game console wars. Wars that would see the likes of Atari, Nintendo, Sony, Sega, and even Microsoft launch consoles and games that would continue to push the envelope on performance, complexity, and visuals.

Not to be outdone, Personal Computer (PC) manufacturers started to offer games as well. The battle between dedicated gaming consoles and PCs would drive all sorts of innovation that not only benefitted the gaming industry, but also other industries like biotechnology.

It may seem strange to think that biotech has benefitted from video game technology, but the same computing challenges to render a 3D, 4K-display environment are similar to those in sequencing the human genome.

That similarity is parallel processing.

Video gaming requires a lot of processing power to render fluid, life-like images on a screen. This task is the burden of the video processor, which takes on the brunt of the calculations from the main CPU.

Here's the thing.

Those video processors are tailor-made to calculate complex equations. To speed things up, they do it all in parallel. Which in English means they have lots of little computers that each process a piece of the screen, all at the same time. This parallel processing makes the images you see on your video game fluid and life-like.

That same video processor can also be used to do other things in parallel like crunch complex equations to sequence DNA. The reason is that this task is exactly the same—lots and lots of data that needs to be crunched by the same equations. Enterprising entrepreneurs have realized this and now the popular video processor company NVidia sells its Graphics Processing Unit (GPU) for all sorts of computation-intensive problems like Artificial Intelligence (AI), big data analysis, image processing, weather forecasting, etc.

I bring up this alternative use of graphics processing because it's this type of crossover use of technology that allows entrepreneurs to create new and exciting products and companies. This sort of creativity, vision, scholarship, and ability to problem-solve using existing and emerging technologies in new and novel ways is how entrepreneurs help make new markets and industries.

Entrepreneurs are always the ones who first see crossover potential and take advantage of the situation before big companies ever see it coming. It's this outside-the-box thinking that has driven gaming outside the console, to the internet, and now into, of all things, to the hiring of employees.

Scoutible is a startup based in San Francisco that uses games to allow its customers to scout for talent. By playing a 20-minute game, Scoutible says it can predict a candidate's job success. It claims that it is two times better than job interviews, three times better than work experience, and four times better than educational levels. These results were based on Harvard and Stanford research studies comparing Scoutible to traditional metrics such as work experience, interviewing prowess, and school attended.

Finally my skills at Tetris will pay off.

Beyond hiring, gaming is making an impact on loyalty programs as well. Airlines and hotels are always looking to use advanced gaming techniques to build loyalty and increase sales. Harris Casinos is a good example of a player loyalty program that links rewards to how much players bet, on tables or on machines, and also to how long they play. This makes it one of the most successful programs in the gambling industry.

In the near term, Virtual Reality (VR) will be the next major technology that will drive gaming to a whole higher level. The technology is new, but moving from Google Cardboard VR to full range-of-motion VR that won't make you nauseous is coming soon. How this happens remains to be seen, but the compute power, innovation trends, and user acceptance are all going in the right direction.

VR is a game-changer (pun intended) for gaming. It allows such a complete immersion into the game world that you feel like you are actually there. This full experience will ultimately even include tactile feedback so that the environment you're in will react to you and you'll be able to "feel" it. Could the "feelies" from *Brave New World* be headed our way?

VR has many other applications besides gaming. From training soldiers to helping patients deal with chronic pain, VR's crossover potential is huge, and entrepreneurs like Howard Rose, co-founder of Firsthand Technology, are leading the way.

Firsthand Technology is not your average VR company. Its primary focus is the use of VR for pain management and the research shows that they're on to something.

V. S. Ramachandran and D. Rogers-Ramachandran first studied VR for pain management back in 1996. What they looked at was how phantom limb pain (i.e., pain from a limb that's not there) can be reduced using a Virtual Reality box. They found a link between synthetic visual images and physical pain.

What does that mean?

It turns out that their Virtual Reality box contained a couple of mirrors that gave an amputee the perception that the missing hand, say, was actually there. When the amputee saw that their lost limb was not "lost" while in the "VR environment," it reduced their pain.

Applications for gaming technology outside the gaming industry show the power of crossover thinking and how "fun and games" can be put to alternative uses. This is exactly what the Ethos means when it says that entrepreneurs "challenge the status quo" and "remain nimble and flexible" because "markets will change and technologies will shift." Sometimes those shifts come from outside a market and creative entrepreneurs seek out those crossover applications to great effect.

Ready Player One.

THIRTY-NINE

Social Media - A Place for Friends

"A brand is no longer what we tell the consumer it is – it is what consumers tell each other it is."
— Scott Cook, founder of Intuit

Humans are social animals. We need human contact to stay sane. More and more, we get this "contact" through social media like Facebook, Twitter, Instagram, and others, which have elbowed their way into our daily lives. In this land rush to make us more connected, lots of companies have put forth products to be the next big thing. The question each company asks itself is, "How can we get people to pay attention to us?" That's what Yik Yak was trying to figure out.

Yik Yak, an anonymous social media app, is a case study in how attracting and retaining users are not enough for a thriving business. That attitude is, like, so 2001 or 2008 when the Wild West of the Internet was just starting out and the social media landscape was a land grab for users. Revenue and profits be dammed!

What separated Yik Yak from a Facebook or even a Twitter was that the anonymous chat app that had been popular with college kids had now given rise to a persistent culture of bullying on its platform. This caused a lot of negative press and a backlash from some users. This was the same kind of challenge that Twitter faced early on, because Twitter users can also be anonymous.

On top of that, Yik Yak had no clear path to monetization. A continuing big problem in the post-boom years of the "we'll make it up on volume" mindset which encourages companies to "capture users by any means necessary and don't worry if you are losing money." That attitude and market forces led to Yik Yak being bought by Square for $1M in April 2017. To put that in perspective, at one point Yik Yak was worth $400M and raised over $70M dollars in VC money. Oh, how the trade winds of social media change.

Twitter had the same problem with monetization but managed to figure it out with ad-based revenue. The jury is still out on whether it can scale to survive because of the unfiltered nature of Twitter (e.g., your Twitter feed is raw as opposed to curated on Facebook). An unfiltered feed makes it harder to target ads to users—something that Facebook has done extremely well. The reason is simple. If you can filter what people see, you can also target what they see. That's a powerful way to get an advertiser's message out there. The more it's seen, the more it will be acted upon.

The bullying dust-up that Yik Yak raised and their problems with monetization are just two of the double-edged swords of building a social media platform these days.

On the one hand, you need to build something that's totally unique and different enough to steal away mind-share from Facebook or Twitter or Snapchat. On the other hand, those same features that grow a rapid user base might not lead into ways to grow a viable company.

User acquisition, retention, and monetization are always tough nuts to crack. It's been that way ever since social media began.

Before Yik Yak, Twitter, and Facebook, there were several social media platforms that were all vying for users. The first one to reach the magical one million members was a site called Friendster back in 2002.

Friendster's success kicked off a myriad of knockoff sites like MySpace that would steal from Friendster's customer base by meeting the user demand for more features and functions. In 2011 Friendster tried to rebrand itself as a place for gaming, but is now defunct after suspending operations on June 14, 2015.

Users are the lifeblood of a social network, but you need more than numbers to be successful. As Internet Archaeologist David Garcia, a professor with the Swiss Federal Institute of Technology, found out when he did an autopsy of Friendster in a 2013 article in *Wired Magazine*:

> What [Garcia] found was that by 2009, Friendster still had tens of millions of users, but the bonds linking the

network [users] weren't particularly strong. Many of the users weren't connected to a lot of other members, and the people they had befriended came with just a handful of their own connections. So they ended up being so loosely affiliated with the network, that the burden of dealing with a new user interface just wasn't worth it.

First the users in the outer cores start to leave, lowering the benefits of inner cores, cascading through the network towards the core users, and thus unraveling.

The heart of successful networks in terms of what [Garcia] calls K-cores. These are subset of users who not only have a lot of friends, but they have "resilience and social influence." As these K-cores disintegrated, the whole Friendster thing fell apart.

Garcia's observation is an interesting one for any social media companies to take heed of—the number of *engaged* users matters more than total users. This seems to be the case for one of the competitors to Friendster—Myspace.

Founded in 2003 by Chris DeWolfe and Tom Anderson, Myspace was a side project of a bunch of eUniverse (an Internet marketing company) employees with Friendster accounts who realized they could build a better mousetrap.

Myspace gained popularity with musicians and entertainment fans since musicians would post their upcoming event dates and latest music for fans to check out. This proved to be a great way to attract and retain users since fans of a band have a common bond—liking the same band—and thus will stick around.

Within two short years of operation, Myspace gained the attention of big media companies like Viacom and News Corp, who locked into a bidding war to buy them. In the end, News Corp bought Myspace for $580 million in August 2005. Not a bad exit for only two years' worth of work.

At the time, Myspace had 20M monthly users while its competitor, Facebook, had less than half that.

By April of 2009, though, the story had changed.

Over the preceding four years, Facebook's growth had been exponential while Myspace saw a leveling out and eventual decline.

Around April 2009, Facebook surpassed Myspace and has continued to dominate the social media space ever since.

By 2011 Myspace was at less than 40M users per month (from a peak of close to 80M) and was sold to Specific Media for a mere $35M. So what happened?

Myspace is the perfect example of what happens when passionate, focused, risk-taking, and creative entrepreneurs get replaced by corporate drones that care only about the bottom line. This focus on things like making money, what's the ROI on that feature, or it's not in the approved budget are the reasons entrepreneurs usually don't last long in a corporate environment.

Today Myspace still has 50 million visitors per month and has gotten back to its roots of being the go-to place for music. It has over 53 million tracks and has worked deals with thousands of record labels to allow unlimited, on-demand listening of both established and unsigned artists.

To put that in perspective, Spotify has 30-plus million music tracks and so does Apple Music. Both those services are purely music downloads with no ways for artists to give updates or fans to post comments. Also both only list music published by record labels. Myspace is different because of their indie-based and lesser-known artists.

Of the 14.2M artists on the Myspace platform, 14M are unsigned (i.e., independently published or DIY).

The Myspace story is another one that begs the question: What went wrong? For a first-mover in the social media space to fall so far, there has to be some sort of lesson to learn.

Indeed, there seems to be.

But you can't point to any one decision or set of decisions that led to MySpace's demise. Some, like founder DeWolfe, regret not doing what other platforms at the time were doing well:

We tried to create every feature in the world and said, "O.K., we can do it, why should we let a third party do it?" We should have picked five to ten key features that we focused on and let other people [developers] innovate on everything else.

There were simple things we didn't execute well on, like address-book importing. It's a blocking-and-tackling [basic] sort of feature that we didn't have nailed down.

If you couple this with alarmist press notices in 2006 that Myspace was not safe for your kids (there were several high-profile bullying cases), you get a constant firefight to make your product safe at the expense of not innovating and falling behind sites like Facebook. As Danah Boyd, a social networks researcher at Microsoft, puts it, this was the beginning of the end:

Myspace got to a point where they were not innovating technologically. They had to do all technical innovations to address the various panics that are happening. Basically their development cycle turned into one of crisis management, not one of innovation.

Facebook did a fantastic job of hiding behind the panic around Myspace and basically saying, "We're totally safe."

MySpace's inability to build an effective spam filter exacerbated the public impression that it was seedy [prowlers lurking to exploit your kids]. And that contributed to an exodus of white, middle-class kids to the supposedly safer haven of Facebook.

It should be noted that Facebook had the same safety concerns as Myspace, but they owned the PR narrative and avoided the bad press. This, along with their curated content and viral nature of "find your friends," is what propelled Facebook to what it is today.

When the people go, so does the ad revenue that supports your company. This perfect storm of competitors out-innovating you, bad press, and a declining user base made it hard to grow and garner more investment for Myspace.

The cautionary tale of MySpace's fall underscores the idea of what first got you to the Promised Land by growing into a real company might not be sufficient to sustain that company.

Entrepreneurs fight a non-stop, multi-front battle against a range of challenges that are hell-bent on putting them out of business. The self-awareness, integrity, and scholarship recommended by the Ethos will not guarantee success. But it sure helps.

FORTY

E-commerce - Way to Shop!

"If you use your money to create exceptional products and services, you won't need to spend it on advertising."
— Seth Godin, best-selling author

As a child, my family would take us on weekly trips to Sears to look at the latest and greatest tools and gadgets. My dad loved Sears. We bought everything from Sears.

Sears was our fashion center, our home improvement club, our mechanic, and our entertainment provider. This love affair with Sears started with the Sears catalog.

Since the age of eight, I loved reading the Sears catalog. For me it was the best way to glimpse all the neat gadgets that you could buy, particularly tools.

For some reason, I loved to look at tools.

The pictures of tools were particularly fascinating since it was a glimpse at what a 108-piece ratchet set looked like. When we went to Sears, I got to see and feel everything—well, almost everything—that was in the magical Sears catalog.

In 1498 the first recorded catalogs were published in Venice to sell books. These catalogs were later expanded to sell things from books to seeds, but were generally not printed en masse. Catalogs started to take off when regular mail services began. Thus the era of the mail order catalog was born.

My beloved Sears catalog was not the first mail order catalog in North America. That honor goes to Tiffany & Company, who in 1845, sent out their first mail order catalog called the "Blue Book," in their signature Tiffany blue.

In an ironic twist of fate, or history repeating itself, when Sears started in 1886, it was only mail order. As demand started to take off, they realized that a traditional brick and mortar presence would boost sales, and they created their first stores in the 1920s.

Jeff Bezos, did you shop at Sears before you created Amazon?

Nowadays the Sears catalog has gone the way of most catalogs—replaced by the infinite variety of online catalogs that is today's e-commerce.

Sites like Walmart.com, Amazon.com, and Jet.com are our online, on-demand catalogs that guide us through the infinite display of products from all over the world. There are also sites like Groupon that bombard us with deal after deal to get us to buy a cream-colored fedora. This new online way to shop has made a big dent in traditional brick and mortar brands, including my beloved Sears.

From 2006 until 2016, the market capitalization change for popular brick-and-mortar retailers were: Best Buy (Down 49%), JCPenney (Down 83%), Kohl's (Down 59%), Macy's (Down 46%), Nordstrom (Down 21%), Sears (Down 95%), Target (Down 15%), and Wal-Mart (Up 2%). And note Amazon (Up 1,910%).

Only Wal-Mart and Amazon grew during that 10-year period. Wal-Mart grew primarily because it expanded into warehouse clubs, while Amazon grew from unique and new product offerings like Alexa, Amazon Web Services (AWS), streaming video, etc. In that sense, it's not "fair" to call Amazon a retailer, but Jeff Bezos is certainly living the Ethos of being visionary, action-oriented, and having passion for making a positive impact on its customers.

These brick-and-mortar retailers seem to have missed the boat like Blockbuster did, first missing it with video rental, then live streaming, then original programming.

It's not the fact that these companies have brick and mortar stores that's the problem. The real problem is not being self-reflective enough to change their mindset to make the shopping experience more pleasant.

That's when someone with an entrepreneurial mindset can come in and disrupt the status quo. Even markets that seem immune to innovation are being disrupted.

Companies like Dollar Shave Club (shaving needs), Casper (mattresses), and Warby Parker (eyeglasses) are redefining the shopping experience and making it a lot more convenient and, dare I say fun, to shop for razors, beds, and eyeglasses. The times they are a-changing, and for the better.

The main reason these new retailers are succeeding against the incumbents is because they are solving problems in creative ways that deliver an experience that customers are craving. It's the classic example of applying the Ethos values of risk-taking by seeking knowledge and hustling to make it all happen.

Think back to the last time you were at an old-time retailer. Apart from Nordstrom or Best Buy or Williams Sonoma, the experience can be kinda depressing.

The floors are usually cluttered with disorganized merchandise. It's hard to find an employee to talk to. The yellow din of the lights feels like a scene out of a retro 70s zombie movie, where you might come upon a gaggle of zombies eating the brains of the slowest clerk. That's not to say it's not beneficial to touch and feel a product, but long gone are the days where a clerk will actually give you some useful information.

Once you do find something, you have to wait in line behind someone who is bound to want a different size, or complain about the price, or forget where they put their checkbook.

Yes, I said checkbook.

That's not a pleasant experience. Now that everything is available online (including groceries), as a retailer you have to step up your game to get people in the store. Which is what Amazon is starting to do with its new brick and mortar stores.

Amazon Go is a grab-and-go store concept where you don't have to check out. The whole store is wired with technology to figure out what you picked up and left with. The whole goal is to make grab-and-go as convenient as one-click shopping online.

No lines.

No fumbling for your card (or checkbook).

No talking to a clearly annoyed clerk.

No hassle.

Pick the stuff you want and leave.

It's like the real-world Amazon Prime. Brilliant!

This type of shopping experience is what Amazon has trained us to expect. The reason the company did not make a profit for the better part of ten years was to get ahead of the retail curve by investing in technologies that make shopping easy and one-click like. Its competitors lacked that vision to invest in those technologies.

Jeff Bezos is a true visionary (or an astute observer of history) and he and his team at Amazon believed that the future of retail was going to change once people got comfortable with online purchases. Once that happened, they could move that awesome experience back into a real store. Let's hope they can pull it off.

Amazon is a great example of innovating a tired old business model. The thing is, you don't need an innovative technology stack or a radical idea like Amazon Prime to win. What you need to understand is your customers and why they shop with you, and that's exactly what Costco understands.

Costco, the warehouse retail giant, began in 1983 and made the concept of warehouse stores so successful that Wal-Mart stole their idea. It has 727 warehouses in nine countries and has no plans to change its business model to be more online.

Rather, it's focusing on enhancing the shopping experience and providing a wider selection of products to its members. Costco does have an online presence but it's to enhance the in-store experience and for business customers to order for delivery.

Countless Wall Street analysts have beaten up CEO Craig Jelinek for the way he runs Costco. They complain that margins are too low and he pays his employees too much, yet Costco is the perfect example of a company that knows what it is down to its core. Jelinek, and all of Costco, lives the part of the Ethos that says, "I know that each day, I must earn the loyalty, respect, and trust of my team and my community."

Craig's vision and tenacity to stick to what you are good at has led the retailer to buck the downward trend that so many other brick and mortar retailers have fallen into.

While other stores have sinking profits, Costco's profits have doubled.

While other stores are shuttering and shuddering in Amazon's wake, Costco has grown revenue an average of 4.6% from 2013 to 2016. Amazon grew on average 22.3% over that same time period, while Wal-Mart grew 0.88%.

There must be something in the water up in Washington state, since both Amazon and Costco are headquartered there.

The way we shop is ripe for disruption and, I for one, applaud companies that make it a lot more enjoyable and economical. I don't know a single person who does not first check online for things they are looking to buy. If they do go into a store, their purchase has already been vetted to determine the best deal, the most convenience, and the best product.

Throughout the years, there have been all sorts of technology upgrades to make the store experience better. None have stuck as much as online shopping experiences.

Lots of companies are innovating in the retail space without the use of cutting-edge technology. Rather, they are rethinking the purchasing experience and making it frictionless. One of the best examples of this drive to not only solve a major problem but also disrupt an industry is online eyeglass company Warby Parker.

Founded in 2010, Warby Parker was the brainchild of some Wharton business school friends who all had the same problem—they kept breaking or losing their glasses all the time.

It's not uncommon to have to pay upwards of $500 or more for a pair of eyeglasses.

Think about that for a second.

The latest and greatest iPhone or Android mobile device costs about that and does so much more. What's the deal with eyeglasses?

That's the exact question Warby Parker founders Neil Blumenthal, Andrew Hunt, David Gilboa, and Jeffrey Raider wanted to answer.

It turns out that eyewear, all kinds of eyewear, is dominated by Luxottica, an Italian company that owns retail outlets like Sunglasses Hut, Lenscrafters, and Pearle Vision. It also owns brands such as Ray-Ban, Oakley, Vogue, Oliver Peoples, Persol, Alain Mikli, Arnette, and REVO. On top of that, it licenses designer brands including Bulgari, Burberry, Chanel, Coach, Dolce & Gabbana, Donna Karan, Paul Smith, Polo Ralph Lauren, Prada, Stella McCartney, Tiffany, Tory Burch, Versace, and Armani. Let's say it's an integrated 7,000-store monster that makes a ton of money because they are the only game in town. Kinda looks ripe for disruption if you are the entrepreneurial type.

That's exactly what Warby Parker did.

Neil, Andrew, David, and Jeff realized that if you could sell direct to customer via the internet (sound familiar?), you could still have a high-quality product but charge less.

How much less?

The average price is $95, which, compared to $500, is a lot more reasonable. The only trick is how to sell prescription eyeglasses online, and that's where they innovated.

On top of the standard free shipping both ways, Warby Parker has a unique Home-Try-On program that allows customers to choose five frames to try on at home for five days—thus taking the friction out of "how do these glasses look on me?"

On top of that, you can upload a photo of yourself to their site and see what the glasses would look like on you. These innovations have made Warby Parker part of the unicorn club with their recent funding round (2015) touting an impressive $1.2B evaluation on revenues upwards of $100M.

This same story has been repeated for companies like Zappos (bought by Amazon for $1.2B in 2009), Dollar Shave Club (bought by Unilever for $1B in 2016), Ebates, a site that gives shoppers cash back for shopping (bought by Rakuten for $1B in 2014), and Trunk Club (bought by Nordstrom for $350M in 2014). So how did these companies live the Ethos to garner such large exits?

All these companies took a critical look at the status quo of doing things and said there has to be a better way. They used drive, determination, tenacity, grit, and scholarship to invent better ways to shop. They exhibited the entrepreneurs' traits, values, and beliefs to challenge competitors, attract talent, and develop the new techniques to make a positive impact in their marketplace.

FORTY-ONE

Transportation – Crash Test Dummies

"Rules are made for people who aren't willing to make up their own."

— General Chuck Yeager, first person to break the sound barrier

In July 1976, the SR-71 Blackbird became the world's fastest airplane with a recorded speed of 2,193.13 MPH.

No plane since has broken that record.

First introduced in 1964, the SR-71 was the brainchild of legendary aircraft designer Kelly Johnson, who worked at Lockheed Martin. For those of you who don't know who Kelly Johnson was, think of him as the Steve Jobs of airplanes.

His lab, called the Skunkworks, produced some of the most advanced aircraft in the world—from the first U.S. jet fighter (P-80 Shooting Star) to the first stealth fighter (F-117 Nighthawk). To this day, the Skunkworks method of locking a bunch of smart people in a room to solve a tough problem is still practiced by all sorts of companies. Steve Jobs used it to create some of Apple's best products.

That's why it's odd that transportation has not seen much innovation since those glory days of aviation.

It's clear that transportation is ripe for disruption.

It's refreshing to finally see startups taking the lead in making travel better, faster, and cheaper. No other startups have exemplified this attitude better than Tesla and SpaceX.

Both Tesla and SpaceX are the longest of the long-odds startups. If you were to tell someone that you were not only going to start a car company, but an electric one at that, they would call you crazy. But then to follow that up by also starting a rocket company? True madness!

Tesla was one of the first car companies to bring electric cars to the market. Tesla also added something else that was equally revolutionary—autonomous driving. Tesla was the first company to put autopilot into a production automobile. This marked a drastic turning point in transportation that companies like Google have been working on for years. Why are these innovations important?

Most people in the U.S. use their cars only five-percent of the time. The rest of the time, your car sits parked doing nothing. That's a pretty crappy ROI for a big investment that dropped in value the moment you bought it.

Autonomous technology changes that.

No more circling for parking. No more "was it 5D or 3D?" when looking for your car. In fact, Tesla wants you to be able to rent out your car when not in use by driving itself to someone who wants to rent it. That's a game-changer for how we will use cars in the future. It's also a whole lot safer to have the car drive than a human.

The funny thing about autonomous technology is, like most advances in transportation, it was not driven by industry. Rather it was the government, via the DARPA Grand Challenge in 2004 that first offered cash prizes to self-driving cars that could successfully navigate a course. This opened the door to developing autonomous vehicles that would be able to first navigate out in the open and then in the urban jungle.

As we discussed before, the government can be either a champion of innovation or its staunchest opponent. The trick is finding the right balance of innovation that is sometimes more art than science. Uber found that out the hard way with its first self-driving car trials in San Francisco that were halted by the state of California. Even Uber needs to play by the rules.

Transportation of all types is highly regulated because of the potential of mass injury and death. To its credit, the National Transportation Safety Board (NTSB) has been a successful government agency for increasing both transportation safety and knowledge by the use of unbiased accident analysis. This has helped cars become safer, and given airplanes the best safety record of any form of transportation.

With advanced autonomous technology, it is hoped that car safety will become as good as airplanes.

The drive for better, safer, more economical, and less environmentally impactful transportation will change our economy forever. It's no real stretch to say that in five to ten years, people won't need to drive their cars. Truck manufacturers like Volvo and Mercedes have already been testing driverless trucks. Uber, Google, General Motors, and Ford are starting to test driverless cars as well.

Vehicle autonomous technology is still in its infancy, but is already affecting the mindset of the driving public. The first Tesla with autopilot was released in October of 2015. That's only 11 years from the first DARPA Grand Challenge lab prototypes to mass production, and the pace of change is only going to increase. The coming innovations will affect all the ways and means of consumer and business travel, and will challenge our personal and society's ability to absorb and accept them.

Autonomous cars and trucks are not the only transportation innovation out there.

Hyperloop One was formed in 2014 by Shervin Pishevar and Josh Giegel to create a new form of transportation (another Elon Musk idea) that will speed you from San Francisco to Los Angeles in 30 minutes.

Hyperloop One is built on the premise that a tube inside another tube, when in a vacuum, can enable rapid transport with low friction losses over great distances. Such a system would be for point-to-point connections only but, again, this opens up an entire new way for people and goods to be moved. As Hyperloop One puts it:

> Hyperloop is a new way to move people and things at airline speeds for the price of a bus ticket. It's on-demand, energy-efficient, and safe. Think: broadband for transportation.

Hyperloop's vision is pretty amazing considering that the original Elon Musk paper was released in 2013. In 2017, they will have a test track ready to go in the Nevada desert. Along with the test track, Hyperloop One will be taking RFPs for a full Hyperloop installation from over 40 states and countries.

When transportation is on-demand, safe, and affordable, it changes the entire dynamic of transportation and transportation ownership.

Why buy a car when you can hail one at a moment's notice?

Uber and Lyft have made this commonplace and it's only going to accelerate when self-driving cars also become a reality. If you live in any large metropolitan area, you can already hail an Uber or Lyft in a matter of minutes for travel within your metro area. That reality all happened within eight years after Uber was founded in 2009 and Lyft's founding in 2012.

The same thing is happening for long distance travel. Why fly when you can be whisked in less time from LA to SF in a pneumatic tube on steroids?

The trick to making all this happen is not just the core technology, but creating the infrastructure to make it possible, affordable, and easy to use.

Hyperloops need electricity to create both their magnetic levitation and their vacuums. Electric cars need batteries to store energy. Societies need cheap and clean sources of energy. Some clever entrepreneurs, not named Elon, have proposed some wide-ranging solutions.

Solar Roadways ran a successful Indiegogo campaign that raised over $2.0M with one of the cleverest and funniest videos I have ever seen. Their idea is to embed solar panels in roadways. This makes total sense since roads are permanently exposed to sunlight and for much of the time not much traffic is on them.

With solar roadways you can collect energy, reconfigure lanes, melt snow, and even wish drivers a happy new year via embedded LEDs that you can program in all sorts of ways. Look out, neighbors, this Christmas I'm going to brighten your commute home with a Clark Griswold level of holiday lights.

Transportation is finally starting to see an increase in vision, tenacity, collaboration, creativity, and, frankly, optimism that there are better, cheaper, and safer ways to transport people and goods around the world. Technology, infrastructure, budget considerations, and government regulations will figure heavily into how, when, and to what degree these innovations will be rolled out.

Perhaps the biggest challenges will be in winning the hearts and minds of people who have always been in control of getting themselves and their goods from A to B. Autonomous vehicles will cause a dramatic shift in employment and in transportation industries. Entrepreneurs in every field will be called upon to help provide the technical, economic, budgetary, and social acceptance needed to make all these innovations a reality.

FORTY-TWO

Search - I'm Feeling Lucky

"There's nothing that cannot be found through some search engine or on the Internet somewhere."
— Eric Schmidt, Executive Chairman of Alphabet, Inc.

Regis McKenna is a marketing guru's marketing guru who most growth hackers today either don't know or could not pick out of a line-up. That's about to change.

Regis is famous for always carrying around a National Blank Book Company 80-sheet 8x10 notebook that he would make handwritten notes in. As Regis recounts in an April 2016 *Fast Company* article, the notes served many purposes:

> I wasn't just taking verbatim notes. They're kind of my sketchbooks for things. I intermix data with my own view, and it blends. Some of them you do with clients, some you do on airplanes after you've left. You have to translate things for clients so they can follow up.

These notebooks captured some of the history of how famous brands like Intel, Genentech, and Apple began marketing their products in the early days. It's a glimpse into how fledgling companies formulated their marketing messages and changed the world. For example, in Regis's notebook was the outline of the marketing plan for Apple when it was first founded. Image what it was like being at the first meeting with Steve Jobs and figuring out how to market Apple—true history in the making.

Regis had certain rules that he followed to make sure his clients would grab the most attention. One such rule was to have your company's name start with the letter *A* so it would be listed first in the phonebook. Today that might not seem like sage advice but, back in the 70s, 80s, and 90s, most people looked up places to do business in the phonebook or, for businesses, the Yellow Pages.

For those too young to remember, the Yellow Pages was a massive listing of companies that could be kept by the rotary phone for when you needed to call someone. It came out roughly once a year and was indexed by the type of business you were looking for. If you wanted a restaurant, you would flip to *R* and look up what you wanted. Needing a tow? The Yellow Pages had your back, under *T*.

There was also the White Pages, which was an alphabetical listing by last name of everyone in your town or area. It also listed businesses, but no one ever used it for that. The Yellow Pages was where it was at and Regis knew that.

His advice was an old-fashioned way to rank high in the search medium of the time, and if you flip through an old phonebook you will see his advice in action.

From "AA Plumbing" to "AAA Pest Control," everyone wanted to be at the top of the search results (category page) because they knew that potential customers were not going to look much past the top three to five entries. It's the same way today with searching on the internet.

Internet searching is now the de facto way consumers find what they are looking for. Hardly a moment goes by that someone is not searching for an article on Google, a toaster on Amazon, or a mint Yogi Berra baseball card on eBay.

Search is everywhere, and being found at the top is king.

Every second there are over 58,000 Google searches for everything you can think of. Those searches are incredibly valuable to brands. In 2016, over $83B was spent on paid searches, up from $73B in 2015. Paid search has become the equivalent of being first in the good old Yellow Pages.

To put that in perspective, paid search started in 2000. That means the revenue from paid search went from $0 to $83B in 16 short years. Back then Google even powered Yahoo's search results. Image that.

As we discussed before, Google was not the first company to do search. That honor goes to Archie back in the 1990s. What Google did was make search both relevant and profitable.

The profitable part does have its price. Not to Google, but to the privacy of users who search. To make search fast and relevant, Google tracks everything that a user searches. It uses this data to refine its algorithms to make them better and more selective on what to show you. This also makes the more popular or relevant sites come up higher on the search list. This is great if that content is high quality and people are clicking on it. This would be like listing companies by customer ratings instead of their name in the Yellow Pages. Can you see how valuable that is for brands?

Even in the Yellow Pages, companies could pay for large or catchy ads that would optimize their "search" results. This is the equivalent of paid search today. This option is valuable for brands because the companies that stand out, other things being equal, are the ones that will be called or clicked on the most. The more times a customer engages, the more business a company gets.

For consumers these paid ads and relevance were easy to figure out. For searching online, it's a little trickier and ripe for gaming the system.

As we discussed, companies used to take advantage of Google's rules and create link farms (lots of links on a page) to fool Google into thinking that their content was more important than other content. These enterprising entrepreneurs gamed the system to drive more organic (non-ad-based results) traffic to their sites. This made them a lot of money because they could charge companies for ads on their high-traffic sites. You can debate the ethics of all this, but it became a huge problem for Google because the value of those results was reduced.

You see, if Google starts to produce bad search results (e.g., results that the searcher finds questionable or irrelevant) then customers won't use Google to search anymore. That has a two-fold effect.

First, it reduces Google's ad revenue and, second, it reduces the quality of their search results.

The Catch-22 is this: search needs users searching to make the algorithms more efficient, and the results need to be of high quality so users keep searching.

To get more searches, you need to attract more people to your platform. In order to attract more people, your results have to be high quality and clickable. If you get that wrong, people will go to other sites or use other search mechanisms. It's always about quality. Like social media, you need to keep users on your site or things go south. That's not lost on Google.

High quality search is why Google constantly changes its search algorithms to weed out sites that only do a great job of Search Engine Optimization (SEO)—like Mahalo did as we discussed before. It's important to stay relevant since Google isn't the only game in town.

More people are now going directly to Amazon to look for products to buy. This trend will continue as more and more people spend their time in fewer and fewer applications. I can envision a time where Messaging apps will be the go-to interface for not only communicating with your friends, but also buying tickets to the next Bon Jovi tribute band.

Out of all the technology advancements on the internet, search is the one that makes our lives so much easier. Being able to have the world's information at our fingertips is astounding power. It also presents challenges that some search companies are trying to address.

The most important challenges are privacy and governmental access to personal and private information. Services like DuckDuckGo (discussed in Part One) have challenged Google by not tracking a user's search history—thus making a more private search that returns results more aligned to what *you* want instead of what the search engine wants to show you. This is a classic example of responding to customers' demands by providing a whole different experience than the status quo. It's also an example of seeking knowledge (scholarship) to find a creative way to solve a pressing need.

FORTY-THREE

The Experience Economy - Couch Surfing Mavericks

"Advertising is a tax you pay for being unremarkable."
— Robert Stephens, founder of Geek Squad

Jennifer Hyman's journey as an entrepreneur can be summarized by the first time she pitched her company, Rent the Runway, an online store to rent the latest fashions, to a big Boston VC firm:

> When Hyman was about to get to the part where she explained how many inventory turns [how many times you can rent an item] she could get from a Diane von Furstenberg, one of the men interrupted the presentation, cupped her hand in his and said, "You are just too cute. You get this big closet and get to play with all these dresses and can wear whatever you want. This must be so much fun!"

As we discussed before, this type of response to a female entrepreneur is all too common and is one reason the Ethos states that:

> All under my leadership are given equal and unbiased opportunities to succeed. I lead myself and my

company so that everyone involved is safe from harassment, bullying, and exploitation.

It's important that we as entrepreneurs hold ourselves to a higher standard so that situations like what Jennifer had to endure go away. Thankfully, that VC's unacceptable attitude did not deter Jennifer. Rather, she used it as inspiration.

Entrepreneurs come up against all sorts of barriers, stereotypes, and prejudices. In a perfect world, it's these challenges that help fuel entrepreneurs to build great companies. In Jennifer's case, the condescending comment ignited her drive to not only to do that, but to finally shatter the glass ceiling by being a runaway success—pun intended. She lived the Ethos by believing in her vision enough to get past the awkwardness caused by that clearly sexist comment to focus on building a creative solution to a big problem—the shift from owning things to having experiences.

The idea behind Rent the Runway is simple in concept yet complex in execution. The concept is to buy designer dresses wholesale and rent them via the web for a night or two at a fraction of the purchase price.

Simple idea, yet getting the 65,000 dresses and 25,000 accessories to their five million members is daunting. That's why their 280 employees are an eclectic mix of talent ranging from data scientists, fashion stylists, app developers, logistics experts, and apparel merchandisers.

What Rent the Runway represents is an old idea redone in a new way. There have always been places to rent tuxedoes and, in Asia, it's common to rent your wedding dress. These types of services are finding a new and eager customer base in millennials who have come of age in the sharing and on-demand economy.

Instead of "owning" things, they "rent" or "experience" them.

This new consumer streams music on Spotify, watches original shows on Netflix, hails a car on Uber, rents a room on Airbnb, and now keeps their wardrobe fresh on Rent the Runway.

The experience economy is the latest market to thrive on ubiquitous access to the internet. This ease of internet access is how web-based companies can build up and scale. The poster child for this type of marketplace is Airbnb.

Recall that we discussed Airbnb in the chapter on Tenacity (Chapter 24) because of the creative way they raised money and their profile by selling breakfast cereal. There is a lot to learn about how Airbnb began and scaled its business.

Founded in 2007 by roommates Joe Gebbia and Brian Chesky, Air Bed & Breakfast was a way for the pair to afford to pay rent in expensive San Francisco. The idea came to them because a big design conference was coming to town and hotels were either all booked up or going for an exorbitant amount of money. So they bought three air mattresses, put up a simple website, and hosted their first two guests for $80 a night.

The idea of renting out a room or even swapping your house or apartment is nothing new. People have been doing that for years whether it's a co-owned condo in Maui or an extra bedroom you have to lease out to make your monthly rent.

The big idea that made Airbnb take off was making the process of hosting and being a guest simple and seamless. In the past, this was the hardest part of the whole deal. Airbnb made anyone with a room and a mobile phone able to own a B&B business.

Marketplaces like the ones Rent the Runway and Airbnb make possible are part of the growing experience economy. Consumers (mostly millennials) want to buy experiences instead of owning stuff. That's why the Airbnbs and Rent the Runways of the world are growing at such a rapid rate—experiences matter more and more to people.

This experiencing rather than owning things has done even more than just allow entrepreneurs to create businesses. It's also enabled those entrepreneurs to then outsource part of that business. That's exactly how Superhost, an outsourced hosting service for Airbnb hosts, came about.

Superhost was founded by twin brothers Amiad and Koby Soto in Israel, where they encountered problems renting out their apartments on Airbnb. They loved the Airbnb idea yet they saw that hosting might not be for everyone. The idea they had was simple. They wanted to take the hassle out of being a host. These hassles included picking guests, organizing house cleaning, and getting urgent phone calls in the middle of the night from frantic guests trying to find the key—all the normal challenges of running a B&B. People loved the idea and signed up.

With their initial success, the brothers moved to San Francisco after being accepted into the famous startup accelerator, Y Combinator.

At the time, San Francisco's Mission district was the most successful Airbnb neighborhood so they decided to prove their idea the old-fashioned way. Their customer acquisition strategy was to walk around Dolores Park with a sign saying "Do You Host Airbnb?" The strategy paid off and soon they had 120 customers (half of them in San Francisco) who wanted to use their services.

Like all good Y Combinator startups, the name had to change and contain a Y. Nowadays, Guesty is a 21-person company with thousands of hosts using their services. Their service has expanded past Airbnb listings and now a host can manage all their property in one place. Guesty has become essentially an online property management company.

The brothers' hustle for new customers, self-determination to work hard, and their vision to find a better way are perfect examples of living the Ethos.

The experience economy perfectly captures the spirit of living the Ethos. It was built with collaboration between companies providing infrastructure (cellular, cloud, and internet), device companies (Apple, Samsung), and other service providers (Uber, Lyft, Airbnb, et al.) to create businesses that never existed before.

The next level in the experience economy is what companies like Tencent (one of China's e-commerce giants) and Rappido (Movile's e-commerce platform in Latin America) are trying to do on their platforms. Namely, to put all Online to Offline (O2O) user needs in one place. Jonathan Shieber of TechCrunch puts it in perspective:

> Similar in scope to what Tencent has done with WeChat in China and what Line has done in Korea (or what Alphabet has done in India with Areo), Rappido is hoping to launch its marketplace allowing folks to order tickets, top up their minutes, and get food or groceries through a single messaging point of access.

> It's a big idea for e-commerce, and one that doesn't really have a corollary in the U.S. yet (Facebook Messenger is trying).

The entrepreneurs who are building the experience economy have the perfect storm of technology, culture, and capital to help fuel their creativity, passion, competitiveness, and vision to change how the world works. Throw in a healthy mix of competitors and a rapid customer feedback loop (ratings), and you get an environment poised for rapid growth.

As with any new marketplace, there have been missteps in creating the experience economy and several companies were not always playing by the rules. The wonderful thing is that the marketplace had within it the self-correcting means for customers and the community to hold those companies accountable. The sharing economy is a good template for how a community keeps its members honest.

Companies like eBay, Amazon, Uber, Airbnb, and Yelp hold both vendors and customers accountable by allowing public feedback of the experiences had by both. At times, this can be gamed but, overall, this two-way feedback keeps everyone honest and in check.

It's through this peer and community feedback, the glue that holds the experience economy together, that a culture is held to a higher standard. As entrepreneurs we also need to hold ourselves to a higher standard of morals and ethics because of the critical role we play in society and the fact that we too will get feedback from society that can reflect on all of us. When an entrepreneur behaves badly it's bad for all of us. With the internet and 24/7 news, there is no longer any place to hide.

Warrior cultures like the Spartans, Samurai, Mongols, and Romans understood the importance of winning with honor in the ultimate game of life and death. While entrepreneurship is hardly that, the lessons from those warrior cultures help shape our ideas of duty, honor, loyalty, service, camaraderie, and respect for one's opponents.

The traits, values, and beliefs of *The Entrepreneur Ethos* are the entrepreneur's guide to fulfilling our destiny to build businesses that make a positive impact on the world while we build an independent life that completes us.

By following *The Entrepreneur Ethos*, our ideas and achievements can be fully realized and accomplished.

By following *The Entrepreneur Ethos*, we earn the loyalty, respect, and trust of our team, our community, and our society.

By following *The Entrepreneur Ethos*, we win with honor.

EPILOGUE

The Pace of Change Is Accelerating

"The pace of change and the threat of disruption creates tremendous opportunities."

— Steve Case, entrepreneur

Change is inevitable. As entrepreneurs, we know that the only way we will truly be successful is if we change the world around to our point of view.

We fight this battle daily.

We wrestle the status quo to the ground, or vice versa.

Without this fight, the world could not move forward.

The whole point of *The Entrepreneur Ethos* is to give entrepreneurs the framework to fight the good fight. It's meant to embrace the challenges of change and to put forth a unique way to take on the world.

Over the last several decades, the pace of change has been accelerating and the world is now a much different place than it was a generation ago. No better illustration of that are the top publicly traded companies.

If you look at the top five publicly traded companies (by market cap) over the last 15 years, you can see what I mean.

In 2001, the top five (in order) were General Electric, Microsoft, Exxon, Citibank, and Wal-Mart.

In 2016, the top five were Apple, Alphabet (Google), Microsoft, Amazon, and Facebook.

The change from the top companies in the old economy (manufacturing, energy, retail) to the technology companies in the new economy all happened within the blink of an eye. The next wave is hot on its heels and Uber is leading the way.

Uber was founded in 2009 and in 2016 had $6.5 billion in revenue. Uber completely changed the way we get around and will continue to disrupt the $4 trillion dollar logistics market.

Our world has so many other technologies that are getting ready to disrupt our society just like Uber.

Technologies like Artificial Intelligence (AI), Virtual Reality (VR), the Internet of Things (IoT), block chain technology (cyber-currencies like Bitcoins), drones, robots, and autonomous technology (self-driving cars) will force society to rethink how we live, work, and play.

Each one of these technologies has a lot of potential for entrepreneurs to change the world, as long as considerations are given for their impact on society. The most important of these impacts is how the human workforce will be altered. Once technology is able to perform the majority of human work, what will humans do? This question is yet another big opportunity for entrepreneurs to explore.

It's vital that entrepreneurs consider *The Entrepreneur Ethos* as they build out these new capabilities. It's important to weigh the moral and ethical outcomes of the accelerating pace of change. The entrepreneurial community, being in the vanguard, needs to consider the implications of new technologies and capabilities. Society has traditionally been ill equipped to absorb all the changes brought by technological advances and their unintended consequences.

Just look at what's happening in manufacturing in the U.S. Contrary to popular opinion, most manufacturing jobs are being taken over by automation and not by outsourcing to other countries. This major technology disruption has deep social impacts since all those idled workers will need to be retrained and transitioned to new work.

The same can be said for autonomous technology (10% of U.S. males drive for a living) and AI stock trading (computers are better than human traders). Pretty soon, all these jobs will go away.

Before that happens, the entrepreneurial community needs to remain inclusive and help people cultivate entrepreneurial skills. This is important to ensure that there will be enough new entrepreneurs to use their old-world and newly acquired skills to bring new technologies to market in a responsible way and to create innovations that make a positive impact on society.

The future is full of the promise of change. For some, these are scary times filled with fear, uncertainty, and doubt about how they will fit in. For entrepreneurs, it's an exciting time, the best of times.

Entrepreneurs need to embrace *The Entrepreneur Ethos* so they can guide society in the best ways possible to take on the challenges of the 21st century and beyond.

Summary of the Entrepreneur Ethos

1. Failure is an option, but never the end result.
2. Integrity is my middle name.
3. Seeking the truth will guide my decisions.
4. The journey is my reward.
5. Being an entrepreneur is an honor I must earn daily.

Acknowledgments

This book would not be possible without the fantastic support of my late wife Jane. She always encouraged me to write my truth and for that I'm eternally grateful. Even though we are no longer together, my love, you are always in my heart.

To Mark McGuinness and Greg Marcus, who read the initial drafts of the manuscript and gave me valuable feedback.

To my editors Dennis Sides and Victoria Clark Wang, who helped me refine my voice and bring *The Entrepreneur Ethos* to life.

To Kevin Holmes, for writing such a wonderful Foreword and building Founders Network—a truly unique resource for entrepreneurs.

To Tim Yin, Brett Fox, Jane Bolander, Geoff Zawolkow, Mark McGuinness, Catherine Bartolomei-Smith, Dale Berman, Marvin Raab, Daniel Kan, Jason Cohen, Eric Eggers, Melissa Hanna, Andrea Barrica, Chris Klundt, Jonathan Shih, Joel Runyon, Ankkit O. Aggarwal, Anand Sanwal, Nathan Rose, Jon Naster, Sam Parr, Katherine Krug, Michelle Mazzara, J.F. Gauthier, Yan Huang, Brandon Foo, Ravi Kurani, Allison Martin, Eduardo Henrique, Michael Clarke, and Philip Thomas, for allowing me to interview you. Your insights and stories were inspiring and an invaluable contribution to *The Entrepreneur Ethos*.

Thanks to The Hustle, CB Insights, and LAUNCH Ticker for your daily inspirations and invaluable research. Every single entrepreneur needs to subscribe to all of them.

I am especially thankful to all my Sheepdog workout brothers and sisters. It's rare and wonderful to find a group of people who not only take care of each other, but also look out for the common good. Each of you is like family to me.

About the Author

Jarie Bolander is an engineer by training and an entrepreneur by nature with over 20 years of bringing innovative solutions to market, such as Bluetooth, USB, RFID, and Semiconductor DNA sequencing. He is currently the co-founder and COO of Lab Sensor Solutions (LSS), a digital health company that is applying sensor technology to track the temperature and location of perishables to prevent spoilage. LSS has had the honor of being part of startup accelerators 500 Startups and Launch Pad Digital Health.

Prior to founding Lab Sensor Solutions, Jarie was at Ion Torrent—a third-generation DNA sequencing company that was bought by Life Technologies for $750 million. Ion Torrent was the first company to productize semiconductor-sequencing technology to achieve the $1,000 genome.

Before Ion Torrent, Jarie was founder and VP of Research and Development for Tagent—an innovative RFID company that created breakthrough technology that integrated antennas on silicon to achieve small, compact form factors.

Prior to forming Tagent, Jarie was at Cypress Semiconductor, where he was the technical project manager for WirelessUSB, a pioneering new wireless standard that made going wireless as simple as wired USB.

He holds an MBA in Technology Management from the University of Phoenix and a BS in Electrical Engineering from San Jose State University.

He is also inventor or co-inventor on over ten patents and has published three other books: *Frustration-Free Technical Management*, *#ENDURANCE Tweet—A Little Nudge to Keep You Going*, and *Business Basics for Entrepreneurs*.

You can read his thoughts on management and entrepreneurship via his blog, *http://www.thedailymba.com* and follow him on Twitter @TheDailyMBA.

Source Notes

Introduction

Alba, Davey. "Ellen Pao Ends Her Lawsuit Against Kleiner Perkins." Wired. September 10, 2015. https://www.wired.com/2015/09/ellen-pao-ends-lawsuit-kleiner-perkins/.

O'Connor, Clare. "Binary Capital Cofounder Knew Of Justin Caldbeck's History Of 'Bad Behavior'." Forbes. June 26, 2017. https://www.forbes.com/sites/clareoconnor/2017/06/26/binary-capital-cofounder-knew-of-justin-caldbecks-history-of-bad-behavior/#49530ac14f4a.

Kosoff, Maya. "Mass Firings at Uber as Sexual Harassment Scandal Grows." The Hive. June 06, 2017. http://www.vanityfair.com/news/2017/06/uber-fires-20-employees-harassment-investigation.

O'Connor, Clare. "Dave McClure Out As Day-To-Day Lead At 500 Startups After Sexual Harassment Accusations." Forbes. June 30, 2017. https://www.forbes.com/sites/clareoconnor/2017/06/30/dave-mcclure-out-as-day-to-day-lead-at-500-startups-after-sexual-harassment-accusations/.

Part One — Challenging The Status Quo

Yourself - The Struggle Within

Pressfield, Steven. The war of art: break through the blocks and win your inner creative battles. New York: Black Irish Entertainment, 2012.

Runyon, Joel. "The Entrepreneur Ethos Questionnaire." Telephone interview by author. June 8, 2016. CEO of IMPOSSIBLE

Hanna, Melissa. "The Entrepreneur Ethos Questionnaire." Telephone interview by author. May 25, 2016. CEO of MCH Ventures

Pressfield, Steven. Do the work!: overcome resistance and get out of your own way. Place of publication not identified: The Domino Project, 2011.

Klundt, Chris. "The Entrepreneur Ethos Questionnaire." Telephone interview by author. June 3, 2016. CEO of StudyBlue

Friends & Family - The Company You Keep

Shih, Jonathan. "The Entrepreneur Ethos Questionnaire." Telephone interview by author. June 7 2016. CEO of Decisive Health

Eggers, Eric. "The Entrepreneur Ethos Questionnaire." Telephone interview by author. May 17 2016. Digital Health Consultant

Beerman, Dale. "The Entrepreneur Ethos Questionnaire." Telephone interview by author. May 4, 2016. CEO of Pacifica

Yu, Arry. "5 Lessons My Mother Taught Me About Business." The Huffington Post. April 21, 2016. http://www.huffingtonpost.com/businesscollective/5-lessons-my-mother-taugh_b_9751852.html

Talent - Finding the Crazy Ones

Alsever, Jennifer. "Fighting co-founders doom startups." CNNMoney. February 24, 2014. http://money.cnn.com/2014/02/24/smallbusiness/startups-entrepreneur-cofounder/.

Cohen, Jason. "The Entrepreneur Ethos Questionnaire." Telephone interview by author. May 16, 2016. Founder & CTO of WPEngine

Suster, Mark. "How I Invest – Both Sides of the Table." Both Sides of the Table. May 27, 2016. https://bothsidesofthetable.com/how-i-invest-9d8266a62d3e#.af2lfgs4a.

Zawolkow, Geoff. "The Entrepreneur Ethos Questionnaire." Telephone interview by author. April 21, 2016. CEO of Lab Sensor Solutions

Sanwal, Anand. "Multiple Startup Job Offers? Here's 9 Data-Driven Tests To Help You Pick Which Startup To Work For." CB Insights Research. November 5, 2016. https://www.cbinsights.com/blog/startup-job-offer/.

Duhigg, Charles. "What Google Learned From Its Quest to Build the Perfect Team." The New York Times. February 27, 2016.

http://www.nytimes.com/2016/02/28/magazine/what-google-learned-from-its-quest-to-build-the-perfect-team.html.

Barr, Alistair, and Mark Bergen. "One Reason Staffers Quit Google's Car Project? The Company Paid Them So Much." Bloomberg.com. February 13, 2017. https://www.bloomberg.com/news/articles/2017-02-13/one-reason-staffers-quit-google-s-car-project-the-company-paid-them-so-much.

Gruber, John. "Fuck-You Money." Daring Fireball. February 2, 2017. http://daringfireball.net/linked/2017/02/13/fuck-you-money.

Technology - Then Magic Happens

"StackShare helps developers find and decide on the best tools and services." StackShare. July 24, 2017. http://stackshare.io/

"The last Kodak moment?" The Economist. January 14, 2012. http://www.economist.com/node/21542796.

"Kodak." Wikipedia. July 26, 2017. https://en.wikipedia.org/wiki/Kodak.

Brachmann, Steve. "The Rise and Fall of the Company that Invented Digital Cameras." IPWatchdog.com | Patents & Patent Law. November 01, 2014. http://www.ipwatchdog.com/2014/11/01/the-rise-and-fall-of-the-company-that-invented-digital-cameras/.

Murphy, Mike, and Akshat Rathi. "All of Google's-er, Alphabet's-companies and products from A to Z." Quartz. August 10, 2015. http://qz.com/476460/here-are-all-the-alphabet-formerly-google-companies-and-products-from-a-to-z/.

"What The Rise Of Supercharged Messaging Apps Means For CMOs." Forbes. April 21, 2016. http://www.forbes.com/sites/onmarketing/2016/04/19/what-the-rise-of-supercharged-messaging-apps-means-for-cmos/.

Technique - Practice Makes Perfect

Relan, Peter. "Where Webvan Failed And How Home Delivery 2.0 Could Succeed." TechCrunch. September 27, 2013. http://techcrunch.com/2013/09/27/why-webvan-failed-and-how-home-delivery-2-0-is-addressing-the-problems/.

Klundt, Chris. "The Entrepreneur Ethos Questionnaire." Telephone interview by author. March 3, 2016. CEO of StudyBlue

Bartolomei-Smith, Catherine. "The Entrepreneur Ethos Questionnaire." Telephone interview by author. April, 27, 2016.

Cohen, Jason. "The Entrepreneur Ethos Questionnaire." Telephone interview by author. May 16, 2016. Founder & CTO of WPEngine

Williams, Matt. "SpaceX Just Put The Coolest Garden Gnome Ever In Its Front Yard." Universe Today. August 27, 2016. http://www.universetoday.com/130432/spacex-just-put-coolest-garden-gnome-ever-front-yard/.

Wasserman, Norm. "The Founder's Dilemma." HBR. February 1, 2008. https://hbr.org/2008/02/the-founders-dilemma.

Timing - Missed It by That Much

"Timeline of web search engines." Wikipedia. July 15, 2017. https://en.wikipedia.org/wiki/Timeline_of_web_search_engines.

"Internet/Broadband Fact Sheet." Pew Research Center: Internet, Science & Tech. January 12, 2017. http://www.pewinternet.org/data-trend/internet-use/internet-use-over-time/.

"You Snooze You Lose - Lessons from the Fall of Blockbuster." BizzVenue. March 05, 2015. http://bizzvenue.com/snooze-lose-lessons-fall-blockbuster/.

Satell, Greg. "A Look Back At Why Blockbuster Really Failed And Why It Didn't Have To." Forbes. September 21, 2014. http://www.forbes.com/sites/gregsatell/2014/09/05/a-look-back-at-why-blockbuster-really-failed-and-why-it-didnt-have-to/.

Sanwal, Anand. "The Entrepreneur Ethos Questionnaire." Telephone interview by author. July 21, 2016. CEO of CBInsights

Yin, Tim. "The Entrepreneur Ethos Questionnaire." Telephone interview by author. December 25, 2015. CEO of TN Technologies

Aggarwal, Ankkit O. "The Entrepreneur Ethos Questionnaire." Telephone interview by author. June 19, 2016. CEO of HydeWest

Akhmechet, Slava. "RethinkDB: why we failed." defstartup.org. January 18, 2017. http://www.defstartup.org/2017/01/18/why-rethinkdb-failed.html.

Customers - No Better Friend

"Here's what I learned hanging out with Jason Fried." danshipper.com.

July 24, 2017. http://danshipper.com/heres-what-i-learned-hanging-out-with-jason-fried

Eggers, Eric. "The Entrepreneur Ethos Questionnaire." Telephone interview by author. May 17 2016. Digital Health Consultant

Competitors – Makes the Pie Bigger

"Historical Chronology." Avis | Rent a Car. Accessed July 29, 2017. https://www.avis.com/en/about-avis/company-information/historical-chronology.

Parekh, Rupal. "After 50 Years, Avis Drops Iconic 'We Try Harder' Tagline." Ad Age. August 27, 2012. http://adage.com/article/news/50-years-avis-drops-iconic-harder-tagline/236887/.

Stevenson, Seth. "Was "We Try Harder" the Most Brilliant Ad Slogan of the 20th Century?" Slate Magazine. August 12, 2013. http://www.slate.com/articles/business/rivalries/2013/08/hertz_vs_avis_advertising_wars_how_an_ad_firm_made_a_virtue_out_of_seco nd.html.

"Auto Rental Factbook 2016." Auto Rental News. July 29, 2017. http://www.autorentalnews.com/fileviewer/2229.aspx.

Griffith, Erin. "Driven In The Valley: The Startup Founders Fueling GM's Future." Fortune. September 22, 2016. http://fortune.com/cruise-automation-general-motors-driverless-cars/.

"Lyft Is Gaining on Uber as It Spends Big for Growth." Bloomberg. April 14, 2016. http://www.bloomberg.com/news/articles/2016-04-14/lyft-is-gaining-on-uber-as-it-spends-big-for-growth/.

Buhr, Sarah. "Lyft, Now Worth $5.5 Billion, Hops Into The Autonomous Car Race With General Motors." TechCrunch. January 04, 2016. https://techcrunch.com/2016/01/04/lyft-now-worth-5-5-billion-plans-to-get-into-the-autonomous-car-race-with-general-motors/.

Hickman, James. "Uber, Lyft continue to grow at expense of taxis, rental cars." TheStreet. January 21, 2016. https://www.thestreet.com/story/13430707/1/uber-lyft-continue-growth-among-business-travelers-taxis-rental-cars-see-share-decline.html.

"Taxicabs of New York City." Wikipedia. July 26, 2017. https://en.wikipedia.org/wiki/Taxicabs_of_New_York_City.

"2014 Taxi Cab Fact Book" New York City Government. 2014. http://www.nyc.gov/html/tlc/downloads/pdf/2014_taxicab_fact_bo

ok.pdf.

"Demographics of New York City." Wikipedia. July 27, 2017.
https://en.wikipedia.org/wiki/Demographics_of_New_York_City.

Frizell, Sam. "Uber and Taxi History: NYC Cab Expert Warns Regulation Is Necessary." Time. November 19, 2014.
http://time.com/3592035/uber-taxi-history/.

"The Tyranny of the Taxi Medallions." Priceonomics. Accessed July 29, 2017. https://priceonomics.com/post/47636506327/the-tyranny-of-the-taxi-medallions.

"DuckDuckGo." Wikipedia. July 29, 2017.
https://en.wikipedia.org/wiki/DuckDuckGo.

Investors - Those Who Make the Rules

Fox, Brett. "The Entrepreneur Ethos Questionnaire." Telephone interview by author. March 14, 2016. CEO Coach

Limey, Yankee Sabra. "Towards a VC code of conduct." yankeesabralimey.tumblr.com. January 15, 2014.
http://yankeesabralimey.tumblr.com/post/73395704448/towards-a-vc-code-of-conduct.

Shen, David. "Qualities of an Awesome Investor - The Web and the World of Business," August 10, 2016.
http://www.dshen.com/blogs/business/archives/qualities_to_be_an_awesome_investor.shtml.

Government - Here to Help You

"Mr. Smith Goes to Washington." Wikipedia, July 26, 2017.
https://en.wikipedia.org/w/index.php?title=Mr._Smith_Goes_to_Washington&oldid=792432589.

Badenhausen, Kurt. "The Best Countries For Business 2015," December 16, 2015.
https://www.forbes.com/sites/kurtbadenhausen/2015/12/16/the-best-countries-for-business-2015/#3b4fc4b795d6.

Vanham, Peter. "Which Countries Have the Most Venture Capital Investments?" *World Economic Forum*, July 28, 2015.
https://www.weforum.org/agenda/2015/07/which-countries-have-the-most-venture-capital-investments/.

Shane, Scott. "Why Venture Capital Deals Stay in Silicon Valley,"

Entrepreneur, November 2, 2015.
https://www.entrepreneur.com/article/252225.

Weissmann, Jordan. "Think We're the Most Entrepreneurial Country In the World? Not So Fast - The Atlantic." *The Atlantic*, October 2, 2012.
https://www.theatlantic.com/business/archive/2012/10/think-were-the-most-entrepreneurial-country-in-the-world-not-so-fast/263102/.

Housel, Morgan. "When You Change the World and No One Notices." *Collaborative Fund*, September 3, 2016.
http://www.collaborativefund.com/blog/when-you-change-the-world-and-no-one-notices/.

Squires, David, and Chloe Anderson. "U.S. Health Care from a Global Perspective," October 8, 2015.
http://www.commonwealthfund.org/publications/issue-briefs/2015/oct/us-health-care-from-a-global-perspective.

"ObamaCare Facts: Facts on the Affordable Care Act." *Obamacare Facts*, n.d. https://obamacarefacts.com/obamacare-facts/.

"E-Residency." *E-Estonia*, n.d. https://e-estonia.com/solutions/e-identity/e-residency/.

Wallison, Peter. "Hey, Barney Frank: The Government Did Cause the Housing Crisis - The Atlantic," December 13, 2011.
https://www.theatlantic.com/business/archive/2011/12/hey-barney-frank-the-government-did-cause-the-housing-crisis/249903/.

Alloway, Tracy. "Why Would Anyone Want to Restart the Credit Default Swaps Market?" *Bloomberg Professional Services*, May 11, 2015, sec. Import - Professional (3/16/2017).
https://www.bloomberg.com/professional/blog/why-would-anyone-want-to-restart-the-credit-default-swaps-market/.

"Community Reinvestment Act." *Wikipedia*, July 21, 2017.
https://en.wikipedia.org/w/index.php?title=Community_Reinvestment_Act&oldid=791571290.

"About TARP." *U.S. Department of the Treasury*.
https://www.treasury.gov/initiatives/financial-stability/about-tarp/Pages/default.aspx.

Part Two — Traits

Passion - Kick the Tires and Light the Fires

Fish, Genevieve. "This Entrepreneur Turned Her Passion Project Into a $300 Million Business." *MyDomaine*, November 11, 2015. http://www.mydomaine.com/female-entrepreneur-suja.

"Clif Bar & Company: Feed Your Adventure®." *CLIF*, n.d. http://www.clifbar.com/our-stories/company/history.

"Clif Bar: Gary Erickson." How I Build This: Clif Bar NPR. October 3rd, 2016. https://www.npr.org/player/embed/495815443/496081302

Raab, Marvin. "The Entrepreneur Ethos Questionnaire." Telephone interview by author. May 6, 2016. Founder of Lab Sensor Solutions

Roth, Carol. "Not Every Creation or Passion Project Should Be a Business," Entrepreneur. April 29, 2015. https://www.entrepreneur.com/article/245604.

Newport, Cal. "Do Like Steve Jobs Did: Don't Follow Your Passion," Fast Company. September 20, 2012. https://www.fastcompany.com/3001441/do-steve-jobs-did-dont-follow-your-passion.

Discipline - The Wood Does Not Chop Itself

"111 Of The Biggest, Costliest Startup Failures Of All Time." *CB Insights Research*, June 22, 2017. /research/biggest-startup-failures/.

Clarke, Michael "The Entrepreneur Ethos Questionnaire." Telephone interview by author. February 22, 2017. CEO of Top Locker Media

Tam, Pui-Wing, and Mylene Mangalindan. "Pets.Com Will Shut Down, Citing Insufficient Funding." *Wall Street Journal*, November 8, 2000, sec. Tech Center. http://www.wsj.com/articles/SB973617475136917228.

Johnson, Zac. "The History of The Huffington Post [Infographic]." *Business 2 Community*, August 19, 2016. http://www.business2community.com/infographics/history-huffington-post-infographic-01636158.

Sarno, David. "A Brief History of the Huffington Post - Latimes." *Los Angeles Times*, February 7, 2011.

http://articles.latimes.com/2011/feb/07/business/la-fi-huffington-post-timeline-20110207.

"HuffPost." *Wikipedia*, July 29, 2017. https://en.wikipedia.org/w/index.php?title=HuffPost&oldid=7928838 40.

Fehrenbacher, Katie. "How A Tech Billionaire's Biofuel Dream Went Bad." *Fortune*, December 4, 2015. http://fortune.com/kior-vinod-khosla-clean-tech/.

Hiltzik, Michael. "President Obama Schools Silicon Valley CEOs on Why Government Is Not like Business," LA Times October 17, 2016. http://www.latimes.com/business/hiltzik/la-fi-hiltzik-obama-silicon-valley-20161017-snap-story.html.

Yarow, Jay. "CHART OF THE DAY: The Startup Curve - Business Insider," March 15, 2012. http://www.businessinsider.com/chart-of-the-day-the-startup-curve-2012-3.

Problem Solving - Houston, We Have a Problem

"Space Shuttle Challenger Disaster." *Wikipedia*, July 23, 2017. https://en.wikipedia.org/w/index.php?title=Space_Shuttle_Challeng er_disaster&oldid=791930927.

Feynman, R.P.: "Volume 2: Appendix F - Personal Observations on Reliability of Shuttle from the Report of the PRESIDENTIAL COMMISSION on the Space Shuttle Challenger Accident: NASA." June 6, 1986. http://history.nasa.gov/rogersrep/v2appf.htm

O'Brien, Chris. "Zenefits CEO David Sacks on His Bold Bet: Less than 10% of Employees Accepted 'The Offer.'" *VentureBeat*, June 21, 2016. https://venturebeat.com/2016/06/20/zenefits-ceo-david-sacks-on-his-bold-bet-less-than-10-of-employees-accepted-the-offer/.

Manjoo, Farhad. "Zenefits, a Rocket That Fell to Earth, Tries to Launch Again - The New York Times." *The New York Times*, October 12, 2016. https://www.nytimes.com/2016/10/13/technology/zenefits-a-rocket-that-fell-to-earth-tries-to-launch-again.html.

Manjoo, Farhad. "Zenefits' Leader Is Rattling an Industry, So Why Is He Stressed Out? - The New York Times," September 20, 2014. https://www.nytimes.com/2014/09/21/business/zenefits-leader-is-rattling-an-industry-so-why-is-he-stressed-out.html?_r=0.

Confidence - Not Cockiness

Reingold, Jennifer. "Southwest's Herb Kelleher: Still Crazy after All These Years." *Fortune*, January 14, 2013. http://fortune.com/2013/01/14/southwests-herb-kelleher-still-crazy-after-all-these-years/.

"8 Herb Kelleher Quotes That Will Teach You Everything You Need To Know About Life." *Free Enterprise*, March 21, 2014. https://www.freeenterprise.com/8-herb-kelleher-quotes-will-teach-you-everything-you-need-know-about-life/.

"Herbert D. Kelleher." Southwest Airlines Newsroom. July 25, 2017. http://swamedia.com/channels/Officer-Biographies/pages/herb_kelleher

"Our History - By Date." Southwest Airlines Newsroom. July 25, 2017. http://swamedia.com/channels/By-Date/pages/history-by-date

Baremetrics. "Subscription Analytics & Insights for Stripe, Braintree, Recurly and Chargify." July 25, 2017. https://baremetrics.com/

Herbert, Alex. "Talking Talent With 4 Successful Silicon Valley CEOs | Drobo," December 7, 2016. http://www.drobo.com/3155-2/.

Balluck, Kyle. "CEO Who Raised Drug Price 4,000 Percent Arrested." Text. *TheHill*, December 17, 2015. http://thehill.com/blogs/blog-briefing-room/news/263553-report-ceo-that-raised-drug-price-4000-percent-arrested.

Horowitz, Aaron, and Julia Smith. "Martin Shkreli Convicted of Securities Fraud, Conspiracy." *CNNMoney*, August 4, 2017. http://money.cnn.com/2017/08/04/news/martin-shkreli-verdict/index.html.

Disis, Jill. "Lawmakers Say EpiPen Hikes Made Mylan Executives 'Filthy Rich' - Sep. 21, 2016." *CNN Money*, September 22, 2016. http://money.cnn.com/2016/09/21/news/companies/mylan-epipen-house-oversight-committee/.

Reuters. "Mylan's CEO Will Testify Over EpiPen Price Hike." *Fortune*, September 14, 2016. http://fortune.com/2016/09/14/mylan-ceo-epipen/.

Lopez, Linette, and Lydia Ramsey. "Mylan CEO Heather Bresch Congressional Hearing on EpiPen - Business Insider," September 21, 2016. http://www.businessinsider.com/mylan-ceo-heather-bresch-house-oversight-committee-hearing-epipen-2016-9.

Seiter, Courtney. "The Humility-Confidence Seesaw: The Untold Secret of Great Leaders - Chicago Tribune," October 30, 2015.

http://www.chicagotribune.com/bluesky/hub/ct-buffer-humility-confidence-leadership-bsi-hub-20151030-story.html.

Focus – Deadlines Focus the Mind

"OODA Loops: Understanding the Decision Cycle," n.d. https://www.mindtools.com/pages/article/newTED_78.htm.

McKay, Brett, and Kate McKay. "OODA Loop: A Comprehensive Guide | The Art of Manliness," September 15, 2014. http://www.artofmanliness.com/2014/09/15/ooda-loop/.

Kan, Daniel. "The Entrepreneur Ethos Questionnaire." Telephone interview by author. May 16, 2016. COO of Cruise Automation GM

Chun, Janean. "Cathy Hughes, Radio One: From Teen Mom To Media Mogul." *Huffington Post*, September 26, 2012, sec. Huffington Post. http://www.huffingtonpost.com/2012/08/17/catherine-hughes-radio-one_n_1798129.html.

Benner, Katie. "Warned of a Crash, Start-Ups in Silicon Valley Narrow Their Focus - The New York Times." *New York Times*, August 28, 2016. https://www.nytimes.com/2016/08/29/technology/warned-of-a-crash-start-ups-narrowed-their-focus.html.

Competitiveness - Where Do I Sign Up?

McGuiness, Mark. "The Entrepreneur Ethos Questionnaire." Telephone interview by author. April 25, 2016. Author & Creative Coach

"The 50 Greatest Business Rivalries of All Time | Fortune.Com." *Fortune*, March 21, 2013. http://fortune.com/2013/03/21/the-50-greatest-business-rivalries-of-all-time/.

Schlossberg, Mallory. "Dunkin' Donuts Vs. Starbucks Map - Business Insider." *Business Insider*, January 12, 2015. http://www.businessinsider.com/dunkin-donuts-vs-starbucks-map-2015-1.

"Disruptive Innovation." *Clayton Christensen*, July 10, 2012. http://www.claytonchristensen.com/key-concepts/.

Velayanikal, Malavika. "Google-Backed Freshdesk Takes on Salesforce with a New Tool." *Tech in Asia*, June 22, 2016. https://www.techinasia.com/google-backed-freshdesk-takes-on-salesforce-with-freshsales.

Awkwardness - Waiting to Be a Swan

Richards, Carl. "Learning to Deal With the Impostor Syndrome - The New York Times." *New York Times*, October 26, 2015. https://www.nytimes.com/2015/10/26/your-money/learning-to-deal-with-the-impostor-syndrome.html?_r=0.

Warrell, Margie. "Afraid Of Being 'Found Out?' How To Overcome Impostor Syndrome," Forbes. April 3, 2014. https://www.forbes.com/sites/margiewarrell/2014/04/03/impostor-syndrome/.

Hamm, John. "Why Entrepreneurs Don't Scale." *Harvard Business Review*, December 1, 2002. https://hbr.org/2002/12/why-entrepreneurs-dont-scale.

Warrell, Margie. Stop Playing Safe: Rethink Risk: Unlock the Power of Courage: Achieve Outstanding Success. Wiley, 2013.

Henrique, Eduardo. "The Entrepreneur Ethos Questionnaire." Telephone interview by author. February 17, 2017. Co-founder of Movile.

Grit - Hard Is What Makes It Great

Chen, Walter. "Why You Should Hire People Toughened by Failure, Not Those Coddled by Success." *Entrepreneur*, August 7, 2014. https://www.entrepreneur.com/article/236026.

"Catherine L. Hughes: Black Entrepreneurs, Black CEO, Black Executive, Black Billionaires, Entrepreneur Profile." *Black Entrepreneur Profile*. Accessed July 29, 2017. https://www.blackentrepreneurprofile.com/profile-full/article/catherine-l-hughes/.

Holiday, Ryan. *The Obstacle Is the Way: The Timeless Art of Turning Trials into Triumph*. Tim Ferriss, 2014.

Rose, Nathan. "The Entrepreneur Ethos Questionnaire." Telephone interview by author. September 8, 2016. CEO of Assemble Advisory

Kurani, Ravi. "The Entrepreneur Ethos Questionnaire." Telephone interview by author. February 3, 2017. CEO of MySutro

Greene, David. "'How I Built This': Cathy Hughes On Radio One." *NPR.Org*, September 27, 2016. http://www.npr.org/2016/09/27/495595080/how-i-built-this-radio-one.

Chun, Janean. "Cathy Hughes, Radio One: From Teen Mom To Media Mogul." *Huffington Post*, September 26, 2012, sec. Huffington Post.

http://www.huffingtonpost.com/2012/08/17/catherine-hughes-radio-one_n_1798129.html.

"Urban One." *Wikipedia*, July 1, 2017.
https://en.wikipedia.org/w/index.php?title=Urban_One&oldid=78842
3291.

Engber, Daniel. "Angela Duckworth Says Grit Is the Key to Success in Work and Life. Is This a Bold New Idea or the Latest Self-Help Fad?," May 1, 2016.
http://www.slate.com/articles/health_and_science/cover_story/201
6/05/angela_duckworth_says_grit_is_the_key_to_success_in_work_a
nd_life_is_this.html.

Essig, Todd. "625,000 Reasons To See Grit As Key To Success." *Forbes*, September 26, 2013.
https://www.forbes.com/sites/toddessig/2013/09/26/625000-
reasons-to-see-grit-as-key-to-success/#54bcbd334514.

"Research." *Angela Duckworth*, n.d. http://AngelaDuckworth.com/.

Part Three — Values

Integrity - When No One Is Watching

"Elizabeth Holmes." Forbes. July 29, 2017.
http://www.forbes.com/profile/elizabeth-holmes/.

Carreyrou, John. "Hot Startup Theranos Has Struggled With Its Blood-Test Technology." The Wall Street Journal. October 16, 2015.
http://www.wsj.com/articles/theranos-has-struggled-with-blood-
tests-1444881901.

"E-mails reveal concerns about Theranos's FDA compliance date back years." The Washington Post. December 02, 2015.
https://www.washingtonpost.com/news/wonk/wp/2015/12/02/inte
rnal-emails-reveal-concerns-about-theranoss-fda-compliance-date-
back-years/

Griswold, Alison. "Sexual harassment is finally starting to topple Silicon Valley's powerful male elite." Quartz. July 04, 2017.
https://qz.com/1020790/sexual-harassment-is-finally-starting-to-
topple-silicon-valleys-powerful-male-elite.

Kiel, Fred. "Return on Character: The Real Reason Leaders and Their Companies Win." *HBR*, April 7, 2015.

https://hbr.org/product/return-on-character-the-real-reason-leaders-and-their-companies-win/16899-HBK-ENG.

"Regulators Warn Testing Startup Theranos over Lab Conditions." *AP News*, n.d. https://apnews.com/3ec32eb4a282451896f1fdff4114ff81/regulators-warn-testing-startup-theranos-over-lab.

"Top 10 Crooked CEOs." *Time*, n.d. http://content.time.com/time/specials/packages/article/0,28804,1903155_1903156_1903152,00.html.

Fisher, Anne. "In Business, Nice Guys Finish First. Yes, Really." *Fortune*, n.d. http://fortune.com/2015/04/01/character-leadership-business-success/.

Kim, Penny. "I Got Scammed By A Silicon Valley Startup." *Startup Grind*, August 28, 2016. https://medium.com/startup-grind/i-got-scammed-by-a-silicon-valley-startup-574ced8acdff#.fulfmrlxx.

Natanson, Hannah. "VCs Draft Code of Conduct to Battle Sexual Harassment." *The Information*, July 5, 2017. https://www.theinformation.com/vcs-draft-code-of-conduct-to-battle-sexual-harassment.

Scholarship – I'm a Wander

"IBM Watson Health - IBM Watson for Oncology." *IBM Watson Health*, January 1, 2017. https://www.ibm.com/watson/health/oncology-and-genomics/oncology/.

Cha, Ariana Eunjung, and Shelly Tan. "Watson's next Feat? Taking on Cancer." *Washington Post*, n.d. http://www.washingtonpost.com/sf/national/2015/06/27/watsons-next-feat-taking-on-cancer/.

"FACT SHEET: Investing in the National Cancer Moonshot." *Whitehouse.Gov*, February 1, 2016. https://obamawhitehouse.archives.gov/the-press-office/2016/02/01/fact-sheet-investing-national-cancer-moonshot.

Huang, Yan. "The Entrepreneur Ethos Questionnaire." Telephone interview by author. December 15, 2016. CEO of Press Release Jet

"The Digital Hospital: 80+ Companies Reinventing Medicine In One Infographic." *CB Insights Research*, October 11, 2016. /research/digital-health-medicine-market-map-company-list/.

"About | Chan Zuckerberg Initiative." *The Chan Zuckerberg Initiative*, n.d. https://chanzuckerberg.com/about.

Chaykowski, Kathleen. "Chan Zuckerberg Initiative Promises To Spend $3 Billion To Research And Cure All Diseases." *Forbes*, September 21, 2016. https://www.forbes.com/sites/kathleenchaykowski/2016/09/21/chan-zuckerberg-initiative-invests-3-billion-to-cure-disease/.

Action-oriented – Don't Wait For An Invitation

Naster, Jon. "The Entrepreneur Ethos Questionnaire." Telephone interview by author. October 20, 2016. CEO of Hack the Entrepreneur

Parr, Sam. "The Entrepreneur Ethos Questionnaire." Telephone interview by author. October 23, 2016. CEO of Hustle Time Media

Sanwal, Anand. "The Entrepreneur Ethos Questionnaire." Telephone interview by author. July 21, 2016. CEO of CBInsights

Runyon, Joel. "The Entrepreneur Ethos Questionnaire." Telephone interview by author. June 8, 2016. CEO of IMPOSSIBLE

Independence – Means Running Your Race

Miller, Ben. "For-Profit Colleges Went Astray, Should Return to Their Roots (Essay) | Inside Higher Ed." *Inside Higher Ed*, May 30, 2014. https://www.insidehighered.com/views/2014/05/30/profit-colleges-went-astray-should-return-their-roots-essay.

"U.S. Student Loan Debt Statistics for 2017." *Student Loan Hero*, March 10, 2017. https://studentloanhero.com/student-loan-debt-statistics/.

"232 Startup Failure Post-Mortems." *CB Insights Research*, June 9, 2017. /research/startup-failure-post-mortem/.

Griffith, Erin. "Fraud in Silicon Valley: Startups Show Their Unethical Underside." *Fortune*, December 28, 2016. http://fortune.com/silicon-valley-startups-fraud-venture-capital/.

Solomon, Brian. "Zenefits CEO Parker Conrad Resigns Amid Scandal." *Forbes*, February 8, 2016. https://www.forbes.com/sites/briansolomon/2016/02/08/zenefits-ceo-parker-conrad-resigns-amid-scandal/#445517218314.

Risk-taking – High Wire Act

"Man on Wire (Official Movie Site) - Starring Philippe Petit, Jean
François Heckel and Jean-Louis Blondeau - Available on DVD - Trailer,
Pictures & More." Accessed July 30, 2017.
http://www.magpictures.com/manonwire/.

Sanwal, Anand. "The Entrepreneur Ethos Questionnaire." Telephone
interview by author. July 21, 2016. CEO of CBInsights

Barrica, Andrea. "The Entrepreneur Ethos Questionnaire." Telephone
interview by author. May 26, 2016. CEO of O.school

Weissmann, Jordan. "Entrepreneurship: The Ultimate White Privilege?
- The Atlantic." *The Atlantic*, August 16, 2013.
https://www.theatlantic.com/business/archive/2013/08/entreprene
urship-the-ultimate-white-privilege/278727/.

Tenacity - Bulldog Is My Middle Name

"The 13 Y Combinator Startups Worth Over $50 Billion." *CB Insights
Research*, January 5, 2015. /research/y-combinator-startup-
valuation/.

Mazzara, Michelle. "The Entrepreneur Ethos Questionnaire." Telephone
interview by author. December 7,2016. Founder & CEO of Luvafoodie

"Entrepreneurs anonymous." The Economist. September 20, 2014
http://www.economist.com/news/business/21618816-instead-
romanticising-entrepreneurs-people-should-understand-how-hard-
their-lives-can

Roz, Guy. "Airbnb: Joe Gebbia." *NPR.Org*, October 17, 2016.
http://www.npr.org/podcasts/510313/how-i-built-this.

"The Airbnb Founder Story: From Selling Cereals To A $25B Company."
Get Paid For Your Pad, September 18, 2015.
https://getpaidforyourpad.com/blog/the-airbnb-founder-story/.

"About Us - Airbnb," n.d. https://www.airbnb.com/about/about-us.

Nazar, Jason. "14 Famous Business Pivots." *Forbes*, October 8, 2013.
https://www.forbes.com/sites/jasonnazar/2013/10/08/14-famous-
business-pivots/.

Lunden, Ingrid. "Songbird Sings Its Last Tune As Music Service Runs Out
Of Money And Plans To Shut Down June 28 | TechCrunch," June 14,
2013. https://techcrunch.com/2013/06/14/songbird-sings-its-last-
tune-as-music-service-runs-out-of-money-and-plans-to-shut-down-
june-28/.

Parkin, Simon. "Worms or Bust: The Story of Britain's Most Tenacious Indie Games Company." *Ars Technica UK*, June 9, 2016. https://arstechnica.co.uk/gaming/2016/06/history-of-team17-and-worms/.

Hustle - Don't Hate the Playa, Hate the Game

"Hustle Con: An Event for Non-Technical Startup Tactics." *Hustle Con*, n.d. http://hustlecon.com/.
Parr, Sam. "The Entrepreneur Ethos Questionnaire." Telephone interview by author. October 23, 2016. CEO of Hustle Time Media
"About Us | Google," n.d. //www.google.com/intl/en/about/.
Battelle, John. "The Birth of Google." *Wired*, August 1, 2005. https://www.wired.com/2005/08/battelle/.
"10 Unusual Things I Didn't Know About Google (Also: The Worst VC Decision in History)." *Altucher Confidential*, March 17, 2011. http://www.jamesaltucher.com/2011/03/10-unusual-things-about-google/.

Collaboration – The Blind Leading the Blind

"History of Free and Open-Source Software." *Wikipedia*, July 1, 2017. https://en.wikipedia.org/w/index.php?title=History_of_free_and_open-source_software&oldid=788436494.
"Timeline of Open-Source Software." *Wikipedia*, May 16, 2017. https://en.wikipedia.org/w/index.php?title=Timeline_of_open-source_software&oldid=780630300.
Gauthier, J.F. "The Entrepreneur Ethos Questionnaire." Telephone interview by author. December 8, 2016. CEO of The Startup Genome
Schwartz, Barry. "Jason Calacanis: Google's Matt Cutts Killed Mahalo & Wants Revenge." *Seroundtable.Com*, July 3, 2014. https://www.seroundtable.com/jason-calacanis-revenge-google-matt-cutts-18794.html.
Ha, Anthony. "Jason Calacanis' Mahalo Is Reborn As Mobile News App Inside." *TechCrunch*, n.d. http://social.techcrunch.com/2014/01/27/inside-mobile-news-launch/.
Hudson, John. "Google's Billion-Dollar Algorithm Change: Winners and Losers - The Atlantic." *The Atlantic*, March 8, 2011.

https://www.theatlantic.com/technology/archive/2011/03/biggest-winners-and-losers-out-googles-algorithm-change/348685/.

Gannes, Liz. "Mahalo Lays Off 25 Percent for Shift to Apps From Video." *AllThingsD*, October 26, 2011. http://allthingsd.com/20111026/mahalo-lays-off-18-for-shift-to-apps-from-video/.

Goldman, David. "Google Algorithm Change Shifts Billions in Ad Spending - Mar. 8, 2011." *CNN Money*, March 8, 2011. http://money.cnn.com/2011/03/08/technology/google_algorithm_change/index.htm.

Etherington, Darrell. "LinkedIn Battens Down The Hatches On API Use, Limiting Full Access To Partners." *TechCrunch*, February 12, 2015. http://social.techcrunch.com/2015/02/12/linkedin-battens-down-the-hatches-on-api-use-limiting-full-access-to-partners/.

Dignan, Larry. "LinkedOut: CRM Companies Squawk over LinkedIn's API Policies." *ZDNet*, April 24, 2014. http://www.zdnet.com/article/linkedout-crm-companies-squawk-over-linkedins-api-policies/.

Wagner, Kurt. "LinkedIn Is Sharing Less With Developers." *Recode*, May 12, 2015. https://www.recode.net/2015/5/12/11562548/linkedin-is-sharing-less-with-developers.

Part Four — Beliefs

Visionary - The Forest Through the Trees

Bergen, Mark. "The Google X Moonshot Factory Is Struggling to Get Products out the Door." *Recode*, August 29, 2016. https://www.recode.net/2016/8/29/12663630/google-x-alphabet-moonshot.

Bolander, Jane Yin. "The Entrepreneur Ethos Questionnaire." Telephone interview by author. March 19,2016. CEO of JSY PR & Marketing

Thomas, Philip. "The Entrepreneur Ethos Questionnaire." Telephone interview by author. March 20, 2017. CEO of StaffJoy

Fehrenbacher, Katie. "Elon Musk's Vision Includes New Cars, Car Sharing & Approval Of His Deal." *Fortune*, July 20, 2016. http://fortune.com/2016/07/20/elon-musk-master-plan-2/.

Mosher, Dave. "Here's Elon Musk's Complete, Sweeping Vision on Colonizing Mars to Save Humanity." *Business Insider*, September 29,

2016. http://www.businessinsider.com/elon-musk-mars-speech-transcript-2016-9.

Cohn, Chuck. "5 Visionary CEOs and Their Key Traits That Every Leader Should Master." *Entrepreneur*, February 24, 2015. https://www.entrepreneur.com/article/242302.

Musk, Elon. "The Secret Tesla Motors Master Plan (Just between You and Me)," August 2, 2006. https://www.tesla.com/blog/secret-tesla-motors-master-plan-just-between-you-and-me.

Musk, Elon. "Master Plan, Part Deux." *Tesla*, July 20, 2016. https://www.tesla.com/blog/master-plan-part-deux.

Woody, Todd. "Arnold Schwarzenegger's Dream Fuel Makes a Comeback - The Atlantic." *The Atlantic*, May 2, 2014. https://www.theatlantic.com/technology/archive/2014/05/californi a-just-launched-a-hydrogen-car-revolution/361592/.

Musk, Elon. "All Our Patent Are Belong To You." *Tesla*, June 12, 2014. https://www.tesla.com/blog/all-our-patent-are-belong-you.

"Waymo." *Waymo*, n.d. https://waymo.com/.

Lambert, Fred. "Google's Self-Driving Car vs Tesla Autopilot: 1.5M Miles in 6 Years vs 47M Miles in 6 Months." *Electrek*, April 11, 2016. https://electrek.co/2016/04/11/google-self-driving-car-tesla-autopilot/.

Crook, Jordan. "Casper Mattress Startup Lands $13.1 Million Series A | TechCrunch," August 8, 2014. https://techcrunch.com/2014/08/08/casper-mattress-startup-lands-13-1-million-series-a/.

"Designing the Perfect Mattress | Casper®," n.d. https://casper.com/mattresses/design/.

Johnson, Lauren. "Here Are 4 Tips From a Startup That's About to Go Global." *Adweek*, November 6, 2015. http://www.adweek.com/digital/here-are-4-tips-startup-thats-about-go-global-168001/.

Levin-Epstein, Amy. "Mattress Startup CEO Philip Krim Shares His Strategy," April 30, 2014. http://www.cbsnews.com/news/mattress-startup-ceo-shares-his-strategy/.

Burrows, Peter. "By Buying SolarCity, Elon Musk Is Making an Already Difficult Job Much Harder." *MIT Technology Review*, October 11, 2016. https://www.technologyreview.com/s/602487/elon-musks-house-of-gigacards/.

Self-awareness - Know Thyself

"Why Self-Awareness Is Crucial for Entrepreneurs." *Bloomberg*, n.d. https://www.bloomberg.com/news/articles/2012-08-16/why-self-awareness-is-crucial-for-entrepreneurs.

Tjan, Anthony K. "How Leaders Become Self-Aware." *Harvard Business Review*, July 19, 2012. https://hbr.org/2012/07/how-leaders-become-self-aware.

Campbell, Sherrie. "7 Ways Entrepreneurs Can Master Self-Awareness." *Entrepreneur*, October 23, 2014. https://www.entrepreneur.com/article/238754.

"111 Of The Biggest, Costliest Startup Failures Of All Time." *CB Insights Research*, June 22, 2017. /research/biggest-startup-failures/.

"The Top 20 Reasons Startups Fail." *CB Insights Research*, October 8, 2014. https://www.cbinsights.com/blog/startup-failure-reasons-top/

Graham, Paul. "The 18 Mistakes That Kill Startups." *Paul Graham*, October 1, 2016. http://www.paulgraham.com/startupmistakes.html.

Self-belief - I'm Good Enough

Hahn, Fritz. "America Now Has More Breweries than Ever. And That Might Be a Problem." *Washington Post*, January 18, 2016. https://www.washingtonpost.com/lifestyle/food/america-now-has-more-breweries-than-ever-and-that-might-be-a-problem/2016/01/15/d23e3800-b998-11e5-99f3-184bc379b12d_story.html.

"Our Story." *Boston Beer Company*. Accessed July 30, 2017. https://www.samueladams.com/our-story.

Roz, Guy. "Samuel Adams: Jim Koch." *NPR.Org*, July 24, 2017. http://www.npr.org/podcasts/510313/how-i-built-this.

Optimism - Why Not Me? Why Not Now?

Henley, William Ernest. "Invictus by William Ernest Henley." Text/html. *Poetry Foundation*, January 1, 1888. https://www.poetryfoundation.org/poems/51642/invictus.

Holiday, Ryan. "Stoicism Isn't Pessimistic. It's Boldly Optimistic. | RyanHoliday.Net." *Ryanholiday.Net*, November 2, 2015.

https://ryanholiday.net/stoicism-isnt-pessimistic-its-boldly-optimistic/.

Foo, Brandon. "The Entrepreneur Ethos Questionnaire." Telephone interview by author. January 19, 2017. CEO of Polymail

Entis, Laura. "Entrepreneurs: Your Irrational Optimism Is Necessary." *Entrepreneur*, February 14, 2014. https://www.entrepreneur.com/article/231549.

Wong, Kyle. "Why Startup Founders Should Be Optimistic." *Forbes*, August 20, 2014. https://www.forbes.com/sites/kylewong/2014/08/20/why-startup-founders-should-be-optimistic/.

Shontell, Alyson. "Marc Andreessen Asks This Optimistic Question Every Time He Critiques A Startup." *Business Insider*, October 20, 2014. http://www.businessinsider.com/marc-andreessen-on-optimism-and-startups-2014-10.

Bohanes, Michal. "Seven Lessons I Learned from the Failure of My First Startup, Dinnr." *Medium*, August 17, 2014. https://medium.com/indian-thoughts/seven-lessons-i-learned-from-the-failure-of-my-first-startup-dinnr-c166d1cfb8b8#.x613dcrbl.

Vaynerchuk, Gary. "There's No 'Undefeated' in Entrepreneurship." *Gary Vaynerchuk*, December 6, 2016. https://medium.com/@garyvee/theres-no-undefeated-in-entrepreneurship-c405ee5dbc07#.qiyxf63it.

"Joe Montana." *Wikipedia*, July 12, 2017. https://en.wikipedia.org/w/index.php?title=Joe_Montana&oldid=790202389.

"The Catch (American Football)." *Wikipedia*, July 8, 2017. https://en.wikipedia.org/w/index.php?title=The_Catch_(American_football)&oldid=789672240.

Freeman, Eric. "Stephen Curry Can't Stop Making Half-Court Buzzer-Beaters." *Yahoo Sports*, March 9, 2016. https://sports.yahoo.com/blogs/nba-ball-dont-lie/stephen-curry-can-t-stop-making-half-court-buzzer-beaters-072525599.html.

Flexibility - Be Comfortable Being Uncomfortable

Horowitz, with Ben, Jason Rosenthal, and Sonal Chokshi. "A16z Podcast: Startups, Pivots, Culture, and Timing (Oh Shit!) – Andreessen Horowitz," n.d. http://a16z.com/2017/02/19/startups-pivots-culture-decisions-timing/.

Abdou, Jenna. "How to Make Flexibility Your Startup's North Star - 33voices." *33 Voices*. Accessed July 30, 2017. https://www.33voices.com/posts/how-to-make-flexibility-your-startups-north-star.

"Barnes & Noble History | B&N INC." *Barnes & Noble Inc*, August 23, 2016. http://www.barnesandnobleinc.com/about-bn/heritage/.

Martin, Allison. "The Entrepreneur Ethos Questionnaire." Telephone interview by author. February 5, 2017. CEO of UDoTest

Loayza, Jun. "Premature Scaling Killed Us." *PM the Hard Way*, June 2, 2015. http://www.junloayza.com/startup-tips/premature-scaling/.

"Dick's Sporting Goods Is Evolving into a Tech Company." *The Hustle*, November 29, 2016. https://thehustle.co/dicks-sporting-digital.

"DICK'S Team Sports HQ | Youth Sports Made Easy," n.d. https://teamsportshq.dsg.com/.

Weinberger, Matt. "9 Hot Startup Pivots - Business Insider," April 16, 2015. http://www.businessinsider.com/9-hot-startup-pivots-2015-4.

"The 20 Reasons Startups Fail" CB Insights Research. https://www.cbinsights.com/research-reports/The-20-Reasons-Startups-Fail.pdf

Self-determination - Fall 7 Times, Stand Up 8

"The Legend of Cliff Young: The 61 Year Old Farmer Who Won the World's Toughest Race." *Elite Feet*. Accessed July 30, 2017. https://elitefeet.com/the-legend-of-cliff-young.

"End of the Road for Cliff - National - Smh.Com.Au." *The Syndey Morning Hearld*, November 3, 2003. http://www.smh.com.au/articles/2003/11/03/1067708126175.html.

Creativity - Have No Fear of Perfection

"Inside Silicon Valley's Robot Pizzeria." *Bloomberg.Com*, n.d. https://www.bloomberg.com/news/articles/2016-06-24/inside-silicon-valley-s-robot-pizzeria.

"Pizza Saver." *Wikipedia*, July 12, 2017. https://en.wikipedia.org/w/index.php?title=Pizza_saver&oldid=790219739.

Wilhelm, Alex. "DocuSign Raises $233M Series F At $3B Valuation | TechCrunch." *TechCrunch*, March 12, 2015.

https://techcrunch.com/2015/05/12/docusign-raises-233m-series-f-at-3b-valuation/.
"Official Site Of The Original Squatty Potty® Toilet Stool," n.d. https://www.squattypotty.com/.
Squatty Potty. *This Unicorn Changed the Way I Poop - #SquattyPotty.* Accessed July 30, 2017. https://www.youtube.com/watch?v=YbYWhdLO43Q.
Oran, Nicole. "Shark Tank Takes a Bathroom Break with Squatty Potty." *MedCity News*, November 17, 2014. http://medcitynews.com/2014/11/shark-tank-heads-toilet-squatty-potty/.
"Chubbies Shorts." *Chubbies Shorts*, n.d. https://www.chubbiesshorts.com/.
Marshall, Carla. "How Many Views Does a YouTube Video Get on Average?" *Tubular Insights*, February 2, 2015. http://tubularinsights.com/average-youtube-views/.
You, Jia. "Gecko-Inspired Adhesives Allow People to Climb Walls." *Science | AAAS*, November 18, 2014. http://www.sciencemag.org/news/2014/11/gecko-inspired-adhesives-allow-people-climb-walls.

Part Five — Dents in the Universe

Cloud Computing - Software Eats the World

"The Canva Story." *About Canva*, January 30, 2015. https://www.canva.com/our-story/.
Andreessen, Marc. "Why Software Is Eating The World." *Wall Street Journal*, August 20, 2011, sec. Life and Style. https://www.wsj.com/articles/SB10001424053111903480904576512250915629460.
Patel, Jeetu. "Software Is Still Eating the World | TechCrunch." *TechCrunch*, June 7, 2016. https://techcrunch.com/2016/06/07/software-is-eating-the-world-5-years-later/.
"It's Not Easy Being Google." *The Hustle*, January 27, 2017. https://thehustle.co/google-other-bets.
Hof, Robert. "Marc Andreessen: Now, Software Is Programming The World." *Forbes*, n.d.

https://www.forbes.com/sites/roberthof/2016/07/12/marc-
andreessen-now-software-is-programming-the-world/.

Audio Streaming - Pretty Fly for a White Guy

Swash, Rosie. "Frank Zappa Invents Filesharing Business Model ... in
1989 | Music | The Guardian." *The Guardian*, April 9, 2009.
https://www.theguardian.com/music/2009/apr/09/frank-zappa-
invents-filesharing-model.
Masnick, Mike. "Did Frank Zappa Come Up With A Business Plan For File
Sharing In 1983?" *Techdirt.*, April 8, 2009.
https://www.techdirt.com/articles/20090405/1806484395.shtml.
Steele, Billy. "Universal Music Group Is Reportedly Done with
Streaming Exclusives." *Engadget*, August 15, 2016.
https://www.engadget.com/2016/08/25/universal-music-group-
streaming-exclusives-report/.
Shaw, Lucas, and Adam Satariano. "Spotify Is Burying Musicians for
Their Apple Deals - Bloomberg." *Bloomberg*, August 26, 2016.
https://www.bloomberg.com/news/articles/2016-08-26/spotify-
said-to-retaliate-against-artists-with-apple-exclusives.
Nieva, Richard. "Ashes to Ashes, Peer to Peer: An Oral History of
Napster." *Fortune*, September 5, 2013.
http://fortune.com/2013/09/05/ashes-to-ashes-peer-to-peer-an-
oral-history-of-napster/.
Shaw, Lucas. "The Music Industry Is Finally Making Money on
Streaming." *Bloomberg.Com*, September 20, 2016.
https://www.bloomberg.com/news/articles/2016-09-20/spotify-
apple-drive-u-s-music-industry-s-8-first-half-growth.
Farivar, Cyrus. "10 Years of Podcasting: Code, Comedy, and Patent
Lawsuits." *Ars Technica*, August 13, 2014.
https://arstechnica.com/information-technology/2014/08/10-years-
of-podcasting-code-comedy-and-patent-lawsuits/.
"How Many Podcasts Are There? State of the Podcast 2015." *Myndset*,
October 27, 2015. http://myndset.com/2015/10/how-many-
podcasts-are-there/.

Video Streaming - See What's Next

"Netflix, Reed Hastings Survive Missteps to Join Silicon Valley's Elite."
Bloomberg.Com, n.d.

https://www.bloomberg.com/news/articles/2013-05-09/netflix-reed-hastings-survive-missteps-to-join-silicon-valleys-elite.

Zambelli, Alex. "A History of Media Streaming and the Future of Connected TV | Media Network | The Guardian." *The Guardian*, March 1, 2013. https://www.theguardian.com/media-network/media-network-blog/2013/mar/01/history-streaming-future-connected-tv.

McLain, Tilly. "A Brief History of Streaming Video." *Streaming Video Blog*, February 12, 2016. https://www.ustream.tv/blog/streaming-video-tips/a-brief-history-of-streaming-video/.

Tassi, Paul. "'Game of Thrones' Sets Piracy World Record, But Does HBO Care?" *Forbes*, n.d. https://www.forbes.com/sites/insertcoin/2014/04/15/game-of-thrones-sets-piracy-world-record-but-does-hbo-care/.

Tassi, Paul. "You Will Never Kill Piracy, and Piracy Will Never Kill You." *Forbes*, February 3, 2012. https://www.forbes.com/sites/insertcoin/2012/02/03/you-will-never-kill-piracy-and-piracy-will-never-kill-you/.

"NO. The Grand Tour Is NOT The Most Pirated TV-Show in History." *TorrentFreak*, December 13, 2016. https://torrentfreak.com/no-the-grand-tour-is-not-the-most-pirated-tv-show-ever-161213/.

McAlone, Nathan. "Growth of Streaming Services Outpacing Traditional Cable - Business Insider." *Business Insider*, April 11, 2016. http://www.businessinsider.com/growth-of-streaming-services-outpacing-traditional-cable-2016-4.

Flanagan, Graham. "Why Sean Parker's Plan to Stream Movies Still in Theaters for $50 Could Work." *Business Insider*, March 16, 2016. http://www.businessinsider.com/sean-parker-movies-streaming-spielberg-jj-abrams-netflix-screening-room-2016-3.

Montgomery, Mike. "With Screening Room, Sean Parker Shows He's Become A More Mature Entrepreneur." *Forbes*, June 2, 2016. https://www.forbes.com/sites/mikemontgomery/2016/06/02/with-screening-room-sean-parker-shows-hes-become-a-more-mature-entrepreneur/.

Coons, Ted. "OTT At a Tipping Point, Poised for Rapid Growth." *Streaming Media Magazine*, 20160826. http://www.streamingmedia.com/Articles/ReadArticle.aspx?ArticleI D=113176.

Moren, Dan. "Why Apple Is Making Its Original TV Content Push Now." *Macworld*, January 13, 2017.

http://www.macworld.com/article/3157688/streaming-services/why-apple-is-making-its-original-tv-content-push-now.html.

Do-It-Yourself - You can do it

Reader, Ruth. "A Brief History of Etsy, from 2005 Brooklyn Launch to 2015 IPO." *VentureBeat*, March 5, 2015. https://venturebeat.com/2015/03/05/a-brief-history-of-etsy-from-2005-brooklyn-launch-to-2015-ipo/.

"Etsy, Inc. Reports 39% Revenue Growth in the Second Quarter 2016," August 2, 2016. https://investors.etsy.com/news-and-events/press-releases/2016/08-02-2016.

Bowen, Ken. "Value Prop: How Radio Shack Lost Its Way by Losing Sight of Its Ideal Customer."*MarketingExperiments: Research-Driven Optimization, Testing, and Marketing Ideas*, March 16, 2015. https://marketingexperiments.com/value-proposition/how-radio-shack-lost-sight-of-its-ideal-customer.

"About." Kickstarter. July 26, 2017 https://www.kickstarter.com/about

"BetterBack - Perfect Posture Effortlessly" Kickstarter https://www.kickstarter.com/projects/1123408990/betterback-perfect-posture-effortlessly

"BetterBack - Perfect Posture Effortlessly." *Indiegogo*, n.d. https://www.indiegogo.com/projects/1498660.

Parr, Sam. "We've Just Closed Another Round of Funding - And Want You to Join," January 15, 2017. https://thehustle.co/funding.

Gaming – Ready Player One

"Video Game History Timeline | The Strong," n.d. http://www.museumofplay.org/about/icheg/video-game-history/timeline.

"The Video Game Revolution: History of Gaming | PBS." Accessed July 30, 2017. http://www.pbs.org/kcts/videogamerevolution/history/.

Nelson, Graham. "The History Of Video Games, By The Numbers." *Huffington Post*, July 10, 2015, sec. Tech. http://www.huffingtonpost.com/entry/the-history-of-the-biggest-video-games-ever-by-the-numbers_us_559edf12e4b096729155d0b9.

Minotti, Mike. "Video Games Will Become a $99.6B Industry This Year as Mobile Overtakes Consoles and PCs." *VentureBeat*, April 21, 2016.

https://venturebeat.com/2016/04/21/video-games-will-become-a-99-6b-industry-this-year-as-mobile-overtakes-consoles-and-pcs/.

"Pong-Story : Who Did It First ?" Accessed July 30, 2017. http://www.pong-story.com/inventor.htm.

"S&H Green Stamps." *Wikipedia*, July 24, 2017. https://en.wikipedia.org/w/index.php?title=S%26H_Green_Stamps&oldid=792103024.

"Play Games | Get Scouted." *Scoutible*, n.d. http://www.scoutible.com/.

"About VR – Firsthand Technology." Accessed July 30, 2017. https://firsthand.com/about-vr/.

Ramachandran, V.S. and Rogers-Ramachandran, D. "Synaethesia in phantom limbs induced with mirrors" http://cbc.ucsd.edu/pdf/Synaesthesia%20in%20Phantom%20Limbs%20-%20P%20Royal%20Soc.pdf

Minotti, Mike. "2016 Saw $30.3 Billion in Gaming Mergers, Acquisitions, and Investments." *VentureBeat*, January 26, 2017. https://venturebeat.com/2017/01/26/2016-saw-30-3-billion-in-gaming-mergers-acquisitions-and-investments/.

Bush, Michael. "Why Harrah's Loyalty Effort Is Industry's Gold Standard." *Ad Age*, October 5, 2009. http://adage.com/article/news/harrah-s-loyalty-program-industry-s-gold-standard/139424/.

Social Media - A Place for Friends

Reader, Ruth. "Users Aren't Enough: Why Yik Yak Is The Latest Casualty Of A Changing Market." *Fast Company*, December 9, 2016. https://www.fastcompany.com/3066457/startup-report/users-arent-enough-why-yik-yak-is-the-latest-casualty-of-a-changing-market.

Yarow, Jay. "CHART OF THE DAY: The Fall Of MySpace - Business Insider." *Business Insider*, June 29, 2011. http://www.businessinsider.com/chart-of-the-day-the-fall-of-myspace-2011-6.

Shields, Mike. "MySpace Still Reaches 50 Million People Each Month - CMO Today - WSJ." *The Wall Street Journal*, January 14, 2015. https://blogs.wsj.com/cmo/2015/01/14/myspace-still-reaches-50-million-people-each-month/.

Williams, Rhiannon. "Apple Music vs Spotify: How Do the Two Streaming Services Compare?" *The Telegraph*, March 17, 2016.

http://www.telegraph.co.uk/technology/2016/03/17/apple-music-vs-spotify-how-do-the-two-streaming-services-compare/.

Gillette, Felix. "The Rise and Inglorious Fall of Myspace." *Bloomberg.Com*, June 23, 2011. https://www.bloomberg.com/news/articles/2011-06-22/the-rise-and-inglorious-fall-of-myspace.

Kolodny, Lora. "Yik Yak Shuts down after Square Paid $1 Million for Its Engineers." *TechCrunch*, April 28, 2017. http://social.techcrunch.com/2017/04/28/yik-yak-shuts-down-after-square-paid-1-million-for-its-engineers/.

McMillan, Robert. "The Friendster Autopsy: How a Social Network Dies." *Wired*, February 27, 2013. https://www.wired.com/2013/02/friendster-autopsy/.

Erickson, Christine. "7 Companies That Could Have Been Facebook." *Mashable*, May 17, 2012. http://mashable.com/2012/05/17/companies-before-facebook/.

E-commerce - Way to Shop!

"History of the Sears Catalog," n.d. http://www.searsarchives.com/catalogs/history.htm.

Pahwa, Divya. "The History of the Catalog." *Divya Pahwa*, August 15, 2014. https://medium.com/@pahwadivya/the-history-of-the-catalog-b5334841e941#.db7tstgzz.

"Costco CEO Craig Jelinek Leads the Cheapest, Happiest Company in the World - Bloomberg." *Bloomberg*, n.d. https://www.bloomberg.com/news/articles/2013-06-06/costco-ceo-craig-jelinek-leads-the-cheapest-happiest-company-in-the-world.

Lee, Timothy B. "How Amazon Innovates in Ways That Google and Apple Can't." *Vox*, December 28, 2016. https://www.vox.com/new-money/2016/12/28/13889840/amazon-innovation-google-apple.

"Sears Is Dying, 'Fast Fashion' Is Thriving." *The Hustle*, December 30, 2016. https://thehustle.co/sears-fast-fashion.

Insights, C. B. "Bad News for Google, Great News for Amazon h/t @scotwingopic.Twitter.Com/5s2hdKxmt2." Tweet. *@CBinsights*, January 7, 2017. https://twitter.com/CBinsights/status/817874817953267712.

Roz, Guy. "Warby Parker: Dave Gilboa & Neil Blumenthal." *NPR.Org*, December 26, 2016. http://www.npr.org/podcasts/510313/how-i-built-this.

Peterson, Hayley. "Why Sears Is Failing and Closing Stores - Business Insider." *Business Insider*, January 8, 2017. http://www.businessinsider.com/sears-failing-stores-closing-edward-lampert-bankruptcy-chances-2017-1.

Touryalai, Halah. "Ray-Ban, Oakley, Chanel Or Prada Sunglasses? They're All Made By This Obscure $9B Company." *Forbes*, July 2, 2013. https://www.forbes.com/sites/halahtouryalai/2013/07/02/ray-ban-oakley-chanel-or-prada-sunglasses-theyre-all-made-by-this-obscure-9b-company/.

Sun, Leo. "Could Warby Parker Be Worth More Than Luxottica One Day? -." *The Motley Fool*, July 10, 2016. https://www.fool.com/investing/2016/07/10/could-warby-parker-be-worth-more-than-luxottica-on.aspx.

Denning, Steve. "What's Behind Warby Parker's Success?" *Forbes*, March 23, 2016. https://www.forbes.com/sites/stevedenning/2016/03/23/whats-behind-warby-parkers-success/.

Bellafante, Ginia. "At Warby Parker, a Sense of Exclusion in a Low Price." *The New York Times*, May 20, 2016, sec. N.Y. / Region. https://www.nytimes.com/2016/05/22/nyregion/at-warby-parker-a-sense-of-exclusion-in-a-low-price.html.

Primack, Dan. "Unilever Buys Dollar Shave Club for $1 Billion." *Fortune*, July 19, 2016. http://fortune.com/2016/07/19/unilever-buys-dollar-shave-club-for-1-billion/.

Henry, Alan. "Subscription Shaving Showdown: Harry's vs. Dollar Shave Club." *Lifehacker*, August 7, 2016. http://lifehacker.com/subscription-shaving-showdown-harrys-vs-dollar-shave-1784723579.

Friedman, Lindsay. "Behind a $100 Million Mattress Startup, Casper Co-Founder Shares Advice on Finding Success as an Entrepreneur." *Entrepreneur*, June 8, 2016. https://www.entrepreneur.com/article/277168.

"Dollar Shave Club Acquisition: Where Does It Stack Up Against Past E-Commerce M&A?" *CB Insights Research*, July 21, 2016. /research/top-e-commerce-startup-acquisitions-dollar-shave-club/.

Transportation - Crash Test Dummies

Sciullo, Maria. "'Oh My God, This Is the Future': First Passengers Get Taste of Self-Driving Uber | Pittsburgh Post-Gazette," September 20,

2016. http://www.post-gazette.com/business/tech-news/2016/09/20/Some-Uber-riders-getting-the-self-driving-experience-for-themselves/stories/201609210024.

Obama, Barack. "Barack Obama: Self-Driving, Yes, but Also Safe | Pittsburgh Post-Gazette," September 19, 2016. http://www.post-gazette.com/opinion/Op-Ed/2016/09/19/Barack-Obama-Self-driving-yes-but-also-safe/stories/201609200027.

Zakrzewski, Cat. "Daimler Invests In 'Last Mile' Robotic Delivery Startup." *Wall Street Journal*, January 12, 2017, sec. Pro Private Markets. http://www.wsj.com/articles/daimler-invests-in-last-mile-robotic-delivery-startup-1484224207.

"Classic Underdog Story." *The Hustle*, February 3, 2017. https://thehustle.co/clean-energy-2020.

Upbin, Bruce. "Digging Into The Hyperloop's Impact on Transport Economics." *LinkedIn Pulse*, January 31, 2017. https://www.linkedin.com/pulse/digging-hyperloops-impact-transport-economics-bruce-upbin.

"15 Fascinating Facts About The SR-71 Blackbird." *HistoryInOrbit.Com*, April 21, 2015. http://www.historyinorbit.com/15-fascinating-facts-about-the-sr-71-blackbird-the-fastest-plane-on-earth/.

"Skunk Works® · Lockheed Martin." Accessed July 30, 2017. http://www.lockheedmartin.com/us/aeronautics/skunkworks.html.

Neil, Dan. "Could Self-Driving Cars Spell the End of Ownership?" *Wall Street Journal*, December 1, 2015, sec. Life. http://www.wsj.com/articles/could-self-driving-cars-spell-the-end-of-ownership-1448986572.

"The DARPA Grand Challenge: Ten Years Later," March 14, 2014. https://www.darpa.mil/news-events/2014-03-13.

Chafkin, Max. "Uber Debuts Its First Fleet of Driverless Cars in Pittsburgh." *Bloomberg.Com*, August 18, 2016. https://www.bloomberg.com/news/features/2016-08-18/uber-s-first-self-driving-fleet-arrives-in-pittsburgh-this-month-is06r7on.

Bradley, Ryan. "10 Breakthrough Technologies 2016: Tesla Autopilot." *MIT Technology Review*, n.d. https://www.technologyreview.com/s/600772/10-breakthrough-technologies-2016-tesla-autopilot/.

"Hyperloop One." *Hyperloop One*, n.d. https://hyperloop-one.com/.

Arieff, Allison. "Opinion | Can a 700 M.P.H. Train in a Tube Be for Real?" *The New York Times*, May 19, 2016, sec. Opinion.

https://www.nytimes.com/2016/05/19/opinion/can-a-700-mph-train-in-a-tube-be-for-real.html.
"Solar Roadways | Indiegogo." Accessed July 30, 2017.
https://www.indiegogo.com/projects/solar-roadways#/.

Search - I'm Feeling Lucky

McCracken, Harry. "Regis McKenna's 1976 Notebook And The Invention Of Apple Computer, Inc." *Fast Company*, April 1, 2016.
https://www.fastcompany.com/3058227/regis-mckennas-1976-notebook-and-the-invention-of-apple-computer-inc.
"Paid Search Ad Spend Worldwide 2017 | Statistic." *Statista*, n.d.
https://www.statista.com/statistics/267056/paid-search-advertising-expenditure-worldwide/.
"History of Search Engines - Chronological List of Internet Search Engines (INFOGRAPHIC) | WordStream." Accessed July 30, 2017.
https://www.wordstream.com/articles/internet-search-engines-history.

The Experience Economy - Couch-Surfing Mavericks

Loper, Nick. "15 Apps That Let You Join the Sharing Economy."
Lifehack, October 23, 2014.
http://www.lifehack.org/articles/technology/15-apps-that-let-you-join-the-sharing-economy.html
Bercovici, Jeff. "Airbnb, Snapgoods and 12 More Pioneers Of The 'Share Economy.'" *Forbes*, n.d.
https://www.forbes.com/pictures/ehfk45edlgm/airbnb-snapgoods-and-12-more-pioneers-of-the-share-economy/
Kessler, Sarah. "The 'Sharing Economy' Is Dead, And We Killed It."
Fast Company, September 14, 2015.
https://www.fastcompany.com/3050775/the-sharing-economy-is-dead-and-we-killed-it.
Bertoni, Steven. "How Mixing Data And Fashion Can Make Rent The Runway Tech's Next Billion Dollar Star." *Forbes*, August 20, 2014.
https://www.forbes.com/sites/stevenbertoni/2014/08/20/how-mixing-data-and-fashion-can-make-rent-the-runway-techs-next-billion-dollar-star/.

"Airbnb's Ambitious Second Act Will Take It Way Beyond Couch-Surfing." Vanity Fair. November 2016. http://www.vanityfair.com/news/2016/11/airbnb-brian-chesky.

Carson, Biz. "How 3 Guys Turned Renting an Air Mattress in Their Apartment into a $25 Billion Company." *Business Insider*, February 23, 2016. http://www.businessinsider.com/how-airbnb-was-founded-a-visual-history-2016-2.

Said, Carolyn. "Airbnb Spawns Array of Companies to Aid Hosts." *SFGate*, March 2, 2014. http://www.sfgate.com/business/article/Airbnb-spawns-array-of-companies-to-aid-hosts-5282838.php.

Goebel, Bryan. "S.F. Transportation Officials Blame Uber, Lyft for Traffic Congestion." *KQED News*, December 14, 2016. https://ww2.kqed.org/news/2016/12/13/s-f-transportation-officials-blame-uber-lyft-for-traffic-congestion/.

"About Us - Get To Know The Guesty Team." *Guesty*, n.d. https://www.guesty.com/about/.

"Airbnb: The Growth Story You Didn't Know." *GrowthHackers*, n.d. https://growthhackers.com/growth-studies/airbnb.

"From Uber To TaskRabbit: Where Valuations Stand Today In The On-Demand Economy." *CB Insights Research*, October 25, 2016. /research/on-demand-ecommerce-valuations/.

Shieber, Jonathan. "With $53 Million in New Funding, Movile Looks to Become the Tencent of Latin America." *TechCrunch*, July 10, 2017. http://social.techcrunch.com/2017/07/10/with-53-million-in-new-funding-movile-looks-to-become-the-tencent-of-latin-america/.

Epilogue – The Pace of Change is Accelerating

Desjardins, Jeff. "Chart: The Largest Companies by Market Cap Over 15 Years." Visual Capitalist. August 12, 2016. Accessed July 22, 2017. http://www.visualcapitalist.com/chart-largest-companies-market-cap-15-years/.

Campoy, Ana, Youyou Zhou, and Christopher Groskopf. "Donald Trump believes manufacturing equals prosperity. Our data analysis proves him wrong." Quartz. July 21, 2017. Accessed July 22, 2017. https://qz.com/1027934/donald-trump-believes-manufacturing-equals-american-prosperity-our-data-analysis-proves-him-wrong/.

"Global 3PL Market." Armstrong & Associates. Accessed July 22, 2017. http://www.3plogistics.com/3pl-market-info-resources/3pl-market-information/global-3pl-market-size-estimates/.

"Uber (company)." Wikipedia. July 18, 2017. Accessed July 22, 2017. https://en.wikipedia.org/wiki/Uber_(company).

CPSIA information can be obtained
at www.ICGtesting.com
Printed in the USA
FSHW011716011219
64447FS